ERDOGANOPHOBIA

Manufacturing Hate And Political Fear: A Case Study

ABDÜLKADİR ÖZKAN

kopernik

ABDÜLKADİR ÖZKAN: Journalist and writer. He was born in 1980 in Istanbul. He graduated from Istanbul Bilgi University, Faculty of Communication. He began his journalism career at *Yörünge* journal as a reporter. He worked as a foreign news editor at İhlas News Agency. After working as a news coordinator for *Turkish News Weekly* in Sydney, Australia for two years, he worked as a news editor in Thailand, Hong Kong, China and Indonesia. He lived in Lebanon, Jordan and Dubai for three years, right after the assassination of Lebanon's Prime Minister Refik Hariri. He continued to write weekly columns in the *TNW*. He served as editor-in-chief of the *Global Research* journal. His expertise lies in media and intercultural relations and Marshall McLuhan's theories on media. He served as the press adviser to Professor Mehmet Görmez, director of the Presidency of Religious Affairs, in 2010, and as the press counselor to Professor Nabi Avcı, minister of education in 2014. He was appointed as chief adviser to the prime minister in 2015. Currently, he is a board member of the Turkish National Commission for UNESCO, general secretary of the Islamic Culture and Arts Platform, board member of the European Diplomats Association, director of the Cultural and Arts Studies Center, and general secretary of the Democracy for Everyone Enterprise. He has good command of English. He is married with three children.

First published by Kopernik Inc.
®Abdülkadir Özkan 2018

Editor-in-Chief: Abdülkadir Özkan
Advisor: Prof. Halil Berktay
Series Editor: Dr. Yaşar Çolak
Director: Dr. Cengiz Şişman
Copy Editing: Peter Klempner
Design: Ali Kaya
Application: Sinopsis

Kopernik Publishing House
Kopernik Inc.
108 Olde Towne Avenue Unit: 308 Gaithersburg Maryland 20877 - USA
www.kopernikpublishing.com

Certification no: 35175
ISBN: 978-975-2439-36-8
First Edition: January 2018
Second Edition: July 2018

Printed in ISTANBUL
Bilnet Matbaacılık ve Yayıncılık A.Ş.

ISTANBUL - LONDON - NEW YORK – WASHINGTON DC

ERDOGANOPHOBIA

Manufacturing Hate And Political Fear: A Case Study

ABDÜLKADİR ÖZKAN

kopernik

CONTENTS

SECTION TWO
THE AK PARTY ERA

FOREWORD

R ecep Tayyip Erdoğan is also known as Leader, Master, Sir, Conqueror of Davos, and World Leader while the opposition calls him the New Sultan and Dictator. Regardless of the angle, regardless of in which ideological frames it is analyzed, Erdoğan being the greatest success story after Mustafa Kemal Atatürk in the history of Turkish politics is an undebatable fact. The significant contributions he has made to Turkey's democratization, his pragmatism that has completed Islamism's – "Muslim politics" – integration with the system, his determination which has succeeded in turning conservative democracy into a political doctrine against Islamism, and his reformist goals that have ensured Turkey's neo-liberal economic, societal and cultural transformation, are only some of the headlines that render Erdoğan one of the most important political actors in Turkish politics. Therefore, a history of politics written without taking Erdoğan into consideration from multiple angles would not make it possible to understand Turkey's critical democratization and transformation processes.

Although Erdoğan is compared in the general sense to Adnan Menderes and Turgut Özal – both important figures of

Turkish right-wing politics – his characteristic qualities differ greatly from theirs. Thanks to his political style that is formed with the impact of the center-right tradition's traumatic interim period experiences, Erdoğan is, beyond dispute, the most rational, reformist, and pragmatic political figure in the country's right-wing politics. Erdoğan is also the most criticized and debated figure in Turkish political history. In addition to all these characteristics, Erdoğan is an important politician who has been able to show the courage to challenge the status quo on a global scale. As much as he dared to break the idols of the established order in Turkey, he is a powerful leader who exclaimed to sovereign powers in the name of the oppressed, that "the world is bigger than five", who made the world accept that the New Turkey is now a noteworthy actor against oppression and oppressors. As a requirement of the nature of politics, it would be a mistake to ignore Erdoğan's political mistakes and flaws. Such an approach, before anything else, is against the nature of subjects. Despite his harshening political discourse, with all his mistakes and flaws, Erdoğan is an important figure raised by Turkish politics in whom almost an entire society – including the majority of opposition circles – have hope for the future.

His oppositional spirit, protest identity, ideological understanding that does not tolerate oppression and never favors the oppressor, has in recent times turned Erdoğan into the target of the sovereign powers in the West. The Western paradigm, which projects that political Islam will fail vis-à-vis modernity, has almost felt itself defeated due to Erdoğan's political achievements. As such, a systematic manipulation policy was started against Erdoğan. The established status quo that is disturbed by the New Turkey goal in internal politics has never held back from supporting the West's anti-Erdoğan sentiment. The animosity for and opposition to Erdoğan, which gives his harshening and changing discourse as an explanation and taking the form of a "phobia" for the last few years fueled with anti-Turkish and anti-Muslim sentiment through escalating hatred for Erdoğan, shows that we are face to face with a serious problem. Diagnosing the West's anti-Erdoğan sentiment at the point reached, as a disease, and calling this disease "Erdoganophobia", is the correct approach in terms of conceptualizing the matter. Hence, the objective of this study is, while investigating the hidden causes for this new disease that has formed in both domestic and foreign politics with an analytical method, to make reference to the historical and philosophical foundations of the matter in the context of the East-West conflict.

Although what is conceptualized in the study in various forms as anti-Erdoğan sentiment, fear of Erdoğan, and "Erdoganophobia" has become an interesting fact today, the model of protest politics Erdoğan has brought forward since the mid-1970s points to the first stage that those who have an established order were uneasy about. While conservative Islamist politics has been significantly visible in Turkish political life since the 1990s, the political line represented in the early 2000s changed the dimension with a unique inversion and set the grounds for anti-Erdoganism and fear of Erdoğan to grow further. The West's phobic outbursts aimed at Erdoğan, who is at the peak of his political maturity, especially after 2009, the perception operations trying to present Erdoğan with terms such as "dictator" and "authoritarian", find basis in Islamophobia. Therefore, the recent history chronology here presents the phases of anti-Erdoganism from the 1970s to the present, the fear of Erdoğan, and, in the final analysis, Erdoganophobia.

This study, while developing different angles in relation to Erdoğan's political career and characteristics, also tries to take a socio-political and socio-economic picture of Turkey's adventure with democratization. This book, which has no academic pretension but is still the result of a meticulous study, should be taken into consideration as a reading of recent political history reading centered on Erdoğan

I would like to thank everybody who supported me with their criticism and ideas in the completion of this study, especially my esteemed teacher, Professor Nabi Avcı, and my dear brother Cüneyd Zapsu. I am also grateful to friends who read the text once it was completed and made various corrections and noted what was missing, and my dear wife who provided her full support.

January 2018, Ankara
ABDÜLKADİR ÖZKAN

INTRODUCTION

A GENERAL PICTURE

French political scientist Professor Olivier Roy says in his much-discussed thesis in the early 1990s that political Islam, in line with the teachings of Hassan al-Banna and Abul A'la Mawdudi, has failed. To ground his thesis, published as a book, *The Failure of Political Islam*,[1] he makes reference to the traumas experienced in Islamic communities, listing political failures with specific examples from Algeria, Iran, Afghanistan, and Pakistan. However, throughout the book, Roy asks the reader what modern political Islam suggests to Muslim societies. Roy, who suggests that Islamism's area of influence has not yet ended, that political Islam may one day come to power but the result will be disappointing, sees the ideology of political Islam as unable to make new room for itself against modernism, and that is the reason behind this failure. When presenting the proposition that political Islam is unsuccessful, he excludes Turkey as an example. However, in an article he wrote in 2004, identifying the AK Party as the "democratizing face of Islam",[2] he likens it to the conservative

---

[1] Olivier Roy, *The Failure of Political Islam*, I. B. Tauris & Co Ltd, New York 1994.

[2] Yalçın Akdoğan, *Modern Türkiye'de Siyasî Düşünce İslâmahk*, İletişim Yayınları, 2004, p. 630: "The AKP represents the democratization of Islam and is, at this point, in the same position as the Christian Democrats in Europe. Compare Mr. Erdoğan with Bavarian PrşnePrime Minister in Germany. They have a lot

parties in Europe and contends that the AK Party does not represent political Islam. However, Erdoğan's changing and radicalized[3] political language and style after 2007 is interpreted in Western media as a shift from conservative democracy toward radical political Islam. This change will be perceived as a transformation process that will justify those who choose to stand distant from Erdoğan and the AK Party due to their Islamist origin.[4] As the point reached by the discourse on Islamism that is altered through the AK Party's definition of what a conservative democrat is, the strain of political Islam[5] Erdoğan represents, and the West's shifts in discourse that have been revealed in time are outlined in the upcoming pages. As for now, through the reference from Roy will do.

Without a doubt, the greatest success story in Turkish political history in the last century is Mustafa Kemal Atatürk. His opponents recognize the fact that he was a political genius as much as his supporters do. Yet, the other political leaders who contributed to establishing democracy after Atatürk left should also be given credit. However, it is commonly accepted that one of them is a significant milestone in Turkish politics. That is Recep Tayyip Erdoğan, who left his mark on Turkey's last 15 years with his unfamiliar political style. It would neither be realistic nor an objective approach to identify Erdoğan, like the opposition, as only a politician stuck inside

---

in common. They are both conservative and advocate free market economy and technology. They want religion and the state to be kept seperate, but Mr. Stoiber advocates keeping the crucix symbol to at schools, while Mr. Erdoğan wants the hijab to be allowed at schools. One is Muslim, the other is Chritsian, yet they are very close." Roy, 2004.

[3]   Valeria Talbot, *The Uncertain Path of the "New Turkey"*, ISPI, New York, 2015.

[4]   Graham Fuller's writings were critical in the depiction of the AKP as an Islamic party. "Freedom and Security: Necessary Conditions for Moderation," *American Journal of Islamic Social Sciences*, 22/3 (Summer 2005), pp. 23-24.

[5]   Beyond being a term the AK Party developed for itself, this definition was used to refer to the term Islamist, which the Western intelligentsia refers to when talking about the AK Party and the National Outlook tradition.

tight molds, a leader in love with the presidency, or a populist political figure. As much as Erdoğan is an important actor
who has been able to reach the evolutionary stages of Turkey's goal of democratization of the last 150 years to a noteworthy level, he is also a brave and determined politician who
is able to test the people's pulse and whose predictions are to
the point. In addition to being a reformist who has been able
to turn the concept of a conservative democrat – which entered literature with Turgut Özal – into a sustainable political
discourse, alongside his Muslim identity, he is a strong, revolutionary leader who has dared to break the molds of tutelage
and challenged the idols of the system. Despite all these qualities, Erdoğan is also probably one of the most criticized figures in Turkey's political history. Therefore, it is not possible
to understand and analyze Turkey's adventure with democratization without him.

It is possible to say that Erdoğan's character of dominant,
determined leadership and God-given charisma are the underlying factors behind his unstoppable rise and success that
started in his youth. However, does the fact that the anti-Erdoğan sentiment that gained an international dimension, accompanied by the allegations of authoritarianism that escalated with systematic efforts in both domestic and foreign policy in recent years that is currently at the level of a phobia
have any relationship to the theories that predict the failure
of political Islam? How should this new situation we are facing be defined? What are the truths behind the systematic
fear campaign that has reached a phobia today? Why is it that
Western politics, which sang Erdoğan's praises until the mid-
2000s, feel the need today to make a change in its discourse?
Why do his political opponents in Turkey and his interlocutors in the West fear Erdoğan? Are the increasing accusa-

tions against him for becoming authoritarian coincidental? Is Erdoğan an uncriticizable leader? Is his bold political tone, which forces the limits of diplomacy, the reason behind this phobia? Or is it the concern that the transformation of the mindset of the political line led by Erdoğan in the last two decades might set an example for other Islamic societies?

In order to answer these questions, it is necessary to analyze Erdoğan's political life in sections. Erdoğan became acquainted with the National Outlook during his youth and his relationship with Necmettin Erbakan gives crucial cues to Erdoğan's political roots. The National Outlook era coincides mostly with the shaping of Erdoğan's political discourse and political mind. The protest spirit he possesses surfaced in the early years of the National Outlook. His initial ideological divergence against the prominent figures of the National Salvation Party and Welfare Party caused him to be commemorated among the innovators that Korkut Özal led. In fact, it is evident that he has a crucial paradigm incompatibility with the innovators led by Özal. He was perceived as the prince of Erbakan, and the spoiled child of the house. They did not want him to come to the fore and be visible. On the other hand, the protective attitude of Erbakan, the leader of the National Movement, was not welcomed by its senior figures. The initial place, in which many years later anti-Erdoğanism sentiment eventually turned into a phobia, is in fact his home, where he was born and where his ideologies were shaped. It is of great importance to take note of the point that it is unnatural to claim that the protest stance Erdoğan has adopted throughout his political life is correct and reasonable. It is for this reason that the portrait of Erdoğan that we are trying to illustrate is one that, from time to time, has a humane aspect that includes his shortfalls and mistakes. In fact, it is built on a political profile in which this aspect dominates from time to time.

The National Movement tradition rejects the discourse of a Western mobilized idea of the politicization of fundamentalism and Islamism that is born as a result of radicalization, and thus separates itself from such definitions. As it believes the definition Islamism is produced from the perspective of orientalism and does not represent the national and native stand within Western molds, it describes itself with concepts of a "Just Order" and "National Outlook". However, this does not change the outlook of the Western world on the National Movement and its political extension, which is Erdoğan's stance. Ever since the initial years of the establishment of the AK Party until 2007, Erdoğan was not perceived as a representative of political Islam in the classical sense. However, the West still prefers to cautiously approach Erdoğan, who has stripped himself from the National Movement garb. With the transformed political discourse after 2008, the line Erdoğan represents is a different version of the thesis of political Islam and Erdoğan is accepted as a new populist, Islamic, political leader. Although Erdoğan rejects this definition from a different perspective, it is more comprehensible to analyze the issue from the aspect of the AK Party's relations with the West as an advice of the bankruptcy of political Islam.

The fractures Erdoğan experienced within the National Movement surfaced evidentially during his candidacy while running to be the mayor of Istanbul. His election as mayor came as a surprise. Survey companies were wrong once again.

Erdoğan's political foresight of winning the elections came true and the respected elders of the party were forced to congratulate Erdoğan and his innovative team. His mayorship, which is analyzed in detail in the following pages, became imperiled with his prosecution following his recitation of a poem in Siirt on December 6, 1997. The prosecution's decision was declared that he was charged under Turkish Criminal Act 312/2 for the crime of "[d]iscriminating and inciting hatred against class, race, religion, sect or regional differences", and following an appeal of the court decision, it was declared that Erdoğan would never be able to return to politics. He was isolated during this period and his expectations of support from his party were shattered. In the opinion of Vural Savaş, the High Court Prosecutor, the political traditions that Erbakan and Erdoğan represented showed them to be "blood-sucking bats". Furthermore, a case was opened to shut down the Welfare Party with the claim that they were dragging the country into a civil war. On January 16, 1998, the Constitutional Court ordered the shutdown of the Welfare Party on the grounds of involvement and "actions against the secular principle of the Republican system". It was not only Erdoğan, but also the strongest party of the National Outlook Movement, the Welfare Party, that took its share from the practices of those traumatic days. Both Erdoğan and Erbakan were banned from politics. The politics of the National Movement then continued on with the establishment of the Virtue Party. An imperative development contrary to the norm took place during the 1st Virtue Party Congress that was held on May 14, 2000. Abdullah Gül was brought to the fore by the "innovative" wing up against the candidate Recai Kutan, who was chosen by Erbakan to become the Chair of the party. This was considered to be the second oppositional move in the National Outlook tradition following the first, which took place during the party congress on October 15, 1978, when Korkut Özal left the lists, so to say. *Birikim* magazine, which had a leftist-socialist perspective, reported this innovative step that took place within the National Outlook tradition after 20 years with the following: "The Virtue Party Congress: The Democracy Virus Infiltrates the Virtue Party". Shortly, it was deduced that Erdoğan, with his innovative political style, was behind Abdullah Gül's candidacy. Gül lost the election by a small margin. However, the first foundations of the conservative democrat Erdoğan-era that would shape the future of Turkey had been successfully set. The congress in which Recai Kutan and the traditionalists were victorious was recorded as a pyric victory, so to speak.

From this point on, the fracture between Erbakan and Erdoğan turned into complete disengagement. Erbakan, who hardened his opposition to Erdoğan following the formation of the AK Party, called Erdoğan "a pawn who has been brought into power by racist imperialism with the use of all media facilities" and "the subcontractor of the Chaim Nahum doctrine". Eventually, the debates escalate even further, but Erdoğan never used a style disrespectful to his preceptor.

Erdoğan's political life that coincides with the AK Party era is expectant of many important incidents. The strategic alliances formed with the European Union, the U.S., and Israel was not welcomed by the National Outlook factions. In fact, Erdoğan did not have the intention to please the cadres of the former party. His purpose was to fill the vacancy in the center of politics with discourse of conservative democrats. With the trust on his shoulders, he entered an era of balance relations with both internal and external powers. In relation to the solution of the headscarf problem, which was one of the most chronic problems of conservative politics, Erdoğan crossed the touchline, and during a visit to Spain as part of the Alliance of Civilizations program on January 14, 2008, he set the whole process into action as he commented on the headscarf of some women at the program: "Even if they wear a headscarf as a political symbol, will you consider that a crime too? Can you bring a ban against symbols and images? Where in the world do they prohibit this freedom?" On February 23, 2008, with the support of the Nationalist Movement Party, the ban passed through Parliament and was printed in the Official Gazette. This step was presented in the *Hürriyet* newspaper with the headline: "411 Hands Vote Yes for Chaos". Despite the balanced politics Erdoğan insisted on undertaking, all of the requests aimed at solving social problems caused restlessness among the secular members of society. It is for this reason that the mid-2000s were the most critical years in which many large-scale social protests took place in Turkey. The crises that took place in 2007 forced Erdoğan to change his discourse. The problems experienced with President Ahmet Necdet Sezer, the Republic Protests, the State Council attack, the 367 crisis, e-memorandum, the Dolmabahçe meeting, the party closure case, the Ergenekon and Balyoz (Sledgehammer) operations and trials, increasing terrorist attacks, and the Gülen Movement spiraling out of control, all caused Erdoğan and AK Party to become targeted by an extraordinary and controlled agenda. While internal politics is hectic, foreign politics is no different. The "one minute" and Mavi Marmara crises with Israel, the Arab Spring that got out of hand in the Middle East and North Africa from 2009-2010, the withdrawal of single rulers ruling the region for half a century and stepping down from the political stage, and the U.S.' Middle Eastern policies that changed into a completely new dimension all forced Erdoğan's hand in reconsidering the political discourse he had used from the very beginning of his political career. Eventually, all of this negativity in the region causes the AK Party's diplomacy discourse to evolve into "zero neighbors", despite the fact that it set off on a path with the aim of attaining "zero problems with neighbors", and thus, Turkey found itself within a great chamber of fire outside its borders.

In order to truly understand the changes in the AK Party and Erdoğan's political discourse after 2011, it is necessary to analyze the historical, political, and socio-political facts of those years. It is for this reason that a more reliable framework appears if one is to evaluate Erdoğan's political adventures in separately, such as the period before the AK Party up until 2002, and the political terms after 2002. His political style, which changed and transformed after 2007, and which became more evident in 2011, is not different from his political rhetoric following the social upheaval attempts of the Gezi Park protests, the December 17 and 25 judicial coup, and the July 15 military coup attempt – it is not a recently surfaced rhetoric as a result of Erdoğan's character. To illustrate it as pieces that have undergone a transformation over time helps to explain the general picture as a whole. In this regard, due to Erdoğan's realism and sincerity, it is necessary to accept that he is a unique politician who earns continuous support, trust, and social acceptance despite his political discourse. The following sections of this research analyze the changes and transformations in Erdoğan's political discourse and documents the statements of those witnessed it.

SECTION ONE
NATIONAL OUTLOOK ERA

FOOTSTEPS OF CHANGE: 1985 WELFARE PARTY CONGRESS

It was 1983. It had been about three years since the September 12 military coup under Chief of Staff General Kenan Evren's command. The junta had restricted life and democracy to the utmost, and political and economic instability had started to push the limits. On June 1981, the open discussion of political matters was banned. In 1982, with a National Security Council (MGK) decision by the junta administration, discussing the past, present, or future of former politicians was prevented in an almost Orwellian style.[1] Turkey was going through tough times. With the order from Evren, who became president after the coup, Turkey went to the ballot box on November 6, 1983. An unexpected situation emerged when the results were announced. The people had shown their reaction to the interruption of the junta at the ballot box. The Nationalist Democracy Party (MDP) led by military-based Turgut Sunalp, who was considered a favorite in the elections from which known political figures were banned, and for whom Evren made a call of support a night before the election,[2] had faced great defeat, coming in third

---

[1] Eric Jan Zürcher, *Modernleşen Türkiye'nin Tarihi*, İletişim Yayınları, Istanbul 2015, p. 403.

[2] *Milliyet*, November 6, 1983.

with 23.27 percent of the vote. Necdet Calp's Populist Party (HP), representing the left, came second with 30.26 percent of the vote, and former DTP Undersecretary Turgut Özal's Motherland Party (ANAP) – which was given no chance before the election – had won with 45.14 percent of the vote. This unexpected and hard-to-digest victory would lead to an entirely different atmosphere with Özal being tasked on December 7, 1983, to form the 45th government. Özal, who received a vote of confidence with support from 213 members of Parliament, had shattered the dreams of those who had thought he would follow the balance policy of ignoring interim Prime Minister Bülent Ulusu and his team in his first Cabinet.[3]

There were no known political figures in the November 6, 1983 parliamentary elections. Due to political bans, Süleyman Demirel, Bülent Ecevit, Necmettin Erbakan, Alpaslan Türkeş and their parties could not take part in the elections. The Welfare Party (RP), founded upon attorney Ali Türkmen's application on July 19, 1983, was not permitted to take part in the general elections on the grounds that it could not complete its formation. Some party members having been vetoed by the National Security Council was the most concrete reason that delayed the Welfare Party's formation. However, the result remained the same, and the Welfare Party went into the records as the biggest political movement of the National Outlook. Pro-junta circles, however, identified it as "religionist",[4] and as such it could not run in the election. The term of Necmettin Erbakan's political ban was when the change discourse was expressed among the party. The congress in which unvetoed founding member Ahmet Tekdal was chosen chairman

---

[3] Aydın Taşkın, *1960'tan Günümüze Türkiye Tarihi*, p. 347.
[4] Zürcher, *Modernleşen Türkiye'nin Tarihi*, p. 407.

on June 30, 1985,[5] was an important assembly during which the signals of change in the National Outlook line was noticed. The demand for change, which stood out in the congress presided over by Council Chair Hasan Aksay, also drew media attention and was closely followed by the newspapers and magazines of the time. That women were permitted to become party members for the first time and appeared at the congress was a revolutionary change in the National Outlook tradition. *Yankı*, a weekly news analysis magazine known to have a left-wing editorial policy, in 1985, noted the "plentitude of women" at the congress, which it described as "the Welfare Party's Show of Strength".[6]

We will further mention *Yankı*'s exclusive news and the newspaper analyses of the time in upcoming pages, but an important figure drew attention behind the curtain of the change that took place in the 1985 congress. Recep Tayyip Erdoğan, a major milestone in himself in Turkey's political life, took the stage as a 30-year-old politician and the architect behind the change. The correct way to read the change Erdoğan expressed throughout his political journey is through an in-depth analysis of his youth with the National Outlook. As a matter of fact, starting with Erdoğan's protest political stance from the National Salvation Party (MSP) term would be more historically correct. Erdoğan, who ventured into politics in the 1970s in the youth branch by Erbakan's side, discovered politics at an early age during his education at an imam-hatip high school. Getting noticed for being hardworking, Erdoğan first made obvious his reformist attitude at the National Salvation Party's 4th Ordinary Grand Congress in 1978. However, prior to the congress, the unexpected drop in the party's

---

[5] *Sabah*, July 1, 1985.
[6] *Yankı*, July 8-14, 1985, issue 745, pp 20-23.

votes in the June 5, 1977 parliamentary election was targeted with criticisms from a team that included Erdoğan. The number of MSP deputies dropping from 48 to 24 after the election activated intra-party opposition. The reasons behind the failure needed to be determined to take immediate measures. Although the report Erdoğan prepared was presented to party Chairman Erbakan, nothing much changed. The congress assembled a year later. At the October 15, 1978 4th Ordinary Grand Congress, the second eldest member of the Özal family presented a second party assembly list against the list of the National Outlook's natural leader Erbakan.[7] The attitude taken by Özal despite Erbakan was considered by the big shots of the party to be "a plan to conquer from within by taking the MSP from Erbakan".[8] This first demand for change was considered unpleasant and provocative. Korkut Özal's aim was not to drag the party into internal chaos, but to suggest a new and realistic political model free of idealistic and heroic discourses that would take heed of social demands and offer solutions to problems. This suggestion was the clearest indication that Özal's political style was different from that of Erbakan. The congress gathered in a tense atmosphere. Physical fights, from time to time, replaced discussions. Oğuzhan Asiltürk and Şevket Kazan declared Özal and his supporters, who prepared a list against Erbakan, to be traitors. Özal was also prevented from taking the platform and making a speech.

However, the support from Erdoğan, one of the architects of the second list, who was among the delegates in his capacity as Istanbul Provincial Youth Branch president, showing the courage to step out of the National Outlook identity, would leave a mark on the general assembly, and the reform-

---

[7] October 15, 1978 National Salvation Party Congress Minutes.

[8] Ahmet Akgül, *Erbakan Devrimi*, Togan Yayıncılık, Ankara 2011, p. 345.

ist-traditionalist fight that started in 1978 would continue in-
cessantly until the establishment of the AK Party. Journalist
Hüseyin Besli, a close witness of the period, explains the reformist-traditionalist debates surfacing for the first time in
the party and Erdoğan's emergence as follows:

The Erdoğan factor in the 1978 congress

The MSP achieved a success in the 1973 elections both beyond
is own expectations and public opinion predictions, and with
the 48 seats it secured in Parliament, it became a key party that
will solve the power balance in Parliament. Although the Republican elites, primarily the CHP, were not pleased about this,
it ends in the formation of the CHP-MSP coalition government. In the elections held in 1977 upon Bülent Ecevit's breaking the coalition, the MSP was unable to achieve the same previous success. Its votes dropped from 11.8 percent to 8.5 percent and it won 24 seats in Parliament compared to its previous
48. A group among the party wants the reason behind this defeat investigated and hence, those responsible to be determined
and held accountable. Furthermore, they submitted to Erbakan
their demands in relation to making a change in the party administration to prevent the same from happening again and the
party being run with a new mindset.

The group, demanding reform upon Erbakan's silence over
on demands and criticism, prepared a second list with Korkut Özal's initiative in the 4th Ordinary Grand Congress held
on October 15, 1978. Recep Tayyip Erdoğan, who was only 24
years old at the time and among the delegates in his capacity as
Istanbul Provincial Youth Branch chairman, also supported the
second list in the congress. Tayyip Erdoğan was probably the
youngest delegate in that congress hall, but he was very active.
He strongly objected when the headquarters wanted to prevent
his meeting with the delegates. Arguments erupted into phys-

ical contact. Eventually, even though those defending the second list were unsuccessful, being among those who want reform, Tayyip Erdoğan left a strong impression on the delegates and the audience with his averse and challenging attitude and becomes a success in that congress.[9]

1976 Youth Branch Congress

Erdoğan, who became a shining star at the 4th Ordinary Congress, stood out with his dissident in the provincial youth branch elections in 1976, two years before the 4th Ordinary Grand Congress, and became a candidate in spite of the wants of the headquarters. As a surprise candidate in the congress with Kadir Mısıroğlu as council chairman, Erdoğan became provincial youth branch chairman at the age of 22, winning the majority of the vote from delegates. In Hüseyin Besli's words, "Although he has undertaken a heavy responsibility at a very young age, he has no trouble overcoming this responsibility with his self-confidence and his respectability among his circle."[10] However, the political tremors experienced in Turkey in the 1970s, embargo problems, and soured ties with the West following the Cyprus Peace Operation, topped the list as the most important problems standing in the way of the Republic, which was getting ready to celebrate its 50th anniversary. Hence, although the change that took place in the National Salvation Party during this period did not occupy much space on Turkey's agenda, these years in which the slogan "the Islamic movement cannot be stopped" become political discourse, migration from the village to the city was greatly increasing, cities became surrounded by slums, and

---

[9] Hüseyin Besli, and Ömer Özbay, *Bir Liderin Doğuşu Recep Tayyip Erdoğan*, YTY, Istanbul 2014, pp. 41-42.

[10] Besli-Özbay, *Bir Liderin Doğuşu Recep Tayyip Erdoğan*, p. 32.

the new Turkish bourgeoisie started to take the stage, in the 1990s turned into the labor pains of a driving force that would change the future paradigm of politics.

Wind of Change in the Welfare Party

The 1st Ordinary Grand Congress on June 30, 1985, which is considered the footsteps of change in the National Outlook tradition, was revolutionary in terms of women's visibility. Erdoğan, who played an effective role in the organization of the women's branch, was a candidate to become a notable politician in his capacity as provincial chair. *Yankı*, a weekly news magazine of the time published by Mehmet Ali Kışlalı, prepared an exclusive file on the transformation in the Welfare Party:

The Welfare Party's show of strength

A crowd started from the entry to the Atatürk Sports Hall. Most of them were bearded. Some were dressed in shalvars. The "religious party supporters" sitting cross-legged on the grass out in the garden were listening to the RP chairman's speech as they would a sermon. Some wore a white prayer cap over their heads.

A rush of hot air flew out from the entrance to the hall accompanied by the scent of rose oil. The delegates, the audience, the crowd of thousands who flocked from all corners of the country for their party's first grand congress were listening to the chairman's speech in reverence. In contrast to the calmness and monotony of party Chairman Ahmet Tekdal, who was reading the text of the 42-page speech in front of him, the crowd in the hall was excited and enthusiastic. The groups of 50 people that took their places in all corners of the tribunes waved the Welfare Party flags they were carrying throughout the con-

gress. The young men in the hall, the majority of them bearded, carrying green-ribboned staff tags on their right collar, were
trying to excite the crowds in the tribunes. One called out slogans on the microphone, then first the groups in all four corners
of the tribunes repeated the slogan in unison, followed by the
entire hall. One corner called out "crescent", the other corner,
"grain". Then a burst of applause, then long-lasting applause.
When the slogans were over, there was not a peep. Nobody was
outside smoking other than the press staff and guests. All of the
female audience sitting in a section with a large-sized Turkish
flag and the party flag wore headscarves The flags in front of
them somewhat prevent the men from seeing them.

The Welfare Party's first congress has shown that this party also has a dynamic base, even if limited. The base of the once key
party is now strong, faithful. Thus, the RP is a party that cannot be disregarded or ignored. This time, the base is not the old
careless base that has no regard for the world. On the contrary,
it is a more aware party that has a good grasp of the significance
of politics. And most of them are young.[11]

As much as *Yankı* was pointing to the discipline at the
congress, it was saying that the change in the Welfare Party was leading a hard-to-ignore transformation. While the
magazine interpreted the youth who represented the majority in the congress as a dynamic base that "cared about
the world", it did not overlook Erdoğan and the reformist
team's efforts behind the scenes. *Tercüman*, a daily in circulation at the time, also described the congress similarly.
However, the analysis by Semih Ergüç is proof of how distant mainstream media was from Islamist politics and religious society:

[11] *Yankı*, July 8-14, 1985, issue 745, pp 20-22.

Female supporters were also among the guests of the RP's 1st Grand Congress. The female RP supporters were sitting collectively in the tribune right across the presidency council platform. The female supporters sitting under the large-sized Turkish flag and party flag did not remove their headscarves and overcoats despite the intolerable heat inside the hall and watched the congress until the end.[12]

The Erbakan Factor

Overlooking and ignoring the National Outlook's natural leader, Necmettin Erbakan, when analyzing the process of change in the National Salvation and Welfare Parties would be a grave mistake. Therefore, progressing by taking into account the Erbakan factor in the transformation and development process of nationalist, conservative, Islamist politics alone produces the right result. Erbakan, who is said to have "always [had a] problematic relationship with the existing regime as an Islamist leader",[13] had a problem, not with the regime, as thought, but with the political paradigm that drains national-spiritual values produced by the existing system. The National Outlook, which greatly contributed to Erdoğan's ideological formation, was based on a new world idea founded on justice. By objecting to the definition of political Islam, Erbakan introduced a new conceptual context. He rejected the suggestions made by Islamists and orientalists that reduce religion to ideology. In this context, the National Outlook was considered a movement of historic depth that cannot be reduced to modern political ideologies based on the "mindset of giving superiority to truth".[14] The victo-

---

[12] *Tercüman*, July 1, 1985.
[13] Ruşen Çakır, "Necmettin Erbakan: Adaletin Bu Mu Düzen?" *Homopolitikus: Lider Biyografilerindeki Türkiye*, S. Öngider (ed.), Aykırı Yayıncılık, Istanbul 2001, pp. 227-229.
[14] H. Bahadır Türk, *Muktedir, Türk Sağ Geleneği ve Recep Tayyip Erdoğan*, İletişim Yayınları, Istanbul 2014, p. 165.

ry of Manzikert, the conquest of Constantinople, the Battle of Gallipoli and the War of Independence were all won with the National Outlook. The National Outlook is "the people's soul, origin, and the people's essence, self, history, and faith".[15] Erbakan identified Muslims' primary and fundamental duty as taking a side in the fight between truth and fiction, fighting against fiction. He regarded politics as an activity carried out within this context and the fundamental duty of being Muslim. Hence, the meaning derived by fundamentalist, salafist Islamic movements from *jihad* and the suggestion made by Erbakan and the National Outlook tradition will always differ greatly from one another.

Giving dominance to justice over oppression constitutes, in Erbakan's mind, the essence of political activity and the position Muslims take in accordance with this objective as active agents, is critical.[16] Thus, Erbakan said the greatest struggle against the Zionist threat, "which tries to turn Muslims into slaves who only pray", lies in the heart of politics.[17] He did not see politics as coincidental. He believed that all kinds of pressure, oppression and injustice would be eliminated with the efforts of believers. The approaches Erbakan mentioned concerning education, culture, trade, industry, domestic polity, and foreign policy were also built around similar principles.

The political model Erbakan developed, in his own words, emerged as an objection, an opposition to the journey toward Westernization. Journalist Fehmi Çalmuk defines Erbakan's objections as:

---

[15] Necmettin Erbakan, "Medeniyet Davamız," *Davam*, MGV Yayınları, Ankara 2013, pp. 174-175.
[16] Türk, *Muktedir, Türk Sağ Geleneği ve Recep Tayyip Erdoğan*, p. 164.
[17] Necmettin Erbakan, "Yaratılış ve İnsan," *Davam*, MGV Yayınları, Ankara 2014, pp. 26-31.

In contrast to Republican elites' associating the Ottoman Empire's collapse with its inability to adapt to industrialization and religion, Erbakan associates this setback to detachment from religious life. It is because of this that the National Outlook, the political identity brought forward by Erbakan, implies both indigenousness and religiousness. The National Outlook's claims to provide a religious and "local" view to every facet of life from politics to current affairs and industrialization to education. Its emphasis on indigenousness is a unique aspect of Erbakan's movement that distinguishes it from other fundamentalist movements.[18]

Erbakan's harsh criticism of the AK Party and Erdoğan until 2007 notwithstanding, it would not be wrong to make the observation that Erdoğan's indigenousness and nationalness-based discourse politics, which he centralized especially after 2009-2010, and his principle of raising religious youth, bears great similarities to Erbakan's National Outlook philosophy. In this context, analyzing Erdoğan independent of Erbakan and the National Outlook is impossible.

Running for Beyoğlu Municipality Mayor in 1989

Despite being the representative of the intra-party reformists, Erdoğan continued to remain sincere to Erbakan. His objective in leading the reformist movement was a reaction to the political tone and the party's big shots that led to the inability of its political movement to produce a realistic solution policy – close to realpolitik – to the problems of life. Erdoğan, who saw that Erbakan's idealistic and utopic political model was closed to change, steered toward a new course in

---

[18] Fehmi Çalmuk, "Necmettin Erbakan," *Modern Türkiye'de Siyasî Düşünce: İslâmcılık*, İletişim Yayınları, Istanbul 2014, Vol. 6, p. 554.

the early 2000s and, even though he was at odds with the tradition from which he emerged, he succeeded in having the National Outlook philosophy accepted by the perception of the century in a modernization that was in sync with the reality of life, dealing a great blow to the established political culture that was based on controlling the people, which Erbakan described as controlled democracy[19]. Prior to the 1989 local elections, despite the objections of the headquarters and the provincial office, Erdoğan ran for mayor again. His choice of district was Beyoğlu, which the Welfare Party lost in the previous elections by a landslide. Erdoğan explains his candidacy process as follows:

> I applied to run for Beyoğlu Municipality mayor. I saw these elections as an opportunity because I believed the votes we received as the RP to date was a lot under the votes we should be winning. People want to vote for us, but the invisible wall between us prevented us from building a relationship with one another. We just couldn't seem to tear down these walls ever since the 1970s. If we could somehow find a way to build relations with the public, the wall would come down and we would be Turkey's leading party. By taking part in this election, in a sense, I wanted to prove my idea and show that the wall standing between the public and us is indeed not indestructible.[20]

In the Beyoğlu Municipal elections, women once again became visible after the 1985 congress. Women taking an active role in politics and attending workshops was a first in the National Outlook tradition, and hence, it was not welcomed. As a witness of the era, Hüseyin Besli said, "The change in the National Outlook is opposed by significant

---

[19] Necmettin Erbakan, "Türkiye'nin Meseleleri ve Çözümleri", *Erbakan Külliyatı*, Vol. 2, comp. M. M. Uzun, MGV Yayınları, Ankara 2013, p. 383.
[20] Besli-Özbay, *Bir Liderin Doğuşu Recep Tayyip Erdoğan*, p. 43.

names in the party."[21] The traditional group's objections did not concern the likelihood of women's failure in politics, but the problem of whether the implementations of the reformist movement, which was gaining increasing visibility and supporters in the party by the day, were permissible according to conventional Islamic procedures and principles. As intra-party jurisprudence debates were ongoing behind closed doors, Erdoğan continued with his campaign operations with the utmost speed. Without taking heed of the debates, he enabled women to participate in campaign operations on the ground. Journalist Sibel Eraslan, who joined the Welfare Party ranks upon Erdoğan's suggestion, ensured the establishment of the women's branch in 1989. Eraslan, who was educated in law, explained the period of change that allowed women to become organized within the party as follows:

> After graduation, Mr. Tayyip [Erdoğan] invited me in 1989 to the Welfare Party's Istanbul Headquarters for tea. I was unable to practice my profession as I wore the headscarf; I had free time on my hands. I left the party to which I came to drink tea to launch the women's branch operations. Until then, women actually working in the National Outlook tradition were unseen. The objective of the new project drawn up by Bahri Zengin and Tayyip Erdoğan was for the women's branch to be established and work with the organization network. Women who were university graduates would somehow meet with religious women who were not very used to leaving their homes and, like the sleeping giant, the women's dynamo would start working. ... The women's project launched in Istanbul by Mr. Tayyip resonated throughout the country and the women's organization

---

[21] Besli-Özbay, *Bir Liderin Doğuşu Recep Tayyip Erdoğan*, p. 44.

operations that kicked off in 1989 resulted in a massive boost in votes in the 1994 local elections.[22]

The architects of the party's unpredictable victory in the elections were women. Erdoğan explained the process as follows:

> While women determined their areas of duty, we had to pay attention to the worldviews and lifestyles of the people living in the region. The presence of a homogenous structure is out of question in the place we call Beyoğlu. Our sisters in chadors who carried out operations in Okmeydanı and achieved success could not possibly be as successful on İstiklal Avenue or in suburbs like Cihangir and Tophane. In those areas, we hence tasked our non-hijabi sisters. Similarly, we asked our bearded brothers as well as those wearing shalvar to avoid joining the convoys we would position in those areas. Some were upset and cried. I told them that them being upset and crying would upset me as well – greatly so. I said please be patient. Trust me about what I will do and how I will do it and obey my instructions. You will see, we will be the ones laughing at the end of it all.[23]

It is clear from the above statements that pragmatism, which Erdoğan has continued to resort to time and again throughout his political career as an important way out, played an effective role in politics before the 1990s. In upcoming sections, Erdoğan's pragmatism will be studied in greater detail with examples. The process of Erdoğan's candidacy for Beyoğlu mayor was the period in which he was almost declared a disbeliever by the traditionalist faction. While the traditionalists categorized the women working on the ground during the campaign period as non-hijabis and hijabi, a *Le Monde* journalist who was following Erdoğan's election cam-

---

[22]   Besli, and Özbay, *Bir Liderin Doğuşu Recep Tayyip Erdoğan*, p. 65.
[23]   Besli, and Özbay, *Bir Liderin Doğuşu Recep Tayyip Erdoğan*, P. 47.

paign, as though he was aware of the reformist-traditionalist debates and Erdoğan's conservative democrat stance – by
which he would identify himself in the future – wrote: "This
young candidate from the Islamist Welfare Party, who appears to be a 'social democrat', should be followed closely."[24]

On March 26, 1989, the people headed to the ballot box-
es. Erdoğan, who carried out an intense campaign in Beyoğlu,
lost despite receiving 22.83 percent of the vote to Social Democratic People's Party (SHP) candidate Hüseyin Aslan, who won
with 29.29 percent of the vote.[25] Erdoğan's tone, discourse, and
political model in the campaign were promising in terms of
garnering public response in the future. This new model Erdoğan developed by standing up to all criticism, helped increase
the Welfare Party's votes in the Beyoğlu district in the 1984
local elections, which previously stood at 17.71 percent. The
party traditionalists closely followed the developments. Despite facing defeat in the election, Erdoğan and his party gained
from the process. Erdoğan tried his luck again in the October
20, 1991 parliamentary elections. Winning the elections, he received his summary of proceedings. However, due to the electoral system based on the preferential vote principle that was
adopted for the first time,[26] Mustafa Baş, who ranked lower on

---

[24] Besli-Özbay, *Bir Liderin Doğuşu Recep Tayyip Erdoğan*, p. 53.
[25] eski.yerelnet.org.tr/secimler/il_secim.php?ilid=34&yil=1989.
[26] "The preferential vote principles was introduced into the Turkish voting system with
Law No. 306, dated May 25, 1961. However, it has been altered a few times. In this
procedure, a voter cannot make any changes to the candidates on a party's list. Instead, voter make their choice among candidates by placing a special mark (like an X)
specified by the law across the names on the list of candidates presented to them. According to Parliamentary Election Law Article 35, in order for the preferential votes
to change the ranking on the party list and to be taken into account, the valid number
of votes given to the party in that election must be no less than 25%. Otherwise, those
elected from that party are considered elected in accordance with their order on the
party list. In the event the preference marks between the two candidates are equal, the
candidate who is in a higher position on the party list is elected. Since the preference
method takes into consideration the voter's tendency, it was a democratic development. However, that it was bound by certain conditions and that voters were generally
unwilling to vote, did not yield the result expected from this method. However, the

the list, objected to the results. In the review following his objection, it was found that Erdoğan received 9,000 preferential
votes while Baş received 13,000, and thus, Erdoğan's summary
of proceedings was cancelled. Hence, Baş, also from the Welfare Party, won the fight he started against Erdoğan and became a deputy.[27] Erdoğan failed once again to achieve the result he desired from the ballot box and the traditionalists in the
party targeted him. The headquarters keeping silent in the face
of this situation that occurred despite the use of preferential
votes being officially banned ahead of the elections, was understood as the anti-Erdoğan group in the party dominating Erbakan's close circle. Another important detail was noticed once
the election results were announced. The Welfare Party, representative of the conservative, Islamist political movement, increased its vote of 8.57 percent in the 1986 parliamentary elections to 20.01 percent,[28] marking the start of days filled with
concern and fear for the future from secular circles. Journalist
Ruşen Çakır, a close follower of Erdoğan and the Welfare Party, interpreted Erdoğan not being elected as deputy in the 1991
elections as an important fracture in politics:

> I had the opportunity to see that the National Outlook tradi-
> tion, which is generally undermined and ignored, is actually on
> a rise. The majority of those cadres later left their mark on Tur-
> key. ... Recep Tayyip Erdoğan, who left his position as RP Istan-
> bul provincial head and ran as a candidate, was in actuality elect-

tendency in direction of preferential votes being used in the 19th Term Parliamentary
General Election on October 20, 1991 was sensed, and that is what happened. That
the required vote rate to take into account the preferential votes in this term election
dropped to 15% was also a factor that drove voters to use preferential votes. However, the preferential vote principle was later lifted." Professor Burhan Kuzu, "Nasıl
Bir Seçim Sistemi: Siyasî Parti Görüşleri Adalet ve Kalkınma Partisi," http://www.
anayasa.gov.tr/files/pdf/anayasa_yargisi/anyarg23/kuzu.pdf.

[27] Soner Yalçın, *Kayıp Sicil: Erdoğan'ın Çahnan Dosyası*, Kırmızı Kedi, Istanbul 2014,
p. 126.

[28] Yüksek Seçim Kurulu Kararı, *Resmî Gazete*, issue 21038, pp 34-35, November 1,
1991.

ed as Istanbul deputy in 1991. However, his fellow candidate Mustafa Baş, who ranked lower, took advantage of the "preferential vote" practice founded by Özal, and hence left him behind and entered Parliament. Had Erdoğan become a deputy, the fate of politics in Turkey, primarily that of the 1994 local elections, could have changed immensely.[29]

This significant increase in the votes of a conservative-Islamist party was also the sign of an important sociological change in Turkish politics. However, it would be wrong to explain the astronomical rise in the Welfare Party's votes with a change in political discourse alone.

The reason behind National Outlook politics, which centered policies around the two important concepts of justice and honesty – which had become degenerate in the politics of the 1990s – and proposed a priority for an development economic model called Just Order for the public that had been struggling with economic turmoil, as it saw acceptance in the suburbs. This should be sought on the grounds of socio-economic and socio-political instability, which had been difficult for Turkey to overcome. Amid this context, discussing the rise in the Welfare Party's votes within the scope of the rates of migration from villages to the city and demographic change statistics adds a different perspective. This change in Turkish voters will be discussed in greater detail in upcoming sections.

Rumors that Erdoğan Was Preparing for the General Presidency

Erdoğan began to face the traditionalist wing of the National Outlook more often in the 1990s. The environment was

[29] rusencakir.com/30-YILDAN-HATIRLADIKLARIM7-20-Ekim-1991-Genel-Secimleri-Baraja-karsi-Erbakan-Turkes-ittifaki/5110.

tense before the provincial congress planned for January 11, 1992. The Central Office would veto some people on the list of 50 that the provincial organization had prepared and sent. Traders played into the hands of the claim going around that Recep Tayyip Erdoğan was preparing for the general presidency. The rumormongers' aim was clear: to create an opening between Erdoğan and Erbakan. As a result, it is not hard to guess which faction was involved in circulating rumors in the party or who had mobilized them. Bringing it to the agenda in *Cumhuriyet* newspaper, Ruşen Çakır[30] made it hard for Erdoğan to make a statement. Erdoğan asserted:

> There is obvious, insidious propaganda. One would think I am apparently preparing for the general presidency. These rumors arose after the coalition and election success. ... We have friends who are scratching at this situation. Mustafa Baş and Necdet Külünk are at the top of these. They are making a special effort to spread this rumor. ... We need to suppress this unrest. It is now our duty to bring this matter to the agenda at every opportunity. Do not hesitate to express yourselves openly at meetings and in conversations if I am not comparable to our teachers or that I am not enough.[31]

This move from Erdoğan was important in that it would leave the enthusiasm of those who wanted him to come head to head with Erbakan as National Outlook's natural leader stuck in their throat. Erdoğan did not want to give an alternative political image to that of Erbakan. He knew that power balances are asymmetrical because Erbakan was a domestic and national political figure who until the late 1990s could easily affect not only the National Outlook community, but

---

30 http://www.birikimdergisi.com/birikim-yazi/3956/fazilet-kongresi-demokrasi-virusu-fp-ye-de-sizdi#.WNO-BDvxg_U.

31 Besli, and Özbay, *Bir Liderin Doğuşu Recep Tayyip Erdoğan*, p. 80.

also middle-income Muslims with his idealistic discourse and service politics. At this point, it is worth mentioning the criticism of Erbakan's political Islamist identity as being an enemy of the state, the military, and the secular Republic. Erbakan respected the state despite all his criticism directed at the system. When journalists were asked about their views on the establishment of the Anatolian Federated Islamic State in Germany, he said: "Don't your time, Turkey is a unitary state. The 60 million sons of the homeland are siblings. We do not like such fabricated words like federal or federated."[32] The military did not speak in opposition. It thought that Atatürk was being exploited and made a statement explaining that it is "opposed to the issue of exploiting the issue of Atatürk."[33] It was not Atatürk's beliefs, but Kemalism's practices in Turkey with which he expressed discomfort. Erdoğan and the AK Party would later also use this argument. However, Erbakan's clear position could not prevent the anti-democratic February 28 operations of Kemalist circles that were uncomfortable with the unexpected rise of the National Outlook, using opposition to Atatürk and the Republic as justification. The AK Party and Erdoğan experienced similar interventions up to 2007. However, the success of the AK Party and Erdoğan to parry the interventions, although just barely, is based on a fundamental feature of the characters of the two political leaders. The main difference that set Erbakan and Erdoğan apart was that Erbakan was the most idealist whereas Erdoğan was, and is, the extreme pragmatist leader. It can be concluded that Erdoğan is incomparable to Erbakan as much as he is a target-oriented politician when the practices over the past 15 years are included with the politi-

---

[32] Necmettin Erbakan, "Kahramanmaraş Refah'la Bütünleşmiş," June 28, 1993, *Erbakan Külliyatı*, vol. 5, M. M. Uzun (ed.), MGV Yayınları, Ankara 2013, p. 348.
[33] Türk, *Muktedir, Türk Sağ Geleneği ve Recep Tayyip Erdoğan*, p. 196.

cal model that puts pragmatism before idealism with charismatic leadership.

Professor Yasin Aktay explains this feature for Erdoğan with the help of Ibn Khaldun's concept of *asabiyyah*. He defines Erdoğan's charisma, which represents energy of intellect and emotional concentration generated by severe conditions of crisis, as a fortune in terms of Turkish politics against the modern bureaucracy that tries to bury alive a leadership with charisma that motivates them and excites organizations.[34] However, the anti-Erdoğan opposition,[35] which became clear in politics in the second half of the 1990s, that is, laicist-Kemalist opponents, presented propaganda accusing him of one-man rule during his time as prime minister. Holding the tradition that owes its existence to the many years of politics of "one man" to Erdoğan as "one man" is as tragicomic as it is a worrisome approach on behalf of Turkish politics. Journalist Tanıl Bora likes to define this process as Erdoğanism and present his political doctrine, which he calls Erdoğanism, by equating it with Putinism and the Orban regime in Hungary. As Bora has done, it is necessary to search with a strong skill analysis for the ideological basis for the justification for equating Erdoğan with Putin. It can be said that Erdoğan's new discourse policy developed in diplomacy and political language after 2011 is the basis for such a development. However, accusing Erdoğan of dictatorship and even equating it to marginal examples, as well as being trapped in vicious ideological stereotypes, turns into an argument on which Erdoğan would also base his opposition to the West. Despite Erdoğan's change in discourse, it is not possible to read the opposition in the West independently from the dis-

---

[34] Tanıl Bora, *Cereyanlar, Türkiye'de Siyasî İdeolojiler*, İletişim Yayınları, Istanbul 2017, p. 504.
[35] ibid., p. 505.

courses of political Islam. Since a detailed analysis of the reasons for the opposition to Erdoğan in Turkish politics with the fear of Erdoğan in the West will be discussed in the Political Mathematics section, let us focus on Erdoğan's candidacy for Istanbul Metropolitan Mayor for now.

Intra-Party Objections

The claims that Erdoğan was preparing for the general presidency forced the intra-party opposition to be vigilant against Erdoğan at all times. There also were debates on candidates before the local elections held on March 27, 1994. The Welfare Party, which nominated Bahri Zengin for the 1989 local elections, remained at 10.48 percent[36] with 238,745 votes, led in the Istanbul Metropolitan Municipality, the hardest to win. For that reason, organizations did not want to spend a lot of work for a province that "cannot be won". The party big shots who determined the candidates for Istanbul were accused of being involved. The nominees were Ali Coşkun, Nevzat Yalçıntaş, Temel Karamollaoğlu, and Veysel Eroğlu.[37] It would not be possible for the Welfare Party to win the election with those mentioned by the media such as Zülfü Livaneli, Bedrettin Dalan, and İhsan Kesici. Erdoğan and his team resorted to openly expressing their discomfort concerning this tendency of the Central Office. Ali Taşkıran, a member of Erdoğan's innovative team, at the provincial meeting on March 20, 1993, took the floor and said: "R. Tayyip Erdoğan is also named in a newspaper report on the 1994 metropolitan mayoral candidates. So let's show our candidates without wasting our time. Feyzullah Kıyıklık already said at a meeting that our candidate

---

[36] yerelnet.org.tr/belediyeler/belediye_secimsonuclari.php?yil=1989&belediye-id=128393.
[37] Taha Akyol, "Belediye Görüntüleri", *Milliyet* gazetesi, p. 17, December 28, 1993.

is R. Tayyip Erdoğan. My candidate is R. Tayyip Erdoğan."[38] The fact that Erdoğan's name came to the forefront in the media allowed Erdoğan, who had more support from the base compared to the other candidates in the party, to surefootedly reach the target. However, the ongoing debates centered on *Millî Gazete* increased and Erdoğan turned into an important figure that drew society's attention as much as the rival candidates. Journalist Çakır, who was closely following National Outlook's politics, wrote at that time:

> Meanwhile, the country was in the atmosphere of local elections and it was not possible to predict what the RP could have done in the midterm elections. In fact, without want for conjecture, the RP came from being ignored. But despite the RP's massive media, it even came to some extent through its sabotage. The innovative movement led by Erdoğan played a key role in the rise of the RP. Innovative RP members who emphasized the strategy of leaving the traditional approach that can be summarized as a call to the mosque community by the National Outlook movement, addressing all segments of society, attracted attention by making party and election studies even in discotheques, even in brothels. But the traditionalist wing in the party was uncomfortable. I just had an interview with Sadık Albayrak, the head writer of Millî Gazete, on the days when people such as former model Gülay Pınarbaşı and open-minded pharmacist Filiz Ergün joined Erdoğan's party in the ceremony. In this statement, headlined 'Virus pandemic in RP,' Albayrak described this transfer as viruses that leaked into the Welfare Party computer and said that this computer could easily beat these viruses.[39]

---

[38] Besli-Özbay, *Bir Liderin Doğuşu Recep Tayyip Erdoğan*, p. 99.
[39] http://rusencakir.com/30-YILDAN-HATIRLADIKLARIM8-27-Mart-1994-ye-rel-secimleri-Medyaya-ragmen-ve-medya-sayesinde-RPnin-zaferi/5118.

ANAP's Ali Coşkun, who was in the process of getting ready to move to the Welfare Party, put up his name for nomination, reducing Erdoğan's chances. However, Erbakan took the reactions from the base into consideration despite the objection of party big shots. From the day it was founded, this burning model of populist politics conducted through the National Outlook tradition with the momentum Erdoğan won for the party to the point of taking the Istanbul Metropolitan Municipality, the formation of a consciousness and belief in this direction in the base was in Erdoğan's favor. As the discussions continued, the party's opposing veins were afraid and Erbakan, who saw his political future, abandoned his own candidates and went with Erdoğan. On January 15, 1994, Welfare Party Chairman Necmettin Erbakan announced Recep Tayyip Erdoğan as his party's mayoral candidate for the Istanbul Metropolitan Municipality.[40]

Erdoğan's candidacy was read as the victory of the Istanbul provincial organization. But before that, on October 10, 1993, Erdoğan experienced an important step leading to his candidacy. The Welfare Party's Ordinary Grand Congress convened. That Abdullah Gül and Recep Tayyip Erdoğan were elected to the membership of the MKYK at the congress was a remarkable development. Erbakan's speech at the congress was even more striking. The fact that Erbakan responded to the problems related to the agenda with a new political language was a remarkable development in terms of Turkish politics, saying that "everybody should be able to use their mother tongue", regarding Kurds, who were marginalized by the political parties at the time.[41] Erbakan's first sign was the first shot, which Erdoğan would later present to the

---

[40] http://www.aljazeera.com.tr/portre/portre-recep-tayyip-erdogan.
[41] http://www.surecanaliz.org/tr/article/sener-akturk-kurt-cozumu-acilim-in-sebebleri-sonuclari-ve-sinirlari.

public for the Kurdish Opening in National Outlook policy with the motto of "let mothers not cry". Erbakan's statement on speaking one's mother tongue hit the country's agenda like a bomb. It is clear that this unexpected development was the behind-the-scenes effect of the innovative wing. Eyes were once again turned to Erdoğan. Hüseyin Besli described the developments that took place at that time:

> Although the National Outlook movement is perceived as a monolithic movement when viewed from the outside, it is a political formation that actually contains different thoughts and attitudes in itself and incompatible understandings. Although the top management of the National Outlook movement is composed of people who require strict obedience to instructions, do not tolerate different views, and do not intimidate themselves into questioning, the center of this center, such as R. Tayyip Erdoğan and the Istanbul organization he is heading, does not approve of the "Jacobean", and a vein of importance has always been there. Although this vessel is mostly strangled and blocked, it has sometimes made outgoing conflicts as if it were in the 1978 congress, and now it has become compulsory in the management of the party, without any conflict with the main body, and with some acceleration in the outside world. Erbakan's speech reflects the effects of this process.[42]

Erdoğan Shown as a Candidate

There was only one day left until the end of the nomination period for the March 27, 1994 general elections of local authorities. Erdoğan, who participated in a program of the Rizeliler Foundation, finally got the phone call he expected. It was Ahmet Tekdal. He congratulated him for the final decision on

---

[42] Besli-Özbay, *Bir Liderin Doğuşu Recep Tayyip Erdoğan*, p. 110.

his nomination. Thus, Erdoğan's years began to make their mark on Turkish politics. Critics in the media targeted the political views expressed and election promises made in the presidential candidate nomination process. If the president is elected, it was claimed that the *haremlik-selamhk*[43] practice of gender segregation would be applied to public transportation in accordance with Sharia law, drinking places in Istanbul would be closed, and the sale of liquor would be prohibited. The fear of Erdoğan in society was pumped through religious conservative identity. In fact, Erdoğan's chances against media opponents İlhan Kesici, Zülfi Livaneli, and Bedrettin Dalan were little if any. Nevertheless, the socially accepted political discourse and campaign language disturbed the central media. Erdoğan and his team started working at top speed.

The company that would run the election campaign was Kule Communications, established with the cooperation of communications teacher Nabi Avcı, television personality Özkul Eren, and musician Özhan Eren. Avcı explained the communication strategy they carried out at that time with the concept of Edward Lorenz's *butterfly effect*. The original theory is based on the idea that a small development anywhere in the world can be reflected at unexpected scales in different regions. It mentions that even a flutter of a wing can change

---

[43] The accusations directed against Erdoğan during his Istanbul Municipalality mayoral candidacy continued after the AK Party was established. 2008/1 (Political Party Closure) 30.7.2008 "In order to participate collectively in the funerals of the religious sects from the practice of harem-selâmlık in party meetings, the fundamentalist associations under the name of the conference, the panel, the following statements were made in the justification decision of the closure case against the AK Party in 2008: to be seen as a gathering at the meetings they held, to not crowd the women, to make imams walking around the mosque during the month of Ramadan in the capacity of the mayor, to exploit our holy religion in this way, has become one of the daily activities of the defendant party." Public officials, encouraged by the race to abuse the AK Party at every level from the prime minister to the mayor, gave speeches with religious motifs in every way from fountain openings to forest fires, published circulars, sacrificed animals on the apron of our international airports, and sponsored sectarian meetings.

the state of the atmosphere completely after a certain peri-od of time. Avcı believes that political discourse built on the basis of Erdoğan's honesty and piety and embracing society would create a butterfly effect in politics. But the biggest ob-stacle was the central media of the period. While explaining the attitude of the media at the time, Avcı said, "The media thinks that the election will pass between İlhan Kesici, Zülfü Livaneli, and Bedrettin Dalan, seeing us as a garnish."[44] The central media encoded Erdoğan and the Welfare Party as the weakest link in the election.[45] However, the *Hürriyet* news-paper on February 18 published the headline: "Wow Tayyip Ağa Wow",[46] on the understanding that Erdoğan was not an easy mark, but still attackers increased in the days to follow.

Erdoğan gained the people's sympathy throughout the campaign. His closeness, warmth and sincerity were different for the public. It drew a different profile than usual politicians thanks to his charismatic leadership. On his first impres-sions of Erdoğan, man of letters and writer Bashir Ayvazoğ-lu, wrote:

> You know there are some people from whom on first sight your blood warms – Mr. Tayyip was like that. In a state in which at no time in my life had I felt a closeness to the Welfare Party, but that day I perceived a spiritual relationship between myself and Mr. Tayyip. Perhaps it was an illusion that arises from his cha-risma. Yes, Mr. Tayyip was a young and charismatic man, and he was saying a mouthful. The Kasımpaşa character wrapped

---

[44] Butterfly Effect: The small change in the initial data of a system and its ability to produce large, unpredictable results. One of the works of Edward N. Lorenz is re-lated to chaos theory. He was later famed for the example of weather conditions in which the flutter of a butterfly wing in the Amazon Forest could cause a storm in the U.S. and the flap of a butterfly wing could lead to the formation of a hurricane that could travel around half the world.

[45] Besli, and Özbay, *Bir Liderin Doğuşu Recep Tayyip Erdoğan*, p. 123.

[46] *Hürriyet* gazetesi, February 18, 1994.

over his reading and the Welfare Party, even though he was sticking his head out from the empty spaces. Undoubtedly this side and old footballer showed him a wide range of sympathy and he immediately composed himself.[47]

The Kule Communications team started to make progress for the campaign. Even though public opinion research companies announced Erdoğan in last place for the election, the survey results from Gallup were different. The company prepared an attention-grabbing report on Erdoğan's astronomical rise, but the media ignored it. After the results of the elections were announced, Nabi Avcı said, "The results of the elections were exactly the same as those of *Milli Gazete*. Not only the results, but even the votes cast were guessed correctly."[48] The slogan the communications team was planning to use on the last day of the campaign was, "OK, God willing". On March 27, 1994, the public went to the polls to the accompaniment of the song "The Time of Welfare Has Arrived", which Özhan Eren had recorded. As the results continued to arrive in the late hours, the Welfare Party and its supporters were rejoicing and astonishment held sway across the entire country. The reason for this astonishment was that representatives of a political line defined as conservative-Islamist would govern the two big, important cities of Istanbul and Ankara. The results were regarded as a sustaining defeat in secular circles. Political language development was an important factor that brought electoral victory – reaching working people in the slums, breaking the image of the Welfare Party as the party of hijabs and beards.[49] The next day, Erbakan told members of the press: "March 27 is the Welfare

---

[47] Beşir Ayvazoğlu, *Sîretler ve Sûretler*, Ötüken Neşriyat, Istanbul 1999, p. 220.

[48] Besli, and Özbay, *Bir Liderin Doğuşu Recep Tayyip Erdoğan*, p. 126.

[49] Mehmet Ali Birand, and Reyhan Yıldız, *Son Darbe 28 Şubat*, Doğan Kitap, Istanbul 2012, p. 65.

Party's own victory. The RP has been brought to power. It is clear that the new Turkey is now the Just Order, the National Outlook Turkey."[50] After Erbakan's declarations, secular circles were too sorry to say a single thing. The Republicans and Kemalists whose head was taken by SHP and DSP interpreted the inescapable power march of National Outlook politics as the days when danger bells rang. Instead of analyzing the socio-political and socio-economic change underlying the election results, secular circles and the central media called the military to duty by calling them reactionary with news of a regime threat. Later, some Welfare Party politicians were being driven away and who were "blood will flow, it will be wonderful"[51] and "Mustafa from Salonika, bastard"[52] types spouting nonsense that increased the air of disturbance in society, whereas those who were preparing an operation on conservative and Islamist politics with those justifications led to the process of the post-modern coup Turkey experienced on February 28.

The Appearance of Islamist Politics

Erdoğan, who had not been given the chance during the campaign, began his duty as Istanbul's new şehremini.[53] The first session of the Municipal Assembly was opened with a reading of the Fatiha.[54] This unexpected success was also an important victory for the innovative wing of the party against the tradi-

---

[50]   Milliyet newspaper, March 28, 1994.

[51]   Günseli Önay, "Kan dökülecek, fıstık gibi olacak," May 9, 1997; http://arsiv.sabah.com.tr/1997/05/09/f08.html.

[52]   Milliyet gazetesi, "Hasan Mezarcı, Atatürk'e saldırdı," July 10, 1997.

[53]   Election results: Welfare Party-Recep Tayyip Erdoğan: 25.19% (973,704); ANAP-İlhan Kesici: 22.14% (855,897); SHP-Zülfiye Livaneli: 20.30% (784,693); DYP-Bedrettin Dalan: 15.46% (597,461); DSP-Necdet Özkan: 12.38% (478,612); MHP-Ahmet Vefik Alp: 1.87% (72.211); CHP-Ertuğrul Günay: 1.4% (54.028).

[54]   Turan Yılmaz, Tayyip: Kasımpaşa'dan Siyasetin Ön Saflarına, Ümit Yayıncılık, Ankara, 2001, pp. 84-85.

tionalists. The election victories in Istanbul and Ankara were also indicative of intense conflicts the two wings of the party would experience moving forward. Erbakan faced off against Mehmet Ali Birand and Can Dündar on Show TV to evaluate the election results. To Birand's question: "Will Welfare Party municipalities not have a war for power?" Erbakan answered: "No, no war will happen, because the present government is already insolvent. You know the proverb physician heal thyself. Our cadre of believers in Istanbul is completely different. This pious staff will come from above everything."[55] The support that Erbakan gave to Erdoğan and his team disturbed the traditionalists.

This momentum Erdoğan and the Welfare Party caught in the 1994 local elections attracted attention from other political parties, as well. In particular, ANAP and the DYP, the radical parties of right-wing politics, tried to understand and make sense of the situation after their routing. Then ANAP Chairman Ahmet Mesut Yılmaz considered the success of conservative Islamist politics as a consequence of the reappearance of conservatism and returning to religion all over the world after the collapse of communism. According to Yılmaz, the process depicted in *God Is Back*[56] was also greatly represented in Turkey, which filled the Welfare Party's sails.[57] Journalist Ali Bayramoğlu strained to explain that the astronomical rise the Welfare Party's votes experienced falls on the political right.

> I think the RP's rise is for two reasons. One of them is the extreme tension between the center-right parties. That is, young people

---

[55] https://www.youtube.com/watch?v=Mffx_KREx5A.

[56] John Micklethwait, and Arian Wooldridge, *God is Back: How the Global Revival of Faith is Changing the World*, Penguin Press, New York 2009. Micklethwait and Wooldridge argue that religion/belief in the world awakened toward the end of the 20th century as a rebellion against secularism.

[57] Birand-Yıldız, *Son Darbe 28 Şubat*, p. 66.

who emerged after Özal and Demirel are not able to manage politics well. And I tell you that, in 1994, the sects and religious communities that had voted for the center-right, for the first time in the tradition of the National Salvation Party, the National Order Party, voted for the RP. This is a very important point.[58]

Cause-Conclusion: Haphazard Politics and Unplanned Urbanization

Istanbul is a city that has struggled with major problems due to populist political discourses in the 1990s. It was a place where life had become unlivable as the result of migration from the village to the city, the mushrooming slums and traffic, and infrastructural problems that had reached life-constricting dimensions, air pollution had become a health threat, municipal water did not flow from taps, and garbage had been turned into barricades. Corruption at the İSKİ municipal water administration, which was on everyone's tongues, was the language of all of Turkey, not just Istanbul. It was no longer easily recognized that wide swaths of the public were in search of a safe port as long as the corruption of politics was extensively felt in life. In such a process of searching, along with the Just Order paradigm, an economic program offered to the public through the clean staff of the Welfare Party was an important factor that increased the social legitimacy of the party and its candidates. Erik Jan Zürcher views the Welfare Party and Erdoğan's victory in the 1994 local elections as "the greatest challenge."[59] That the Welfare Party was able to get a 17 percent of the vote and formed a coalition with the MHP in 1991, and then in the 1994 elections received 19.1 percent of the vote on

---

[58] ibid., p. 62.
[59] Zürcher, *Modernleşen Türkiye'nin Tarihi*, p. 424.

its own, can be read as an increase in Islamist votes. Zürcher also takes into consideration the disciplined organizing of the party's innovative wing as much as the party's Just Order program. The rise of the National Outlook drew attention to rising socio-economic causes. The Welfare Party was no longer the party of small business owners; it was the spokesman of the poorest inhabitants of the enormous urban regions emerging through the unification of many neighboring towns. According to Zürcher, the results of the election were an indicator of the importance in Turkey of winning the "amphibious voter" phenomenon similar to many other European countries. This trend would be even more pronounced in the next decade. The secular intellectuals in the big cities panicked after the RP seized the cities, but after a few frenzies arising from angry youth who right after the elections said that it was their turn already, the situation calmed down after a few exasperations and found a base for a *modus vivendi*[60] in cities, even at the national level, which became increasingly disturbing.[61] Commenting on the election results, journalist Çakır said that the ruling party and the central media acting with them would take the blame to the united central parties instead of realizing that a new era had started in Turkey on March 27, 1994, and that they would not accept the facts in the general elections on December 24, 1995, calling it "political obstinacy."[62]

Turkey a Disaster Area

In the early 1990s, Turkey was literally a disaster area. The economic and political tremors that followed one after the oth-

---

[60] The lifestyle that allows people with different opinions and beliefs to coexist until the fight or conflict between them is resolved.

[61] Zürcher, *Modernleşen Türkiye'nin Tarihi*, p. 425.

[62] http://rusencakir.com/30-YILDAN-HATIRLADIKLARIM8-27-Mart-1994-ye-rel-secimleri-Medyaya-ragmen-ve-medya-sayesinde-RPnin-zaferi/5118.

er, coalition governments through which stability could not be achieved, the April 5 decisions that further impoverished the people, escalating terrorism in the southeast, the Sivas massacre, the massacre of 33 people in the village of Başbağlar, the Bingöl attack in which 33 unarmed soldiers who had received their discharge papers were martyred, followed by the Kurdish question that could not be solved in any way, the unsolved murders targeting known figures that could not be prevented, the Susurluk accident, President Turgut Özal's sudden death, the leader crises in center-right politics, and the U.S.' plans to bring democracy to the Middle East as a result of Iraqi leader Saddam Hussein's invasion of Kuwait were all signs of the rough days ahead. The 1990s was a period in which right-wing politics in Turkey depleted itself while the left continued to use populist discourse despite the people, and the people hence sought new choices. Erdoğan getting on the ground at such a time with a political understanding that is relevant to all levels of society, and leading the organization of the Welfare Party (RP) cadres together with the women's branch is an important detail that drew voters' attention. Therefore, seeking the reason behind the RP, the National Outlook line, and Erdoğan's political success in the deep circumstantial conditions is the right approach.

The Unresolvable Kurdish Question

The early 1990s saw terrorism incidents increase in the country. The state changed its approach in the fight against terrorism and switched to a strategy of total war. Thus began the new era in which "Prime Minister [Tansu] Çiller would suddenly order and he would instantly fulfill [the order]"[63] – as then Chief

---

[63]   http://www.hurriyet.com.tr/geriye-o-sozler-kaldi-tak-emrediyor-sak-yapiyo-ruz-27387374.

of General Staff General Doğan Güneş explained. Prime Minister Çiller, who had previously been seeking a moderate solution to the Kurdish question, changed her attitude immediately after the death of Gendarmerie Commander General Eşref Bitlis, who was known for his pro-Kurdish initiative, on February 17, 1993, and the Bingöl massacre on May 24, 1993, was a milestone for Turkey.[64] The gendarmerie commander dying at the time he was about to expose the Kurdistan Workers' Party's (PKK) international relations traffic was a major breaking point for the Kurdish question. Years later, the letter Bitlis had sent to President Özal would help reveal the secret behind his death. In the letter Gen. Bitlis sent to Özal, he said: "Dear President, you should intervene in this matter, otherwise we might be faced with a serious risk and threats in the region that cannot be stopped. ... The American war jets taking off from İncirlik Air Base were discovered to distribute aid to the PKK". Bitlis also included images and wireless conversations documenting that certain commanders in the Poised Hammer forces were helping the PKK terrorist organization.[65] Soon after the letter reached Özal, General Bitlis was assassinated, but it was recorded as pilot error. Based on Bitlis' advice, Özal gathered the National Security Council (MGK) in August 1992 for an extraordinary assembly in Diyarbakır. Following the assembly that was held on August 27, a 27-article memorandum was issued. The memorandum bore traces of the "Codename: Citadel" plan and emphasized that "the fight against terrorism would be carried out within the scope of law" and operations would be conducted "to raise the quality of life of the people of the region."[66] Similar advice stood out in the final declarations of the MGK meetings in the following months.

---

[64] Gökhan Atılgan-Cenk Saraçoğlu-Ateş Uslu, *Osmanlı'dan Günümüze Türkiye'de Siyasal Hayat*, Yordam Kitap, İstanbul 2015, p. 848.

[65] "Eşref Bitlis'ten Özal'a Son Mektup", http://www.ntv.com.tr/turkiye/esref-bitlisten-ozala-son-mektup,Kh57CMBp2EKPtdupFftg5g.

[66] *Milliyet* gazetesi, August 28, 1992, http://gazetearsivi.milliyet.com.tr/Arsiv/1992/08/27.

After General Bitlis' assassination, similar questions were also raised concerning Özal's death. The sudden death of President Özal, who sent a special delegation of five to Damascus shortly before he died, and who was an advocate of extending the cease-fire declared by the PKK and finding a peaceful solution to the problem, wrecked havoc on Turkey's agenda. Thus, Özal's secret operations aimed at the Kurdish initiative were buried for eternity along with him. Hatip Dicle, who spoke on the process years later, said:

> We met with Öcalan and he had said something interesting to us back then. He had said: "Go and give my condolences to his family. We greatly valued Özal. Özal had relentlessly fought against us, but still we highly regarded his last outbursts; we considered them as historic outbursts and declared the cease-fire as he requested. ... Some forces were not pleased about Özal's outbursts and the resolution of the Kurdish question, and Özal was most likely killed."[67]

In his 2012 study, *Mezopotamya Ekspresi* (Mesopotamia Express), journalist Cengiz Çandar wrote about his suspicions concerning Özal's death:

> It was no secret that Turgut Özal was making efforts to solve the Kurdish question. It was also a common opinion that there were forces that did not want the problem to be solved. That the forces in question may have prevented the solution of the problem by eliminating Turgut Özal seemed, to many, like a significant and valid explanation. ... Turgut Özal had not died; he was killed while he was about to solve the Kurdish question. Though, it may never be known, but 33 unarmed soldiers being killed in an ambush on the Bingöl highway on May 24, 1993 – less than 40 days after his death – saw the end of the cease-fire. What Turgut

[67] Birand, and Yıldız, *Son Darbe 28 Şubat*, p. 20.

Özal feared the most and had mentioned to me in his last words had happened. Terrorism returned worse [than before].[68]

Journalist Uğur Mumcu was another whose murder is unsolved as a sacrifice on the path to solving the Kurdish question. Mumcu was an important figure on the left. He was killed in the explosion of C-4 type plastic explosives in his car in front of his Ankara home on January 24, 1993. The suspicion that Mumcu was killed due to certain claims he made in relation to PKK leader Abdullah Öcalan working for Turkey's MİT intelligence agency at one time in his "Kürt Raporu" (Kurdish Report) gained significance. Even though the politicians of the time had said, "Solving the murder is a matter of honor for the state,"[69] Mumcu's murder case joined the other unsolved cases. Mumcu had left Turkey to deal with a period of trauma difficult to overcome for long years with the suspicious deaths of General Bitlis and President Özal while they were seeking a solution to the Kurdish question.

Similar breaking points in the Kurdish issue continued during Erdoğan's time as prime ministry and on to his time as president. The reconciliation period Erdoğan started with the goal of "ending mothers' tears" despite all the political risks, would, through the inconceivable abuses of terrorist partisans, fail again, and Turkey, having come so close to a solution, would continue to be shaken by bad news as in the past.

Rising Value: Welfare Politics

A negative atmosphere was apparent in the December 24, 1995 parliamentary election as well. Yet, Turkey had entered

---

[68] Cengiz Çandar, *Mezopotamya Ekspresi / Bir Tarih Yolculuğu*, İletişim Yayınları, Istanbul 2012, p. 28.
[69] http://www.radikal.com.tr/politika/16-yilinda-mumcu-suikasti-hl-sir-918404/.

a new period in which history was rewritten and the political cards had been reshuffled. When the election results were announced, the Welfare Party won with 21.38 percent of the vote. It was now the determining power in Parliament with 159 deputies.[70] The Welfare Party increased its votes in the general elections held about two years after the local elections, not only in Istanbul and Ankara, but across Turkey. This development was considered a success for Welfare Party municipalities in Turkish politics. The increase in the popularity of conservative political Islam with this unexpected change and transformation in politics led to traumatic times in which the disease of the military regulating politics would recur, disturbing controlled democrats who were directing capable politics.

From the Slums to the Center

Despite the negation of the National Outlook movement led by Erbakan by political and economic elites ahead of September 12, it was still perceived as a structure that was controllable. However, the conflict between the RP and the sociological wave emerging from the base in the second half of the 1980s led to the association of this movement with the regime threat. This sociological wave also led the RP to form strong voter support in cities for the first time in its history, and finally pave the way for its leader to become the first Islamist prime minister. In *1960'dan Günümüze Türkiye* (Turkey from 1960 to Today), the book co-authored by Suavi Aydın and Yüksel Taşkın, the Welfare Party creating hopefulness for the future is considered the greatest success of National Outlook politics in the 1990s. The results of the ballot in which Erdoğan was elect-

---

[70] http://www.ysk.gov.tr

ed Istanbul Metropolitan Municipality mayor and the Welfare Party's political rise are interpreted as follows:

> Istanbul's new Mayor Recep Tayyip Erdoğan from the RP settled in the agenda of the public opinion to stay there. Erdoğan, who represents the young generation of the "elder" founders of the National Outlook line, stood out with his reformist dynamism regarding methods aimed at voters rather than ideologically breaking off from this line. At a time when center parties reduced politics to creating an image by minimizing their differences, the RP insisted on remaining as is and knew how to rise by attaching significance to gaining visibility in mainstream media. ... Their operation style, which led the Istanbul provincial organization to be called reformist, started to be a determining factor in the party as of the 1990s. Similar to the approach before 1980, the party was working to give its members an RP identity rather than an Islamic identity, and striving to build ties with different segments through socio-economic problems. Visiting bars, which the party members previously avoided, to promote the party, was an example of this approach that resonated most in the media.[71]

New Dispute with the Headquarters

The approach to administration Erdoğan took as mayor led to a dispute with the headquarters once again. Erdoğan wanting to work with certain figures the headquarters did not approve of or recognize increased ideological disintegration, but Erdoğan refused to step back and determined his cadre himself.

The psychological tensions between the reformists represented by Erdoğan and the traditionalists were replaced

---

[71] Suavi Aydın, and Yüksel Taşın, *1960'ten Günümüze Türkiye Tarihi*, İletişim Yayınları, Istanbul 2014, p. 415.

with a deep crisis. Şevket Kazan, Oğuzhan Asiltürk, Fehim Adak, Süleyman Arif Emre and Ali Oğuz, who were known to be close to Erbakan and were criticized as the "politburo", were accused of being the lead actors in the opposition formed against Erdoğan. The Welfare Party winning the 1995 general elections allowed intra-party matters to be put on hold. However, the coalition the Welfare Party established with the True Path Party (DYP) on June 28, 1996, did not last long and, secular circles that were disturbed by Erbakan, led Turkey into a period of trauma that they predicted to last "a millennium."

The "Pool" Formula

After coming to power, the Welfare Party made important moves in development. Through the pool budget system method it created, it helped recover the blocked economy that was on the verge of coming to a halt. The opposition welcomed the system developed by Erbakan as well.[72] Erbakan's new cooperation with Muslim countries, his visits to Far Eastern countries, and the D-8 project were critical in this context. Erdoğan in Istanbul and Mayor Melih Gökçek in Ankara implemented important projects that would change the cities' futures. However, all these development moves started to disturb secular-Kemalist groups, as the success of National Outlook cadres created displeasure among them. Interestingly, although President Süleyman Demirel traveled to Romania for the opening of Bayındır Holding Chairman Kamuran Çörtük's hotel, which was well-known for its casinos, and who was in Demirel's "fami-

---

[72] http://odatv.com/erbakanin-basarili-havuz-sistemi-neden-bir-daha-uygulanma-di-1712141200.html.

ly photo", he did not attend Erdoğan's opening of the potable water system that would revive Istanbul.[73] President Demirel's biased stance dragged Turkey to the verge of a new crisis it would struggle to overcome.

Balance Adjustment for the Military

The MGK's February 28, 1997 decision – the February 28 post-modern coup – dragged Turkey into a new political crisis. The Turkish Armed Forces (TSK) attempted to bring the government into line. The decisions at the MGK ended up being an exciting development for the mainstream media, which was disturbed by the Welfare Party's election victory. The next day, news that Prime Minister Erbakan signed the MGK's decisions "like a lamb"[74] spread across the country. National Outlook politics' natural leader was going through perhaps the toughest test in his life. Erbakan, who spoke after the meeting, gave the message, "We are in agreement with the military",[75] for the sake of not disappointing the masses that placed their hopes in National Outlook politics. However, Major General Erol Özkasnak, the MGK secretary-general of the time who referred to Çiller as "that woman", said, "The military is in agreement with those who believe in Atatürk",[76] so as to make clear the TSK's stance against Erbakan. Journalist Ahmet Hakan, who would years later write an article in *Hürriyet* titled, "Bağışla Bizi Erbakan Hoca" (Forgive Us Erbakan Hodja), showed mutiny against the injustice toward Erbakan back then:

---

[73] Interview with Mehmet Erdoğan on *Siyasî Hafıza / Eski Türkiye'den Yeni Türkiye'ye (1996-2016)* üzerine mülâkat, March 2017.
[74] http://www.milligazete.com.tr/bir_iftira_daha_son_buluyor/293177.
[75] http://arsiv.sabah.com.tr/1997/05/29/p09.html.
[76] http://www.hurriyet.com.tr/28-subatin-ustunden-14-yil-gecti-17143455.

The minutes of the February 28 National Security Council Meeting have been revealed. According to these minutes, in that historic National Security Council meeting, Erbakan hodja ... disagreed rather "immediately" to sign his name as claimed. He showed resistance instead of signing "like a lamb" as claimed. He tried to delay it instead of immediately signing it as said. He objected instead of sweating like it was written. ... Following this new situation that emerged in relation to the February 28 MGK ... [n]ow, we can only make up for it if all of Turkey came together to write a poem titled, 'Help From Erbakan Hodja's Spirituality.'[77]

The reaction briefings given by the General Staff in the summer to media representatives were effective in the mainstream media taking a military position. The price of taking a position on the side of democracy was heavy. The implication that soldiers could use weapons and then Internal Affairs Minister Meral Akşener being threatened with "impalement"[78] scared the controlled democrats. Well-known figures of mainstream media and the directors of major nongovernmental organizations made statements in support of the MGK decisions. Fetullah Gülen, who we will discuss in detail in upcoming chapters, also supported the anti-democratic practices of February 28, and said that the MGK is a constitutional institute. Journalist Ertuğrul Özkök, another person who supported the balance adjustment practices, would years later describe those days with an elitist attitude:

Everybody is talking about newspaper headlines now. People in this country started to recite national anthems in stadiums, the lights would be switched off and on in homes in this county, we

---

[77] Ahmet Hakan Coşkun, "Bağışla Bizi Erbakan Hocam," *Hürriyet*, September 26, 2013.
[78] http://www.milliyet.com.tr/o-generali-de-acikladi-gundem-1537413/.

forgot all of these. Now they are asking us to give account in relation to February 28 in relation to Hürriyet's headline, "We Will Use Arms if Necessary". The military gave a briefing to 450 people a day ago, I was there too. One of them came out and openly said, in so and so article of law number who knows what we are given the authority to use weapons.[79]

Added to the TSK's attitude, the circles doubting and concerned about the National Outlook from the very beginning, showing Erbakan and the RP as anti-regime due to the Welfare Party's rapid rise in politics and the political model of the Erdoğan-led reformists that made an impact on the people, the resulting picture is on the history of Turkish democracy. Vural Savaş, the chief public prosecutor of the Supreme Court of Appeals, took advantage of the situation and filed a claim with the Constitutional Court on May 27, 1997, requesting the permanent closure of the Welfare Party based on the claim that "it has become the center of actions in violation of the principles of secularism."[80] According to Savaş, the figures representing the Welfare Party tradition were "blood-sucking vultures."[81] This initiative seemed like the beginning of the end for Welfare Party politics, but it would turn into a new era ushering in the opportunity to raise new cadres that would shape Turkey's future politics.

It would be misleading to claim that the February 28 process was the result of the Welfare Party's excessiveness alone, and to think that it happened because of the attitudes of certain National Outlook politicians on the Constitution. The impact of political, economic and cultural elites, and opposition elites' increasingly intensifying struggles should also

---

[79] Birand, andYıldız, *Son Darbe 28 Şubat*, p. 233.
[80] Erdoğan, *Siyasî Hafıza / Eski Türkiye'den Yeni Türkiye'ye (1996-2016)*, p. 20.
[81] Aydın-Taşın, *1960'ten Günümüze Türkiye Tarihi*, p. 432

be considered as reasons behind February 28. The increase in the popularity of conservative politics that started to rise with Özal also paved the way for the formation of a new Muslim intelligentsia and Muslim bourgeoisie. Secular urbanites started to lose their privileges in education and culture, which increased their concerns that their modern lifestyles were under threat as well as their reactions to political Islam. If need be, democracy could be put on hold to eliminate this threat, which managed to come out of the ballot box each time. And that is exactly what happened.[82]

Interest in Poetry and Provoking the People to Revolt

On December 6, 1997, Erdoğan attended an outdoor meeting organized by the Welfare Party in Siirt and recited a verse from Ziya Gökalp's poem *Asker Duası* (Soldier's Prayer) poem, which is included in school textbooks. Erdoğan, who is able to activate large masses with his oratory skills, was unaware that his interest in poetry since his youth would one day cause him trouble. The minarets, bayonets, barracks, and soldiers mentioned in the poem dropped like a bombshell. His recitation was interpreted as a call for a reactionary move. During the program, Erdoğan said:

> The minarets are our bayonets, the domes our helmets / The mosques are our barracks, the believers our soldiers, even if the skies and ground cracked open, if floods, volcanoes erupted over us, we are such that our forefathers, whose faith we take pride in, never kneeled to anything frightening. What made our forefathers run from victory to victory, from Manzikert all the way to Çanakkale, the deed of Anatolia, the gate of victories, to

---

[82]   Aydın, and Taşın, *1960'ten Günümüze Türkiye Tarihi*, p. 433.

the impassable fortress of faith, is this state of unity of faith my fellow Siirt citizens are currently in.[83]

The events that took place three days after the speech would go on record in the *Siyasi Hafıza* on December 9, 1997, as follows:

> The Chief Public Prosecutor's Diyarbakır Office of the Court of State Security has started an investigation into Istanbul Metropolitan Municipality Mayor Recep Tayyip Erdoğan for reciting a poem by Ziya Gökalp in a speech he made at the outdoor meeting organized in Siirt on December 6 by the Welfare Party's Siirt Provincial Headquarters.[84]

March 20, 1998: New Memorandum

The closure case opened against the Welfare Party on May 21, 1997, followed by Necmettin Erbakan's resignation on June 18, 1997, and the transfer of DYP Chairwoman Tansu Çiller, marking the end of the RP-DYP government. The process of purging the National Outlook started with the political agility of then President Süleyman Demirel, which has been called the "Çankaya Coup" in the literature. Turkey woke up to another coalition government on June 30, 1997, with the Ahmet Mesut Yılmaz as prime minister. The power balances changed, and the Welfare Party, which was supposed to be the biggest partner in the legitimate government, was now in the position of main opposition party. In such a political atmosphere, the poem Erdoğan recited in Siirt on December 6, 1997, brought an end to his adventure as Istanbul mayor. Erdoğan's recitation of the poem was one of the reasons behind the closure of the Wel-

---

[83] *Hürriyet*, December 9, 1997.
[84] Erdoğan, *Siyasî Hafıza / Eski Türkiye'den Yeni Türkiye'ye (1996-2016)*, p. 22.

fare Party. Tough times were near, and the military, which wanted the implementation of the MGK decisions, did not give up its hold on politics. It asked the new government to be quick in implementing the laws restricting everyday life. The government led by Prime Minister Yılmaz and the military fell into conflict, however. The coalition government between the Motherland Party, Democratic Left Party, and the Democrat Turkey Party, which was formed as a junta project, paid the price for the failure to protect democracy on February 28. Chief of General Staff General İsmail Hakkı Karadayı and four commanders of the Armed Forces gave democracy another balance adjustment with a joint statement in which they said: "Fighting terrorism and reactionaryism is the TSK's legal duty. No authority can deter the TSK from this for the sake of political ambition."[85] The military was obviously not happy with the current government.

Erdoğan's Political Life Ends

It seemed impossible in this intense atmosphere for the TSK to tolerate Erbakan and Erdoğan any further. Thus, their purge from politics was expedited. On January 16, 1998, the Constitutional Court, presided over by its president, Ahmet Necdet Sezer, permanently closes the Welfare Party based on the reason that "it has become the center of activities violating the principles of secularism," the party's assets were transferred to the Treasury, and RP Chairman Erbakan and six party members were banned from politics for five years. The pro-February 28 group was steadily nearing their goal and Erbakan was successfully purged. Next

---

[85]   Birand, and Yıldız, *Son Darbe 28 Şubat*, p. 259.

was Erdoğan, who they perceived as a greater threat than Erbakan. On April 21, 1998, Diyarbakır's 3rd State Security Court (DGM) sentenced Erdoğan to one year in prison and fined of 860 TL for the crime of "openly provoking the people to animosity and enmity by pursuing class, race, religion, sect or regional differences," according to Turkish Criminal Law (TCK) 312/2. Taking into consideration Erdoğan's attitude and good behavior in court, his penalty was reduced to 10 months and a fine of 716.66 TL. As a requirement of the Law on Criminal Execution, Erdoğan spent four months in prison. Although the penalty had no legal significance, it had heavy political consequences. Having been charged based on TCK 32, which includes crimes committed against the state, Erdoğan was banned from politics for life. Following the 8th Department of the Supreme Court of Appeals' approval of the sentence on September 23, 1998, the execution of the penalty became effective.

Erdoğan's case file with the State Security Court contained the considerations of the country's reputable and elite lawmakers. Distinguished Professor Sulhi Dönmezer, who said the speech Erdoğan made in Siirt is entirely within the scope of the freedom of thought, said, "It contains no element or characteristic that indicate any propaganda quality aimed at removing the principle of secularism." Another lawmaker, Professor Uğur Alacakaptan, who believes Erdoğan was innocent, expressed his thoughts:

> Taking such legal action cannot be compatible with the principles of the state of law and freedom of thought or the principle of secularism, which is the foundation of the state of the Republic of Turkey.[86]

---

[86] Besli, and Özbay, *Bir Liderin Doğuşu Recep Tayyip Erdoğan*, p. 204.

The Media's Attitude

Mainstream media took a deep breath. The headlines were obvious: "He can't even become a [village] headman!"[87] "His Political Life is Over,"[88] "Shock penalty for Tayyip."[89] Politics was over for Erdoğan, who spread the discourse of change from within the party to the wider community and brought a breath of fresh air to conservative Islamist politics. This result, which the military and secular circles greatly welcomed, also became the quickest shortcut for the traditionalists of the National Outlook to get rid of Erdoğan. Following the decision seen within the party as the failure of the reformists, it was no longer possible for Erdoğan to be an alternative to Erbakan. From now on, he was one of the National Outlook's traditionalist elders.

The penalty Erdoğan faced for reciting a poem disturbed conscientious journalists in the mainstream media. In his column in *Akşam*, journalist Rıza Zelyut asked: "While even Sharia law allows so much freedom of thought, how can our modern and secular law system be so harsh and intolerant, is it possible to understand this?"[90] Journalist Perihan Mağden, currently known for being radically opposed to Erdoğan, said that the penalty hurt the sense of justice: "The court may, as is usually the case, delay the penalty for five years, as a matter of fact, it could have even converted it into a pecuniary fine. No, the DGM sentenced Erdoğan. The penalty imposed on Recep Tayyip Erdoğan offends my sense of justice."[91] There were also figures who used an iron hand in a velvet glove against those – as a matter of fact, against other columnists – who

---

[87] *Radikal* newspaper, September 24, 1998.
[88] *Hürriyet* newspaper, September 24, 1998.
[89] *Hürriyet*, September 24, 1998.
[90] *Akşam*, April 23, 1998.
[91] *Radikal*, April 25, 1998.

defended the penalty imposed on Erdoğan in spite of those who found the penalty unjust despite being distant to National Outlook politics. Ertuğrul Özkök, a controlled journalist of the junta period, defended the penalty imposed on Erdoğan in an article titled "We are clever, not foolish":

> The events we experienced, the developments we witnessed, are pushing us all toward democratic sincerity. They are giving us the duty of behaving sincerely and avoiding provocative attitudes. For example, the words uttered in Siirt. Nobody should dare try and fool [us] that these words were uttered innocently. It is very clear what he meant, who was being targeted and what people were being called to when he said minarets will become bayonets and mosques barracks. We are all smart enough to understand the difference between stating a thought and provoking an action. We are not foolish enough to not understand why places sacred in faith and religion are stated together with bayonets and barracks.[92]

Toward Pınarhisar

There were only a few days left before Erdoğan went to prison following the approval of his sentence. Pınarhisar Prison would not only be holding the future prime minister and president, one of the most important political figures of Republican history, it would also be a political base where the seeds of New Turkey were sown. Erdoğan's sentence was considered in the National Outlook base as a defeat that was hard to digest. It was not only National Outlook voters who reacted against the decision to sentence him, but also the Istanbul voters who had voted for him. The State Council removed his mayorship on November 5, 1998. However, earlier, on September 23, 1998,

---

[92] *Hürriyet* newspaper, April 23, 1998.

Erdoğan organized a press conference with Virtue Party (FP) Chairman Recai Kutan and FP Executive Board members also in attendance to evaluate the court's decision. An angry and upset crowd accompanied Erdoğan. He criticized the politicization of law in his striking speech – as if to signal the position he would reach in politics years later. He said: "This unjust decision given about me is a new milestone for our democracy struggle. It is a new start. Congratulations."[93] The details in Erdoğan's speech, which he ended with: "This is not the end of the song", were also the first signals that he would leave behind his National Outlook identity.

> Everybody in this country who thinks, speaks, provides service has been made to suffer greatly. Now they want to make us suffer too. The approval of this sentence is not the end of everything. As long as I live, I will speak up against injustice and continue to defend the people's law within the context of universal rules of law. I won't be doing this for myself alone; I am going to seek justice for us all, for all of Turkey. This is why I seek the freedom of thought. I am seeking the freedom to be able to speak the truth. I am seeking the administration understanding of honorable people, not mindsets that work like gangs. I am seeking democracy in all ballots across Turkey and in all its territories, not despotism, not oppression. I am seeking it together with my nation – all of them, my brothers and sisters – for my nation. I seek all this also for those who do not think like me, because they too are going to need these values. The institutes of our Republic, the apple of our eye, whose 75th anniversary we celebrated with great joy, should not have been exhausted so ruthlessly. ... Let Tayyip Erdoğan be sentenced, as long as this dear nation is never miserable.[94]

---

[93] Besli-Özbay, *Bir Liderin Doğuşu Recep Tayyip Erdoğan*, p. 213.
[94] http://www.hurriyet.com.tr/burada-bitmez-39039785.

On March 26, 1999, Erdoğan went to Pınarhisar Prison to begin serving his sentence. However, prior to this, an important incident that did not draw much attention took place. October 26, 1998 was the date Erdoğan officially left the National Outlook.[95] The Virtue Party, which was the National Outlook movement's new party following the closure of the Welfare Party, was founded under İsmail Alptekin as chairman. Erdoğan was also among the party members. His sentence approved by the Supreme Court of Appeals, Erdoğan officially left the National Outlook with the notice of resignation he sent to the Virtue Party Istanbul Provincial Headquarters through the Istanbul 10th Notary. This resignation was almost the proof that Erdoğan was now sailing on a brand new course.

Banned Years and the Virtue Party Congress

News leaked through Constitutional Court circles that increased expectations of the closure of the Welfare Party. National Outlook cadres who had previous experience in the area started working to found a new party. A conservative term, expressing Erbakan's National Outlook paradigm would be a determining factor in the new party's name. On February 23, 1998, the Virtue Party was founded with the application of 41 former Welfare Party deputies.

On May 14, 1998, Recai Kutan became Virtue Party chairman by the decision of the council of founders. Kutan, who stood out for his loyal personality, was the party's trustee chairman. The FP was the party of a historic era in which great changes were taking place in National Outlook politics. The reformists nominated a chairman against Erbakan's au-

---

[95] Yalçın, *Kayıp Sicil Erdoğan'ın Çahnan Dosyası*, p. 170.

thority for the first time at the Virtue Party's 1st Ordinary
Grand Congress on May 14, 2000. It was immediately realized that Erdoğan – one of the architects of the reformist
wing – was the one behind the curtain of Abdullah Gül's candidacy. The traditionalists who thought Erdoğan was eliminated from politics were face to face with a new Erdoğan
threat. The big shots of the party, including Erbakan, were
displeased about this process. Erdoğan, who was banned from
politics, when asking for support for Abdullah Gül, said: "This
is a start. This is something new in the tradition of this movement. However, it is necessary for the party's future. The result is not important. Whether we lose or win is unimport-
ant. What's important is to voice all these demands and shake
the authority."[96]

The Virtue Party's 1st Ordinary Grand Congress was held
on May 14, 2000. Erdoğan's fellow politician Abdullah Gül
ran for chairmanship against Erbakan's trustee Recai Kutan.
An argument took place at the congress due to that the executive board allowed chair candidate Kutan to speak at the
platform for an hour and a half, but Gül's speech was limited to 15 minutes.[97] The executive board's decision caused a
disturbance among the delegates. Kutan's lengthy speech was
considered the expression of the displeasure aimed at the reformists. Kutan told the reformists, who he accuses of impa-
tience, that he was "behind the party's wheel", and that while
he is there, it is not possible to please everyone. He addressed
his rival, Abdullah Gül, with the words of Sheikh Edebali,
saying, "Oh son, know to be patient, don't bloom before the
time comes." Continuing addressing Gül, Kutan said: "Pay attention to how the recent developments in our party are be-

---

[96] *Hürriyet*, "Demokrasiye Bak," May 14, 2000, http://www.hurriyet.com.tr/demok-
rasiye-bak-39154160.
[97] http://www.hurriyet.com.tr/demokrasiye-bak-39154160.

ing approached by which groups, who is supporting what and why. There are such people that if they are praising you, then you are on the wrong path in your cause."[98] This pointed statement otherized Gül and the reformists and left a mark on the congress. Abdullah Gül's speech was short. Actually, he was not given the chance to speak long. His message was clear: "It is time for a change in National Outlook politics."[99] According to Gül, the period of "not discussing matters openly" was over and the time had come for the established political understanding that readily pointed out others' flaws to start seeing its own shortcomings.

One of Erdoğan's advisers, Hüseyin Besli, related the reformist wing's reformist outburst at the Virtue Party's congress to Erbakan's failure to show adequate resistance on February 28. Erdoğan, who has at different times throughout his political life faced various open and covert balance adjustments by the military, stood tall by pointing to the national will as a basis, but unlike Erbakan, he did not show stubbornness. Analyzing the opposition voice rising from the FP, Besli interpreted Erbakan siding with the traditionalists as a lack of trust in the party's young cadres.[100]

Surprise in the Congress Results

The voting process at the congress came to an end. When the results were revealed, Recai Kutan, backed by Erbakan, receives 633 votes, and Erdoğan's candidate Abdullah Gül receives 521 votes. Even though Gül lost the election having received support from nearly half of the delegates, the reform-

[98] Virtue Party Congress Minutes, May 14, 2000.
[99] ibid.
[100] Besli, and Özbay, *Bir Liderin Doğuşu Recep Tayyip Erdoğan*, pp 250-252.

ists actually gained. The result was the first victory the reformists won on the path leading to the foundation of the Justice and Development Party (AK Party). Years later, in an interview, Gül said:

> We would be accused of dividing the party and causing disorder out of nowhere, and even betraying the cause. Before anything else, we had to risk facing such absurd accusations. Our history is filled with examples of people who once saw each other as brothers destroy each other following such disintegrations in such organizations.[101]

However, in a twist of fate, Abdullah Gül was next criticized for abandoning his fellow politician Erdoğan after the December 17 and December 25 judicial coup attempted by members of the Gülenist Terror Group (FETÖ) in 2013,[102] and his silence in the 2017 constitutional referendum campaign led to comments such as that he has a new political pursuit.[103]

The Virtue Party shared a fate similar to the other National Outlook parties. The FP's party closure case taken to the Constitutional Court by the Chief Public Prosecutor of the Supreme Court of Appeals, Vural Savaş, concluded on May 7, 1999. The decision did not change. The slogans "Warrior Erbakan", "Wherever Erbakan goes, we go", "This is the army, this is the commander" in the tribunes at the FP's 1st Ordinary Grand Congress, were one of the reasons behind the permanent closure of the Virtue Party on June 22, 2001. The most important incident in the party's closure was the Merve Kavakçı crisis that took place in the Grand National Assembly of the Republic of Turkey (TBMM) on May 2, 1999. Ka-

---

[101] ibid., p.254.
[102] http://www.yenisafak.com/gundem/abdullah-gulun-darbe-komisyonuna-yaniti-bu-yapiyla-iliskim-olmadi-2591575.
[103] http://www.cumhuriyet.com.tr/haber/turkiye/674537/Yandas_yazardan_Abdullah_Gul_e_agir_sozler_ve_tehdit__Kasinmayin.html.

vakçı, who attended the swearing in ceremony at the TBMM wearing a headscarf, faced the reaction of Prime Minister Bülent Ecevit and Democratic Left Party (DSP) deputies, and was forced to leave the General Assembly Hall without taking her oath of office. The closing down of the Virtue Party led to the reformist-traditionalist disintegration within the National Outlook tradition to change course.

Identity Discussions

In order to correctly understand Erdoğan's politics and his view on politics, a few points require close examination. Pragmatism superseding idealism, his embracing the enemy conceptualization[104] that he positions against the national will, and the service politics he presents through concrete data, are the important points we come across throughout Erdoğan's political life. The problems these characteristics created are basically the reason why Erdoğan parted from National Outlook politics. Erbakan's idealism that pushed the limits of rationality was the biggest factor that disconnected National Outlook politics from the flow of life. Erdoğan did not fall into the same mistake and instead shapes his political discourse on realpolitik. This difference is immediately noticed in the details he includes in election declarations. This disintegration within the party is the reason Erdoğan has been a reformist since the 1970s. Seeing that the tone and style used in National Outlook politics allows it to take position in the center, Erdoğan developed a new political paradigm as an alternative to the center-right, which was dealing with a leader crisis. This paradigm would turn into a major instrument that shaped the AK Party's political discourse from its founding to 2008.

---

[104] Bahadır, *Muktedir, Türk Sağ Geleneği ve Recep Tayyip Erdoğan*, p. 211.

Historian Kemal H. Karpat interprets Erdoğan – who he describes as a "new-type populist Islamist leader" – stepping out from the National Outlook identity and drawing himself a path within the concept of a conservative democrat both as the failure of political Islam against political secularism and as the result of the relationship between modernity and Islam in Turkey.[105] However, the change in Erdoğan's political discourse after 2011 is interpreted, contrary to Karpat's evaluation, as a return to his origins.

The National Outlook identity Erdoğan said he stepped out of[106] continued to be discussed following the AK Party coming to power. His rivals, disregarding the change in his politics, were insistent on claiming that the change was a deception.[107] Shortly before the 2007 presidential election, the discussions ignited again. The restlessness of secular and Kemalist circles was at a peak. Prime Minister Erdoğan, who responded to Ali Kırca's questions in relation to the presidential election on ATV, gave answers the identity discussions:

> We are going to look each other in the face with Mr. [Deniz] Baykal. I made a call to keep the doors open. For example, there was no clear picture yet concerning the presidential issue; we didn't know how Parliament would turn out. We were given attitude right away. "From outside the Parliament..." Just stop. Why are you blocking it? When you say it like this, my answer is ready. Why? Because I consider having a candidate from outside Parliament to run for the presidency to be disrespectful, especially to the 550 deputies. I am absolutely against a president from outside Parliament. Just look at Mr. Baykal saying, "An AK

---

[105] Kemal H. Karpat, *Osmanlı'dan Günümüze Elitler ve Din*, Timaş Yayınları, Istanbul 2015, p. 290.
[106] "Erdoğan: "Millî Görüş Gömleğini 28 Şubatta Çıkardık", *Akşam*, August 14, 2003.
[107] http://www.milliyet.com.tr/2003/05/22/siyaset/asiy.html.

Party militant cannot enter Çankaya." He later used that same expression to describe his own party's deputies.

First go and find out from a dictionary what the word militant means. Is this right? All of our deputies are respectable people who do politics within the democratic system. They are not members of a militarist structure. Mr. Baykal does not know what he is saying. He has completely lost it these days. He is probably receiving public opinion surveys. And when he sees these, he goes off the rails. I said once and for all, I have stepped out of the National Outlook identity. Aren't these people of age? Do they not have that maturity? Let the people decide for themselves. If you don't believe this, then we are saying let's ask the people. Then let the people decide.[108]

Erdoğan tried his skillful move, which he always succeeds in, and played the card of asking the people. This card, which the opposition in Turkey struggles to use at times of crisis, is the right move that has always helped Erdoğan win throughout his political life. The identity discussions did not only occupy the agenda of opposition parties, they also created disorder within the AK Party, which included the important figures of right-wing politics. In 2006, the discussions made their way into the newspapers. However, the discussions concentrating on Erdoğan's wife Emine Erdoğan's religious preferences were shameful in the name of Turkey's democratic culture. Mrs. Erdoğan's headscarf was said to indicate that Erdoğan did not step out of his National Outlook identity. In his article, "Erdoğan'ın Gömleği" (Erdoğan's Identity), published in *Sabah* and now collecting dust on the archive shelves, almost interpreting the opposition's feelings, Erdal Şafak wrote:

---

[108] http://www.yeniasya.com.tr/2007/07/21/haber/h3.htm.

The AK Party's DYP-based deputy and Foreign Affairs Committee Chair Mehmet Dülger made his second warning in 10 days through statements published in Sabah this morning. He had voiced the first one last week on Habertürk TV's Basın Kulübü (Press Club) program. He must have thought it did not receive the response it deserved that he brought it up again in an exclusive statement to Sabah. He gave the same message in both. The most important ones can be collected under two groups: 1) Erdoğan and the AK Party's identity, and 2) Mrs. Erdoğan's headscarf and the presidential election.

Between the lines of the messages given in the first group lie the clues of a deep identity conflict in the AK Party: "Just as I came to the AK Party leaving behind my DYP identity, Mr. Tayyip [Erdoğan] did the same by leaving behind his National Outlook identity. However, if he decides to [resume] the National Outlook identity and enter Çankaya, that won't be right. ... Disconnections between groups in the party grew bigger. If they present National Outlook principles to me, we will have a falling out." This statement from Dülger recalled the answer Erdoğan gave last year to a question in relation to claims of setting up pro-National Outlook cadres: "This is the AK Party. We stepped out of our National Outlook identity. But it seems as though certain groups are trying to force us to take up that identity again."

Dülger speaks surely about the relationship between Mrs. Erdoğan's hijab and the presidential election as well: "Either Erdoğan should not run for the presidency or Mrs. Erdoğan should remove her hijab! Reason being: A president who has a hijabi wife coming to Çankaya would shake Turkey!" Under the current conditions, it is an entirely true evaluation. It is true, because one side sees the hijab as an anti-secular threat and the symbol of political Islam, the other sees it as an obligatory act of faith. One side sees it as the weapon used to re-Islamize the community, and the other sees it as a part of freedom of religion. Since both sides are firmly holding to their positions and are afraid to take even a step, reaching an agreement is impossible. As Dülger says, "Either Mrs. Erdoğan will remove her hijab or Erdoğan will forget candidacy!" Period.[109]

These statements from Şafak, which went on record as a document of shame, contain important details to understand the conditions of the period. Evaluating incidents from today's point of view, the critical processes Erdoğan went through in Turkish politics can be seen more clearly.

Erbakan's Criticism of Erdoğan

In the same years, National Outlook leader Erbakan did not back away from making statements targeting Erdoğan, either. Erbakan described AK Party cadres and Erdoğan as "a bunch of children" and expressed his anger in his own way by saying:

> Wasn't this AKP supposed to be the party of the slums? What happened to those in these slums? They are no more. There used to be four dollar billionaires only, now there are 24. It only worked for the dollar billionaires. Who do you think you are fooling? Children? Get out of here. You are all profiteers, you are all profit economists, you are all in favor of unlawful profit, you are all people who oppress the poor.[110]

Erbakan accused Erdoğan of inexperience and lack of knowledge and claimed that he would fail in government because he stepped away from his National Outlook identity:

---

[109] Erdal Şafak, "Erdoğan'ın Gömleği," *Sabah*, January 4, 2006.
[110] Necmettin Erbakan, "Press Conference," May 14, 2003, *Erbakan Külliyatı*, Vol. 4, comp. M. M. Uzun, MGV Yayınları, Ankara, 2013, p. 228.

He can't succeed because he stepped out of his National Outlook identity. As this is the case, the only thing he is doing is
constantly kicking the ball into his own court with the influence of racist imperialism and mediators. The administration
of a country like Turkey, which is in the world's most key loca-
tion, which is the inheritor of the greatest and noblest history
and has the duty of establishing a new world of bliss, cannot be
left in the hands of such a bunch of inexperienced children who
lack knowledge.[111]

It is very clear that similar senseless outbursts in Erbakan's
political experience and his description of Erdoğan and AK
Party cadres as a bunch of children contradicts the youth ideal that National Outlook tried to form through the achievements of Sultan Mehmed the Conqueror who seized Constantinople. However, Erbakan continued to escalate anti-Erdoğan sentiment with his sarcastic tone, and the Republic Rallies organized since 2007 with large groups uniting in
their anti-Erdoğan sentiment, the e-memorandum, the TSK
memorandum to again make a balance adjustment to democracy, the 367 crisis, the Council of State attack, the party closure case, and the Ergenekon and Balyoz (Sledgehammer)
were the outstanding problems of the period.

---

[111] Necmettin Erbakan, "Millî Görüş, Ekonomik Kalkınma ve Herkese Refahı Nasıl
Sağlayacak?" Millî Kurtuluş Konferansları 2, *Erbakan Külliyatı*, Vol. 2, comp. M.
M. Uzun, MGV Yayınları, Ankara 2013, p. 383.

SECTION TWO
THE AK PARTY ERA

THE BEFORE AND THE 2007 FACTION

The leader crises in the deep-seated parties of the center-right, Islamist politics that lost strength after the Kemalist restoration, the political and social problems produced in the last three decades by the bureaucracy, and the piecemeal social engineering projects remaining from interregnums[1] pushed Turkey toward a new political formation. Erdoğan and his reformist cadres who correctly analyzed the socio-political change in the community worked on a new political movement that brings together important figures already in the National Outlook's sociological pool with popular faces from the center-right. A party that is centered on the justice and development, which had suffered from political degeneration, was founded on May 14, 2001, with Erdoğan as chairman. The Justice and Development Party, called the

---

[1] "Piecemeal social engineering" was coined by Popper. See, *The Poverty of Historiscism*, Beacon Press, Boston, 1957, pp 58-70. In his study, *Geleceği Eskitmek AKP ve Türkiye*, Ahmet Çiğdem uses Popper's concept to identify the AK Party's politics. Çiğdem makes the assessment: "It might be possible to grasp the AKP government's choice of doing business through partial packages during this process, rather than taking a totalitarian measure in relation to social and political problems, within this context." However, the study you have in your hands, uses Popper's concept, contrary to Çiğdem, for the secular-Kemalist understanding that doomed Turkey to interim term darknesses. See, Ahmet Çiğdem, *Geleceği Eskitmek AKP ve Türkiye*, İletişim Yayınları, Istanbul, 2014, p. 17.

AK Party by its founders while the opposition has chosen to call it the AKP, took the stage with the promise of making a difference in Turkish politics. Contrary to the Islamic heritage in its origins, it identifies itself as conservative democratic party. However, the West, especially the hawks that gained prominence during U.S. President George W. Bush's administration, developed anti-AK Party reflexes by thinking that an Islamist party cannot make a democratic transformation.[2] Academic Yüksel Taşkın says the West's reflexes need to be sought in the destructive remains of orientalism. Yet, the description of the AK Party as a conservative democratic party in liberal circles in the U.S. and the West was accepted as a noteworthy success story. At this point, the strategic ties the AK Party established with the Western system, the alliance it formed with liberal segments after coming to power on the path of transforming Turkish politics[3] are important factors that helped Erdoğan's integration into the system. Shortly after coming to power, Erdoğan would, with an article he wrote for *The Wall Street Journal*, also increase the alliance with the U.S.,[4] and this pragmatism was perceived as a sign of transformation in economy and other fields of politics in Turkey.[5]

The years after the AK Party was founded was a critical period in which economic and political instabilities started leading society to new pursuits. It would be correct to describe Erdoğan and the AK Party coming to power in a one-party government in 2002 with 34 percent of the vote as a politi-

[2] Yüksel Taşkın, *AKP Devri Türkiye Siyaseti, İslâmcılık, Arap Baharı*, İletişim Yayınları, Istanbul, 2013, p. 11.

[3] İlhan Uzgel, "AKP: Neoliberal Dönüşümün Yeni Aktörü," *AKP Kitabı: Bir Dönüşümün Bilançosu*, Phoenix Yayınevi, Istanbul 2009, p. 12.

[4] Recep Tayyip Erdoğan, "My Country is Your Faithful Ally and Friend," *The Wall Street Journal*, March 31, 2003.

[5] Uzgel, "AKP: Neoliberal Dönüşümün Yeni Aktörü," *AKP Kitabı: Bir Dönüşümün Bilançosu*, p. 20

cal earthquake that has had permanent consequences in terms of Turkey's political history. Erdoğan and the AK Party garnered support of 34 percent of the electorate in the 2002 parliamentary election as a result of voters' intense confidence that he and his party would end corruption and poverty – not because he would establish an Islamic state. Although the impact of the discourse defined by Erbakan as "middle-class Islamism" starting to get old, it can also be traced in Erdoğan's unexpected rise. National Outlook politics, which received more than 30 percent of the vote from Konya in the 1999 parliamentary election, losing its political fortress of Konya with its new party, the Felicity Party (FP), in the 2002 elections to the AK Party, was an important sign.[6] The AK Party's fast entrance to the political domain with tits identity as a conservative democratic party fueled a new debate among Islamist intellectuals.[7] Turkey would see a new period resulting with the evolution of Islamist, conservative politics, as we will discuss in greater detail in the following pages.

Eric Jan Zükher accepts that the 2002 election results were "dumbfounding" and says:

> The elections were held on November 3, 2002, and the results were dumbfounding. Testing the waters had shown the parties in the coalition government had no chance of passing the 10 percent threshold – and that is exactly what happened. This had also shown that the reformist wing of the Islamist movement, Tayyip Erdoğan's AKP, would be the true winner, yet when that day had come, the level of victory had caused surprise. The party had received more than 34 percent of the vote and achieved the absolute majority in Parliament. Deniz Baykal's CHP was the only other party to make it into Parliament with votes bare-

---

[6] Zürcher, *Modernleşen Türkiye'nin Tarihi*, p. 440.
[7] http://www.hurriyet.com.tr/siyasal-İslâm-bitti-yasasin-yeni-İslâmcilik-128061.

ly passing 19 percent. Support for Ecevit had dropped by 96 percent, but the state of opposition New Turkey Party members wasn't so bright either. The True Path Party was the only one from among the traditional parties that came close to the 10 percent threshold.[8]

From Political Islamism to Conservative Democracy

The AK Party has, in Turkish political history, been the party of remarkable changes. Erdoğan holds notable meetings ahead of foundations both in Turkey and abroad, the most critical of which are those in the West and the U.S. The presence of hawkish politicians who took active positions in the White House and rising anti-Islam and anti-Muslim sentiment in the U.S. after the September 11, 2001 World Trade Center attacks made Erdoğan's meetings in the United States more significant. Erdoğan's meeting with Fetullah Gülen in the U.S. where he stayed a couple of days in July 2000 – before coming to power –[9] and his meeting with the American Jewish Committee and Jewish Institute for National Security of America (JINSA) top executives in Washington resonated throughout Turkey. Both the National Outlook base and the neo-nationalists were disturbed by Erdoğan's uncontrollable charisma and the AK Party's fast rise. These important and notable discussions in the U.S. were the reason the AK Party was accused years later by prominent Islamist journalists of "having been founded with the support of neocons."[10] Before moving on to the details of the AK Party's alliances with the West after its foundation, scrutinizing Erdoğan's political preferences that evolved from Islamism to conservative de-

---

[8] Zürcher, *Modernleşen Türkiye'nin Tarihi*, p. 439.
[9] Nuriye Akman, *Zaman* newspaper, March 24, 2004.
[10] Nasuhi Güngör, *Yenilikçi Hareket*, Elips Kitap, Istanbul 2005, p. 111.

mocracy is important in terms of correctly seeing the AK Party's codes, which in the final analysis is a political transformation project that has achieved success on the nationalism, secularism and neo-liberalism[11] axis.[12]

The predominant ideology in Turkey considers Islamism as a rural movement far from the center that tries to be party to the center by any means possible. This view is the one that social scientists in Turkey like the most among Ali Yaşar Sarıbay's National Outlook interpretations and Şerif Mardin's analyses of Islamism.[13] However, fictionalizing the matter merely as a class war or a conflict of interests without dwelling on the political demands of Islamism, does not help in understanding the transformation of Islamism in Turkey, which has evolved into conservative democracy in the past two decades. Although the AK Party formed a legitimate ground for itself as a response to the February 28 defeat, aiming to restore the Islamist community, its success cannot be viewed independently from the socio-political and socio-economic reality of the second millennium as well as global politics, which experienced a change post-September 11.

The Failure of Political Islam (?)

As Yalçın Akdoğan was analyzing the philosophy of the period in which the AK Party was founded, he approached the topic in the same context as Oliver Roy. Akdoğan says the failure of certain experiences presented in the Muslim world during the rise of Islamism paves the way to a new pursuit

---

[11] Metin Sever, "Merkez Sağ Geleceğini Arıyor, 5", *Radikal* newspaper, October 17, 2002.

[12] E. Fuat Keyman, *Türkiye'nin Yeniden İnşası, Modernleşme, Demokratikleşme, Kimlik*, Bilgi Üniversitesi Yayınları, Istanbul 2013, p. 118.

[13] Nuh Yılmaz, "İslâmcılık, AKP, Siyaset," *Modern Türkiye'de Siyasî Düşünce İslâmcılık*, Vol. 6, İletişim Yayınları, Istanbul, 2014, p. 605.

in the 21st century that is more lively, more alive, that has a grasp of the realities of life but essentially holds onto its sensitivities and tries to take part in all facets of life.[14] Years later, when explaining conservative democracy, the philosophy on which the party's political foundation is based, Erdoğan said it is "a modernity that does not exclude tradition, a universality that accepts localism, a rationality that does not reject meaning, a change that is not fundamentalist."[15]

In time, Erdoğan expanded this definition, describing the AK Party as a party that defends the democratic and secular state of law, that considers secularism the guarantee of democracy and the essential principle of social peace, and that is in search of permanent public consensus around the fundamental characteristics of the Republic.[16] Erdoğan's conservative democratic identity re-ignited debates on Islamism along with those on conservatism. Erdoğan has not tried to bring a new definition to democracy; he instead tries to determine a new course for himself through a compound that became included in political literature through Özal.[17]

Akdoğan considers the new course Erdoğan was trying to open by decoupling himself from the traditional line as a major gain in terms of Turkish politics, and explains it as follows:

> Producing such a term is important in a few aspects: 1. Normalizing politics, 2. Establishing a realistic ground for politics, 3. Forming an independent conservative party, 4. Producing an embracive political style. ... The Justice and Development Party, which emerged with its disintegration from the Welfare/Vir-

---

[14] Yalçın Akdoğan, "Adalet ve Kalkınma Partisi," *Modern Türkiye'de Siyasî Düşünce İslâmcılık, C. 6*, İletişim Yayınları, Istanbul, 2014, p. 621.

[15] Bora, *Cereyanlar, Türkiye'de Siyasî İdeolojiler*, p. 478.

[16] Minutes of AK Party meeting in Afyon, August 1, 2001.

[17] Yalçın Akdoğan, *AK Parti ve Muhafazakâr Demokrasi*, Alfa Yayınları, Istanbul, 2004, p. 18.

tue Party tradition, cannot be judged, with its current position and discourse, in the political Islam category. ... As a result, the Justice and Development Party's target group differs from the classic National Outlook parties with its discourse and style and identifies itself as a party of the masses on the center-right. It could be said this effort would result in transformation, but this transformation process is still ongoing. The conservative democrat identity the AKP, which claims to incorporate the universal with the local, traditional with modernity, the state's sensitivities with the people's values, tries to form has a very political significance and importance rather than being scientific.[18]

Academic Hakan Yavuz interprets the AK Party's entry into politics through the public mind instead of Islamic identity as Erdoğan taking a path outside Islamism.[19] The new course Erdoğan opened has allowed the conservative, Anatolian bourgeoisie to gain as much visibility as the transformation of Turkish politics has.[20] This has paved the way to alliances to be formed through the definition of conservative democracy abroad with the West and with liberals on the inside. Based on this, liberal intellectuals considered the AK Party's rise as social modernization beyond being a threat to social order.[21] The change in Erdoğan's political discourse after 2008 led to the gradual deterioration of this alliance. On a different note, contrary to the established perception, there are those who see the AK Party as the pinnacle of Turkish Islamism. Academic Burak Gürel, who identifies Islamist movements as the product of the alliance built by the reli-

[18] Akdoğan, "Adalet ve Kalkınma Partisi," *Modern Türkiye'de Siyasî Düşünce İslâmcılık,* p. 627.
[19] Hakan Yavuz, "Introduction," *The Emergency of a New Turkey: Democracy and the AK Parti,* Hakan Yavuz (ed.), University of Utah Press, Salt Lake City, p. 3.
[20] Uzgel, "AKP: Neoliberal Dönüşümün Yeni Aktörü," *AKP Kitabı: Bir Dönüşümün Bilançosu,* p. 23.
[21] Nilüfer Göle, *Modern Mahrem, Medeniyet ve Örtünme,* Metis Kitap, Istanbul, 1991.

gious bourgeoisie with the working class, makes a comparison between the AK Party and what Ruhollah Khomeini did in Iran:

> Despite all the historical differences between them, the success behind Khomeini in the Iranian Revolution and the AKP in the Turkey of the 2000s are the same: the result of the religious bourgeoisie's ability to gain the support of the lower classes. In contrast to this, the religious bourgeoisie losing its hegemony over the lower classes is the reason behind the Islamist groups in Algeria and Egypt losing the fight for power in the 1990s.[22]

Comparing the AK Party to the Iranian Revolution is not a well-intentioned approach. Gürel likening a political leader who identifies himself within the lines of conservative democracy to Khomeini cannot be considered an objective analysis. It is also helpful to note here that the AK Party has had difficulty in turning its liberal conservatism theory to a political ideology.[23] However, it should also be remembered that Erdoğan uses this method deliberately. The reason the AK Party has been victorious in every election is not the wide acceptance of its liberal/conservative democracy, but its pursuit in the center of politics for which Erdoğan has rolled up his sleeves to represent. The AK Party choosing liberal/conservative democracy while it was more likely and easier for the nationalist-conservatism theory to find a response from the public is also the product of its efforts to position itself in the center of politics, far from marginality and Islamism. Yet, the AK Party's efforts to open a new area for itself within the definition of liberal conservatism was not merely an effort to develop a new political language pure of marginal ideologies,

---

[22] Burak Gürel, "İslâmcılık: Uluslararası Bir Ufuk Taraması," *Neoliberalizm, İslâma Sermayenin Yükselişi ve AKP,* comp. Neşe Balkan-Erol Balkan-Ahmet Öncü, Yordam Kitap, Istanbul, 2013, p. 26.

[23] Hasan Bülent Kahraman, *AKP ve Türk Sağı,* Agora Kitaplığı, Istanbul, 2009, p. 125.

it also included the goal of developing a political tone above ideologies. This should not, however, be understood as a political model that has no ideology. Erdoğan's choice is politically correct, because what he is trying to achieve is actually the most current form of the political stance through which Turgut Özal tried to position himself on the center-right between 1983 and 1987.

It would help to note here that according to Ali Yaşar Sarıbay's interpretation, Özal's venturesome spirit and mentality was very affective in transforming certain concepts and attitudes. For instance, Özal's first reconceptualization was aimed at the state. The state, which, until then, was thought to be a bureaucratic tool of tutelage, started to be defined by Özal as a device that serves the people. As a result, Özal was considered a politician who opened the state to the people. It could be said that Erdoğan resembles Özal in terms of his political model, which challenges the status quo's established order.[24] The tone Erdoğan developed after the first referendum on April 16, 2017 to consolidate the party base led to criticism that he is moving away from Özal's line.

It could be said that Erdoğan's great transformation in politics before 2002 is the result of concerns about the future of Muslim Anatolia, which was attempting only recently to overcome the February 28 trauma. It needs to be accepted that February 28 showed it is not possible to achieve anything by attacking the Muslim part of society through the state and that human resources and funding cannot be increased. AK Party cadres that emerged by separating from the National Outlook, would, in the party's early years, adopt a tone of consensus far from the conflict in accordance with the polit-

---

[24] Ali Yaşar Sarıbay, *Türkiye'de Demokrasi ve Politik Partiler,* Alfa Yayınları, Istanbul, 2001, p. 69.

ical transformation project while Erdoğan's would choose a balance policy until the end of 2007. Hence, Erdoğan, who went through interregnum traumas, said with caution in a statement in 2004:

> Even though we care about religion as a social value, we don't think that doing politics in accordance with religion, or attempting to ideologically transform the administration by way of using religion is right. Religion is a sacred and common value. It should not be turned into an element of political factionalization that could lead to separatism.[25]

It is quite interesting that the first reaction to Erdoğan's statement came from former CIA Near East and Turkey Officer Graham E. Fuller, who is known for his clear opposition to Turkey and Erdoğan and currently for his closeness to FETÖ members. Fuller openly identifies the AK Party, which he claims breeds on Islamic sources in addition to having liberal democratic values, "is, despite being very cautious and careful about not revealing its religious origins, a religious party."[26] Fuller's definition is a confession important enough to disprove claims that the AK Party got support from Fuller during its founding process. The AK Party's strategic alliances with leading world institutes and organizations will be discussed in depth in the upcoming pages, but the statements American historian Daniel Pipes makes when analyzing Erdoğan as an antithesis to claims from certain Islamist, conservative, and neo-nationalist circles that the AK Party is an American project, is the best possible response to how Erdoğan is envisioned behind the scenes by the Western men-

---

[25] *Turkish Daily News,* January 31, 2004.
[26] Graham E. Fuller, "Turkey's Strategic Model: Myths and Realities," *Washington Quarterly,* Vol. 27, No. 3, Washington, 2004, p. 52.

tality. In an article he wrote for *Policy Watch* in 2003, Daniel Pipes describes Erdoğan and AK Party politics as:

> The Justice and Development Party in Turkey may be very different from the Taliban in terms of its methods, but there is no difference in relation to their aims. If this party were also to take complete control over Turkey, it could turn out to be just as dangerous as the Taliban in Afghanistan.[27]

Contrary to Pipes' claims, Erdoğan has achieved important successes during Turkey's democratization process that his interlocutors consider to be milestones. Erdoğan, who, as a matter of fact, has made the greatest development moves in the history of the Republic, is an effective politician who eliminated the biggest obstacle standing in the way of Turkey's democratization by having important chapters opened in the accession negotiation process with the European Union. Although the polemic between Erdoğan and EU leaders during the April 16, 2017 referendum on constitutional changes and a shift to a presidential government system, the diplomatic crisis with the Netherlands and the covert and open messages aimed at steering Turkish politics through Belgium and Germany's terrorist organizations, were the biggest fallouts with the European Union in the last five decades. The inclusion of Turkey as under inspection again as of April 25, 2017 for the first time after 13 years by the Parliamentary Assembly of the Council of Europe (PACE),[28] cannot be interpreted as a decision resulting solely from Erdoğan's changed political discourse. The decision was the result of efforts by Western politicians, who have recently been showing no hesitation to display Erdoğanophobic behavior in order to force Turkey

---

[27] Daniel Pipes, Washington Institute, *Policy Watch*, Vol. 746, April 10, 2003.
[28] http://www.hurriyet.com.tr/son-dakika-avrupadan-flas-turkiye-karari-13-yil-sonra-bir-ilk-40437890.

into an "Erdoğan-less" political design by making Erdoğan a target. Therefore, Erdoğan's tougher discourse and changed political stance cannot be analyzed independently of the rising Erdoganophobia and anti-Turkish sentiment in the West. Even though this tone and style seem to feed one another, the EU's policies over the past 15 years on Turkey show that Western politics is far from displaying an honest stance on Turkey. This being the case, the tone Erdoğan has adopted on Europe, gradually giving prominence to nationalist political discourse, turns into a stance that finds him significant social support both in Turkey and abroad in oppressed regions.

The AK Party's Founding

On August 14, 2001, the AK Party took its place on Turkey's political scene. The 121-member board of founders was a platform of figures from a very diverse social and political background. Erdoğan being party chairman despite being banned from politics turned the party into an important political movement that would steer Turkey's future. Bülent Arınç, Abdullah Gül, Cüneyd Zapsu, Abdülkadir Aksu, Cemil Çiçek, Tayyar Altıkulaç, Abdüllâtif Şener, İsmail Kahraman, Ali Babacan, and Binali Yıldırım were some of the important figures on the board of founders. The AK Party's founding was announced on August 14, 2001, at a press conference held at Ankara Bilkent Hotel with local and foreign press in attendance. Arınç was unable to hold back his tears when Erdoğan took to the platform. The great victory the reformists in the National Outlook tradition won against the traditionalists had, for the first time, taken tangible form. In his speech, Erdoğan described the day the AK Party was established as "the day the leader oligarchy in Turkey collapsed,"[29] and made striking statements at the conference closely followed by Western media:

> Today is an important day. This day is going to go into Turkish political history as the day the leader oligarchy collapsed, the day the leadership understanding that is a representative of the collective mind instead of a leadership based on a monopolistic understanding is established. This day will go into Turkish political history not only as a wish for an intraparty democracy tradition, but also as the day it is sovereign in the form of a change in mindset and compelling regulation rules.

> Today will go into Turkish political history as the day a brand new political organization model that is transparent in every aspect and open to the questioning and inspection of the voters is established. Today is going to go into history as the birthday of the AK Party, which was established by people who are interested in serving [the people], not those who are interested in [holding] office. Happy birthday. From this day onward, nothing in Turkish politics is going to be like it used to be. Have no doubt.[30]

The pro-National Outlook politicians who did not join the Virtue Party following the AK Party's establishment, in the 21st legislative year, reached the number necessary to establish a group in Parliament, and its group president was Manisa Deputy Bülent Arınç. On November 3, 2002,[31] the AK Party achieved one of the greatest successes seen in the history of the Republic at the ballot box. Garnering 34 percent of the vote, it became the strongest political party with 363 out

---

[29] https://www.youtube.com/watch?v=D337eO8tBB0.
[30] *Milliyet*, August 15, 2001.
[31] Parties' vote distribution in the November 3, 2002 Parliamentary General Election: AK Party: 34.42% (363 MPs), CHP: 19.42% (178 MPs), DYP: 9.52%, MHP: 8.35%, Young Party: 7.24%, and 9 independent MPs.

of 550 seats in Parliament after the Democrat Party.[32] However-
er, upon the application from the Chief Public Prosecutor of
the Supreme Court of Appeals, Sabih Kanadoğlu, the Constitutional Court prevented Erdoğan's candidacy due to his being banned from politics. Erdoğan could not serve as a deputy and was unable to take office as prime minister in the 58th
government and would trust his position to Kayseri Deputy
Abdullah Gül, a popular figure representing the previous reformists from the Virtue Party. The parliamentary arithme-
tic through which Arınç was elected TBMM president further increases the worries of concerned segments of society
and politics. With the two important institutes of state being run by important figures from the National Outlook tradition, President Ahmet Necdet Sezer became the last fortress
of the Republic. Acting in accordance with the mission expected of him, President Sezer caused great distress for the
AK Party cadres. Thus began the stagnation period for Erdoğan and the AK Party, which the military took under close
watch. However, this period, during which Erdoğan would
display an admirable performance in spite of the concerned
voters by squeezing into two years the democratization reforms the previous governments were able to achieve in two
decades[33] and making moves that would raise the level of the
Turkish economy – which could be compared to Syria only in
the beginning of the 2000s – to that of EU member Spain,[34]
was Turkey's evolution from a tutelary democracy to a national democracy.[35]

[32] Yalçın Akdoğan, "Adalet ve Kalkınma Partisi," *Modern Türkiye'de Siyasî Düşünce İslâmahk, Vol. 6,* İletişim Yayınları, Istanbul, 2014, p. 625.
[33] Chris Morris, *The New Turkey: The Quiet Revolution on The Edge of Europe,* Granta Books, London 2006, p. 62.
[34] Soner Çağaptay, *The New Sultan, Erdoğan and The Crisis of Modern Turkey,* I.B.Ta-uris, London 2017, p. 5.
[35] Menderes Çınar, *Vesayetçi Demokrasiden "Millî" Demokrasiye,* Birikim Yayınları, İstanbul 2015, s. 10.

A series of meetings were held during the party's establishment. The office rented on Cinnah Road in Ankara was not only a place where the AK Party's foundations were laid, but also where Turkey's future politics was shaped. Erdoğan followed an approach that values the opinions of esteemed political figures as well as the young team. Ömer Çelik, Faruk Koca, Ahmet Toprak, and Yavuz Selim Aras stand out in the young team led by Mücahit Arslan. The young team wanted the party to be established at once. In meetings with both Erdoğan and Gül, they wanted decisions to be made swiftly. The young team's demand was to escape at once the ideological burden of the National Outlook, which they believed was an obstacle stopping them from realizing their political, economic, and social demands.[36] This approach was also the most obvious indicator that the National Outlook identity had been left behind. Thus began the stage in which dialogue was established with different segments of society. Journalist and writer Hasan Bülent Kahraman defined this stage as the rejection of Islam as a political project by AK Party cadres. Kahraman includes the following evaluations in his analysis:

> My claim is that when Abdullah Gül ran for party chair against Recai Kutan, he had severed his ties with political Islam. But did he completely sever his ties with Islam? No. I am not saying anything like that, because Islam has four dimensions in Turkey, which I have been suggesting ever since the start within the scope of these analyses. It has social, cultural, economic and political dimensions. The AKP also maintained its social and cultural ties with Islam, but it cut its ties with Islam at the political level. If you ask whether Recep Tayyip Erdoğan later shifted a little more toward Islam after becoming party chairman compared to Abdullah Gül's project or the mindset in that term, I

---

[36] Besli-Özbay, *Bir Liderin Doğuşu Recep Tayyip Erdoğan*, p. 263.

would say, yes, that is possible. But the reason is completely psychological.[37]

A close witness of the time, Hüseyin Besli, evaluated the AK Party's relations with different constituencies during the establishment process and the dialogue it was trying build with TÜSİAD circles as the result of its pursuit for a more liberal and pluralist identity independent of the National Outlook mentality and the center's political void.

Besli interprets the change in the AK Party and Erdoğan' discourse on this ground. However, the groups in question increased the worries of concerned modernists distant from Erdoğan by repeatedly bringing up Erdoğan's outburst when he said in an interview with Nilgün Cerrahoğlu from *Milliyet* years ago: "Democracy is a tram, we will ride it until we get to our destination and get off when we arrive."[38] Years later, he tried to clarify the matter to Eyüp Can from *Zaman*:

> The assessment that I regard democracy as a means was taken out of context and twisted and presented in different context. I guess, as aims are always seen in Turkey as principal and means as occurrences, my definition of democracy as a means was perceived like an insulting approach. Yet, I am a person who believes in the legitimacy of means as much as that of aims. Regardless of how legitimate and lawful aims are, if they do not have the same legitimacy, no real result can be achieved.[39]

His similar outbursts over time would lead to comments that he "is an ambitious traveler on the road to democracy."[40] Howev-

---

[37] Kahraman, *AKP ve Türk Sağı*, p. 126.
[38] *Milliyet*, July 14, 1996.
[39] *Zaman*, July 20, 2000.
[40] http://www.gazetevatan.com/rusen-cakir-491426-yazar-yazisi-erdogan--demokrasi-tramvayinda-ihtirasli-bir-yolcu/

er, the political model Erdoğan, presented despite the criticism, would in total give the opportunity to the successful political integration of Islamic movements in Turkey with democracy.

Strategic Alliances

The strategic relations Erdoğan established with the West go back to before the AK Party's establishment. The trips Erdoğan made abroad immediately after his release from Pınarhisar Prison also gave direction to the AK Party's establishment process. On July 16, 2000, Erdoğan traveled to the U.S. as a guest of the American Jewish Committee (AJC). The contacts Erdoğan made, having met with the directors of the Jewish Institute for National Security of America (JINSA) during his stay in the U.S., roused the continuing discussions against him in Turkey.[41] The tone used selectively in the media to influence center-right voters was against Erdoğan. *Milli Gazete*, the National Outlook's media outlet, was also among those discussing Erdoğan's contacts in the West.[42] However, the media's opposition unexpectedly increased society's curiosity about Erdoğan. Conservatives were almost sure that the contacts Erdoğan made with Western and Jewish lobbies were all strategic moves. Both the Anatolian Tigers and White Turks expected Erdoğan to follow a world-integrated policy.

Following August 14, 2001, Erdoğan made important contacts abroad acting in his capacity as AK Party chairman. Following the 2002 elections, he attended the EU summit organized in the Danish capital of Copenhagen. He visited 14 countries in a brief period and meets with heads of government and state. The contacts Erdoğan made merely as par-

---

[41] Erdoğan, *Siyasî Hafıza / Eski Türkiye'den Yeni Türkiye'ye (1996-2016)*, p. 39.
[42] http://www.milligazete.com.tr/bu_yaziyi_mutlaka_okuyun/112583.

ty chairman were a first in Turkish political history. It was not long before Erdoğan drew reactions, as he was closely followed in the West and accepted by foreign heads of state. While the opposition in Turkey questioned in what capacity Erdoğan was carrying out these meetings, the answer came from EU Enlargement Commissioner Oli Rehn, who said it was "in the capacity of chairman of a successful party that succeeded in coming to power alone."[43]

Pragmatism and Erdoğan

There is benefit here to take a brief look at how pragmatism turned into practice in Erdoğan's life. The success Erdoğan achieved in the 2002 elections thanks to his charisma along with his changed political discourse was the result of the network of relationships he established both at the domestic and global level. Politics for Erdoğan consists of the collection of services that rehabilitate everyday life. Hence, politics is for Erdoğan a pragmatic means in the philosophy of politics. His philosophical foundation brings him forward as the most pragmatic and least ideological political personality in the history of the Republic. Frankly, this is not coincidental, but rather the result of his conscious choices.

Describing Erdoğan in a *Washington Post* article in 2010, Janine Zacharia wrote: "[He] doesn't seem as much of an ideologue as a pragmatic capitalist trying to make money and create markets." Zacharia explained Erdoğan's pragmatism as follows:

> Since Turkey and Syria eliminated border restrictions several months ago, the crowds of Syrians at the glittering Sanko Park

---

[43] Besli, and Özbay, *Bir Liderin Doğuşu Recep Tayyip Erdoğan*, p. 342.

Mall in this southeastern Turkish city have grown tenfold. Since Turkey and Syria eliminated border restrictions several months ago, the crowds of Syrians at the glittering Sanko Park Mall in this southeastern Turkish city have grown tenfold. Exports from Gaziantep to Syria are booming, and rich Turkish businessmen are stepping up their investments across the border.

"There's no difference between Turks and Syrians", said Olfat Ibrahim, a 35-year-old Syrian construction engineer with bags of goods in hand. She said she has stepped up her visits across the border since the lifting of visa requirements. 'Syria is Turkey.' The thriving trade is a sign of Turkey's rising influence with Syria, part of its effort to reach out to neighboring countries to build economic ties it hopes will also stabilize political relationships and expand its influence in the region. Those efforts, which include business ventures with Iran, illustrate to some extent how futile U.S. efforts to isolate those countries with sanctions have become. They've also raised concerns in Washington and in Israel about whether this key Muslim member of NATO is undergoing a fundamental realignment. Turkey's efforts, however, seem as much about economic expansion as they do about foreign policy, with an aggressive strategy of seeking new markets for Turkish businessmen, many of them backers of Prime Minister Recep Tayyip Erdogan's Justice and Development Party. To some analysts, Erdoğan doesn't seem as much of an ideologue as a pragmatic capitalist trying to make money and create markets. Turkey, meanwhile, is also looking to export some of its cultural influence. Kivanc Tatlitug, a popular soap opera star, has been so effective at promoting Turkey's interests and tourism in the region that during Foreign Minister Davutoglu's recent visit to Bulgaria, 'there was a question whether Turkey, as a government, is promoting these series as propaganda,' Davutoglu said. It is, he said, one thing the government is not doing.[44]

Although Erdoğan's political rivals have from time to time wanted to use his pragmatism against him, the topic having no social base is a striking matter that requires sociological analysis. Erdoğan, who in recent years has faced intense criticism due to the political strategies he developed with Syria, Russia, and the U.S., and the setbacks in the fight against FETÖ, continues to maintain his political charisma.[45]

EU Negotiation Process and the Military

The most strategic success achieved by the AK Party in relations with the West was the restarting of negotiations with the EU in 2004. The EU is an important political area that strengthens the AK Party's legitimacy.[46] Thus, Erdoğan would be often accused of instrumentalizing the EU and democracy.[47] However, Erdoğan made major moves in relation to EU membership, which he has considered critical on the path to Turkey's democratization from the very beginning. Turkey's negotiation process has been interpreted as a critical stage in which democracy and Islamism would adapt

---

[44]   http://www.hurriyet.com.tr/erdogan-ideologdan-cok-pragmatik-bir-kapitalist-14363856

[45]   Ruşen Çakır, "Pragmatizmin Sınırları," March 15, 2017, http://medyascope.tv/2017/03/15/erdoganin-pragmatizminin-sinirlari/

[46]   Burhanettin Duran, "AKP and Foreign Policy as an Agent of Transformation," Hakan Yavuz (ed.) *The Emergence of a New Turkey,* University of Utah Press: Salt lake 2006.

[47]   As the instrumentalization of the European Union membership process is also considered the instrumentalization of democracy, Ahmet Çiğdem criticizes Erdoğan's rapport with the EU. Çiğdem, who takes the criticism a little further, accuses the AK Party of being shameless. Taking into account that Turkey's democratization efforts over the past five decades have taken solid form in the AK Party and Erdoğan era, it would not be wrong to say that this view is a subjective approach that has found a place amid stringent ideological boundaries. See, Ahmet Çiğdem, *D'nin Hâlleri: Din, Darbe, Demokrasi,* İletişim Yayınları, Istanbul 2009, p. 131.

to one another.[48] Erdoğan was aware that the AK Party was on the right track. The first agenda article tackled within the scope of the Copenhagen criteria[49] was the apoliticization of the military. Erdoğan believes that a democracy that could unburden itself from tutelage would carry Turkey to the level of contemporary civilization, and he made every effort for this. Hence, the National Security Council was demilitarized and its secretary-general is now chosen from among civil bureaucrats and not from the military. The number of military members on the board was limited the number of civilian members increased. Similar changes were made in the Supreme Military Council. These changes were a new stage in Turkey in which the tutelage of the military over the state came to an end. The time in which the military considered itself the real owner of the country was left behind. Retired Lieutenant General Atilla Kıyat, who appeared on Star TV's *Arena* program on September 13, 2011, criticized the past reflexes of the military:

> For years, we considered ourselves the sole owner and lover of the country. Hence, we made some mistakes. Please excuse my expression; we stuck our nose into everything. We gave members to the RTÜK, we gave members to YÖK. ... We attempted to run the country through the MGK, and as a matter of fact, we did. The MGK meetings lost their purpose. They turned into monthly meetings in which it checked the government's activities.[50]

---

[48] Morris, *The New Turkey: The Quiet Revolution on The Edge of Europe*, p. 61.

[49] Copenhagen Criteria: The conditions determined at this summit held in Copenhagen, Denmark on June 22, 1993, which the countries that apply for European Union candidacy, are required to be fulfilled in order to be accepted for full membership. In accordance with this, the countries that want to become members of the European Union must reach an adequate level in areas such as the rule of law, democracy, minority and human rights, and economy.

[50] Baskın Oran, *Türk Dış Politikası: Kurtuluş Savaşından Bugüne Olgular, Belgeler, Yorumlar (2001-2012)*, İletişim Yayınları, Istanbul, 2013, Vol. 3, p. 104.

Judicial Tutelage

Another problem that needed to be solved was judicial tutelage. Certain decisions from the judiciary that were clearly in violation of the law brought to the agenda complaints that the judiciary was trying to fill the tutelage void while military tutelage waned. Maximum sentences in political and ideological cases were being given while crimes committed by pro-official ideology circles were sentenced to the minimum, and the sentences handed down in gender-related crimes, femicides, and child molestation were so low to insult the social conscience. This environment rendered judicial reform mandatory. Between 2007 and 2011, various reforms, including the structural change of the Constitutional Court and the Supreme Council of Judges and Prosecutors, were made. However, on February 7, 2012, the Istanbul specially authorized prosecutor called MİT Undersecretary Hakan Fidan, who was present at Erdoğan's Oslo meetings in the capacity of his special representative, to testify as a witness.[51] This was the indication that Turkey was face to face with a new threat. The reforms the government attempted to escape the established tutelage and to create an independent and unbiased judiciary led to an international intelligence-controlled organization that infiltrated capillaries the state to take over the judiciary. The judicial coup attempted by the "Parallel Structure" on December 17 and December 25, 2013, with instructions from Fetullah Gülen, were the clearest indication of the level of abuse in the judiciary.

The EU's Sincerity Problem

Erdoğan's determination to implement adjustment laws was

---

[51] http://t24.com.tr/haber/sabah-oslo-gorusmeleri-yabanci-bir-ajan-tarafindan-cemaate-servis-edildi,250598

praised by Western interlocutors. Erdoğan's attitude toward the EU was clear in the period starting from 2004 through to the monitoring decision in April 2017. However, EU leaders' hesitant policy became effective in Erdoğan's change of discourse. The Cyprus issue with Greek Cyprus at the center despite Turkey's intense efforts, the Readmission Agreement for which the EU has avoided fulfilling its obligations, humanitarian aid for Syrian refugees, and visa liberalization, which has turned into a long-winded story, are all chronic problems between Turkey and the EU. Later, former European Commission Vice President Günter Verheugen would criticize the West's sincerity problem:

> Germany was the one that reported that we should bring Turkey and the EU closer. Each time I called Erdoğan, who was then prime minister, he would ask what more can Turkey do in the area of democratization, and I would make various suggestions. Erdoğan fulfilled all the democratization efforts I suggested. I ask, what changed? Did Turkey change? Or is it us? Now we call Erdoğan a dictator. We are very wrong and mistaken and we must turn from this mistake at once.[52]

It would be unfair to say that the goal of full EU membership the AK Party included in its party program in 2002 failed unilaterally in the ongoing process. It is not possible to evaluate the European Union membership policy considered as the main engine of democratization as the fundamental strategic objective in AK Party governments independent of the diplomatic developments of the time. The causes of the fracture in EU-Turkey (AK Party) relations should be sought in Erdoğan's political discourse that changed after 2011 as well as the fascist political changes on a rise in the West. Al-Ja-

---

[52] http://www.aksam.com.tr/dunya/vatan-haini-can-dundari-yerine-dibine-so-kan-verheugen-turkiyeye-garanti-verilmeli/haber-606012

zeera Türk writer Galip Dalay evaluated the AK Party's attempt to position its EU goal in the center of politics as the caution of a political party that comes from a National Outlook background:

> In its first term in power, the AKP had to fight its political, economic and social inheritance from the 1990s. The heavy policies applied against the high identity demands in the 1990s, responding to the public's objections resulting from the tutelage system with more tutelage like in the system's February 28, 1997 post-modern coup, led the gap between the people and the system/government to a hard, close stage. The Alevis, leftists and liberals, and primarily the Kurds and religious, were faced with serious injustice resulting from the system and had complaints. The AKP, which came to power in such an atmosphere, being aware of the demands of the people and having seen four of its parties close down previously, acted with caution. The formula to meet the people's needs by taking into consideration the sensitivities of the system, the AKP's fundamental strategy in its first term in power, EU compliance laws were all the main engine of the articles of democratization in this period.[53]

Hesitant Politics

Erdoğan's first years in power were praised as a bright and successful term in the history of Turkish diplomacy.[54] Yet, it needs to be accepted that the fractures and rising racist, Islamophobic political discourse in the West after 2007, led relations to evolve into a critical period. The West's changing political attitude toward Erdoğan in this context developed on the axis of

---

[53] Ayşegül Büşra Özkan, "Türkiye'nin Avrupa Birliği Macerası: 2002-2015 Döneminde Yaşanan Gelişmeler," BİRSAM Report, 2015, p. 2.

[54] Kemal H. Karpat, *Kısa Türkiye Tarihi 1800-2012,* Timaş Yayınları, Pstanbul 2016, p. 285.

debates on political Islam. The attitude of Erdoğan – whose political discourse changed after 2007 – toward the West, was considered and praised by AK Party voters as a brave stance. Turkey's relations with the West reaching a critical state by 2016 strengthened the theories that AK Party rule was at the end of the road.[55] However, changing power balances and the strategic alliance period nearing an end in Turkish-U.S. relations forced Erdoğan to join the new world order that includes Russia, China, and Iran. In addition to continuing diplomatic relations with the sides, Erdoğan also continued with his populist political outbursts. He made his Shanghai Five outburst, as if to challenge the anti-Turkey sentiment that was systematically escalated in the EU. This discourse, which is considered as an axis shift, was actually not coincidental. This outburst has been interpreted as Erdoğan using an iron first in a velvet glove against those showing anti-Turkey sentiment. Although his Shanghai Five outburst contained serious problems, Erdoğan said:

> The issue is that Turkey should feel comfortable for once. It should not say the European Union is everything for us. This is my opinion. Some may be criticizing this, but I am only saying my own opinion. For example, I am saying why shouldn't Turkey be among the Shanghai Five? I hope that in the event of a positive development that, in other words, Turkey taking place among the Shanghai Five will allow it to act a lot more comfortably in this regard.[56]

China did not take long to respond: "Chinese Foreign Ministry spokesperson Geng Shuang: We highly regard Turkey's wishes."[57]

---

[55] https://tr.sputniknews.com/politika/201701051026642300-perincek-bati-erdogan/.
[56] http://www.cnnturk.com/dunya/erdoganin-sanghay-beslisi-aciklamasina-rusyadan-ilk-yorum.
[57] http://www.ntv.com.tr/dunya/cinden-turkiyenin-sangay-beslisi-ile-is-birligi-aciklamasina-destek,_ssF5DpbPkGkzuCtG19XTw.

Erdoğan and the AK Party's changing regional politics should be taken into consideration in the context of power balances that were reshaped after the onset of the Arab Spring. Even though the Syrian civil war reaching a dead end, Bashar Assad, who Erdoğan said would not "last three months", turned into a death machine that turned the region into a bloodbath for years, justifying Turkey's theories. In the final analysis, the fractures in the government's Syria policies should also be carefully noted.

The Great Middle East Project (BOP) and the U.S.

The Great Middle East Project (BOP), for which Erdoğan assumed the role as co-chair for a term, is among the matters he is most criticized on by his own base. The project, which conservative circles perceive as the preparation stage for the "Great Israel" project was declared to the public as "ensuring democracy in the Western sense in the Middle East and its near regions, the elimination of terrorism, increasing economic relations, and ensuring economic cooperation to stabilize the region."[58] However, common opinion is that:

> It is a project aimed at preventing the formation of likely forces of the United States of America and the West bloc – of which it has assumed leadership – that may rival it; aimed at renewing the maps drawn in the early 20th century and re-designing the Muslim countries in the region spanning Morocco and Indonesia to ensure control over valuable resources such as oil, natural gas, boron and thorium, and guarantee Israel's security.[59]

Upon these discussions, Erdoğan brought clarity to the

---

[58] http://www.globalresearch.ca/plans-for-redrawing-the-middle-east-the-project-for-a-new-middle-east/3882.

[59] http://sahipkiran.org/2016/09/11/buyuk-ortadogu-projesi-bop/.

matter. He said the Great Middle East Project "is a peace mission that prioritizes regional security."[60] But the project was stillborn. The paradigm shift in the U.S.' regional policies were supportive of BOP-related concerns. The rise of Israel's inhumane policies in Gaza further increased concerns. Erdoğan targeted the opposition parties that brought the matter up as a political item while he was speaking to the AK Party group on January 13, 2009. He criticizes both Israel's feature as an "occupying state" and his disturbance over the criticism turning into anti-Semitism:

> There is some talk going on. They say Erdoğan is the BOP co-chair. The objective of the Great Middle East Project is clear. What can I do if they couldn't read into this or if those who were in position then did not tell this to their chairmen? Turkey's task in the BOP is clear. The BOP was established to preserve peace. But it is a stillborn project. There is nothing that binds us to the BOP. Using this at every chance is nothing other than political exploitation. ... There are those who are disturbed by us voicing our disturbance about the death of civilians, of children. The reason Turkey has mediated between sides until now and has stepped in for cooperation is that it maintains its fair attitude, it is honest and it does not have double standards. We know that if we lose these values, if we do not voice what is right and lawful, the first thing we lose will be our self-respect. ... I am a leader who says anti-Semitism is a crime against humanity. It is impossible for us to have a wrong mindset like he is a Jew, and they are bad, she is a Jew, she is ruthless. He is not a Jew, they are so and so, and support this understanding. Hence, there are those who curse savagery in both Israel and Turkey and around the world. We see them too; we have to see them. I have to say that we also follow with great pleasure and apprecia-

---

[60] *Yeni Şafak* newspaper, January 13, 2009.

tion the Jewish movements that stand against these unlawful attacks. [Concerning criticism of his harsh rhetoric] I guess it isn't harsher than phosphorus bombs. Please excuse me, I am human before anything else, I am a father alongside my duty as prime minister before anything else. We are the children of a civilization whose principle is honesty and righteousness.[61]

As debates continued, a map published in the *Armed Forces Journal*,[62] known for its close ties to the U.S. Armed Forces, dropped like a bombshell. The map, prepared by retired Lieutenant Colonel Ralph Peters, is titled "The New Middle East",[63] and the article contains striking statements. Even though it does not fully comply with the Pentagon's doctrine, it has been claimed the map is used in the NATO Defense Academy's training. The map shows Turkey's eastern and southeastern regions as "Free Kurdistan". The change in Turkey is not the sole detail that draws attention. On the map, Saudi Arabia and Iraq are divided into three parts. Iraq is divided into "Sunni Iraq" in western Iraq and an "Arab Shiite State" in its east and south. The map, placing Kirkuk, Mosul, and the other Turkmen provinces in Kurdistan, led to unrest. Then Chief of General Staff General Yaşar Büyükanıt expressed Turkey's reaction to the map his American counterparts, which the United States Central Command (CENTCOM) is believed to be behind. This irreparable accident encountered in the project he co-chaired left Erdoğan in a difficult situation. However, Ahmet Davutoğlu, then chief adviser to the president in charge of foreign policy, said years later that Erdoğan had assumed the position as co-chair of the "Democracy Aid Group" of which Italy and Yemen are also mem-

---

[61] Grand National Assembly of Turkey AK Party Group Speech, January 13, 2009.
[62] http://armedforcesjournal.com/peters-blood-borders-map/
[63] http://www.globalresearch.ca/plans-for-redrawing-the-middle-east-the-project-for-a-new-middle-east/3882

bers, not the co-chair of BOP.[64] What is more interesting is the arguments that took place within the context of the Great Middle East Project, efforts of the opposition parties to bring it ton the agenda, and the maps leaked to the press. None got any response from the AK Party's base and Erdoğan's momentum in the confidence index always continued upward.

March 1, 2003 Resolution Crisis

Erdoğan considered relations with the West reaching a reasonable level as the requirement of the modernization adventure that began with Sultan Selim III. Just as the regulations made within the scope of the EU acquis contribute to democratization, they also paved the way to the AK Party's social legitimacy. However, the political crises with the U.S. from time to time emerged as an international legitimacy problem. The U.S.' Middle East policy, aiming to give a new form to the region ever since the early 1990s, entered a critical phase with the invasion of Iraq in 2003. Nobody was aware that the operations launched by the White House, promising to bring democracy, would drag the region into a great trauma that it would not be able to overcome for many years. Perhaps they were aware and the developments were part of a plan carried into effect. The U.S., which used arguments of the presence of weapons of mass destruction as grounds, invaded Iraq despite the United Nations deciding against it. Shiite militias executed Iraqi President Saddam Hussein, who was tried in a court set up by invading forces, on December 30, 2006, and the centuries-old Shiite-Sunni conflict ongoing in the region entered the possibly bloodiest period in its history. Years lat-

---

[64] http://www.haber7.com/siyaset/haber/642749-davutoglu-erdogan-bop-es-bas-kani-olmadi

er, former U.S. Secretary of State Colin Powell admitting that the invasion of Iraq was a mistake would be remembered as the "defeat of neocons".[65] The secret behind terrorist organizations continuing their presence in the region today, along with the sociological facts behind the emergence of Daesh-like terrorist groups,[66] are hidden in the process of the invasion of Iraq.

The U.S.'s bid to invade Iraq in March 2003 to topple the Saddam regime indicated an important fracture in Turkish-American relations. The U.S. administration sent the 4th Mechanized Division to the İskenderun port on January 2003, in hopes that Turkey would give them unconditional support. On January 19, U.S. then Chairman of the Joint Chiefs of Staff General Richard Myers came to Turkey. The AK Party government with Abdullah Gül as prime minister did not want to give the impression of a country that it was allowing the opportunity for the invasion of a Muslim country. However, the U.S. administration was absolute in its decision to intervene in Iraq. On February 1, 2003, a delegation led by Ambassador Deniz Bölükbaşı started diplomatic meetings with the U.S. The rough negotiations contributed to Turkey's fight against the PKK, and an agreement was reached on significant topics, including northern Iraq's status. The coordinates of the troops to be deployed in Turkey's southeast within the scope of the memorandum of understanding signed on February 8, 2003, was determined and preparations were completed. The U.S. waited for the result of the resolution vote the government presented to Parlia-

---

[65] Jonathan Schward, "Lie After Lie After Lie: What Colin Powell Knew Ten Years Ago Today and What He Said," 2013, http://www.huffingtonpost.com/jonathan-schwarz/colin-powell-wmd-iraq-war_b_2624620.html

[66] Madawi Al-Rasheed, and Marat Shterin, *Dying For Faith: Religiously Motivated Violence in the Contemporary World*, I.B.Tauris, New York, 2009.

ment for the intervention in Iraq. The resolution was put to a vote in Parliament on March 1, 2003, and was unexpectedly rejected.[67] Hence, the U.S.' 4th Mechanized Division, which had been waiting at the İskenderun port for almost two and a half months for Turkey to take step, had to change its route.

The draft law that would provide the U.S. Armed Forces direct and indirect logistic and military opportunities being rejected in Parliament, with 250 no votes and 264 yes votes, falling short of an absolute majority, was not the result the AK Party expected.[68] Concerning the unexpected result, Erdoğan years later evaluated the rejection of the draft law as a significant loss of position for Turkey's Middle East policy:

> I was in favor of the March 1 resolution. Those who opposed it did not say this. Back then, Bush asked for a favor from me. But unfortunately we were left with the error of our own friends. Had the March 1 resolution passed, it would have gained Turkey a seat at the table. Seeing the horizon is very important. Now, in Syria, this can go as is to a certain point only. We in Turkey have to protect our sensitivities. This airspace is also NATO's airspace. They also need to take the necessary steps. All this is also a test for everyone. We are ready against all kinds of possibilities. The Turkish Armed Forces have all kinds of authority aimed at threats targeting our country.[69]

The Parliament vote had a cold shower effect on the White House. American officials were not late to react, either. The U.S. Army raided the TSK's Special Forces Office in Sulaymaniyah, northern Iraq, on July 3, 2003. Eleven Turkish soldiers were taken under custody in the raid and

---

[67] Oran, *Türk Dış Politikası: Kurtuluş Savaşından Bugüne, Olgular, Belgeler, Yorumlar,* Vol. 3, p. 272.
[68] Grand National Assembly of Turkey, Resolution Minutes, March 1, 2003.
[69] Fikret Bilâ, "Senin Ne İşin Var Suriye'de," *Milliyet,* February 6, 2016.

handcuffed and had hoods placed over their heads. The incident, also known as the "hood crisis", aroused intense anti-American sentiment in Turkey, and Erdoğan's crisis with the U.S. would lead to Turkey being left out of the game in the region. The form of the incident was perceived as a message to the TSK, which the U.S. believed did not take enough of an initiative in the invasion. July 4 being a national holiday in the U.S. made it difficult for Turkish officials to find someone to answer in Washington. Apparently, the U.S. specifically chose July 4. In WikiLeaks documents that surface years later, a note says that the U.S. ambassador to Ankara also had no idea about the incident.[70] The crisis was mended before it escalated any further. Prime Minister Erdoğan reached U.S. Vice President Dick Cheney and asked that the soldiers be released immediately. Hence, the incident ended with the Turkish soldiers released 55 hours later.[71] The gravity of the crisis would become much clearer years later,[72] and the Ergenekon and Balyoz (Sledgehammer) cases in 2007 – which took effect with instructions from Pennsylvania – targeting the TSK would be interpreted as revenge on the TSK.

Then Secretary of State Donald Rumsfeld called the fracture in his 2012 memoire as an embarrassment: "The U.S. administration was sure. But the Turkish parliament did not approve the U.S. transit request by a razor-thin margin. The lack of support by a NATO ally in the region was a serious operational setback as well as a political embarrassment."[73] In

[70]   *Taraf*, April 4, 2011
[71]   Oran, *Türk Dış Politikası: Kurtuluş Savaşından Bugüne, Olgular, Belgeler, Yorumlar*, Vol. 3, p. 272.
[72]   Abdülkadir Özkan, *Modern Zamanların Hasan Sabbahı: Fetullah Gülen*, Kopernik Kitap, Istanbul 2017, p. 156.
[73]   Donald Rumsfeld, *Known and Unknown a Memoir*, Penguin Group, New York 2012, p. 78.

his book, *Decision Points,* former U.S. President George W. Bush said that Turkey let the U.S. down:

> We had been pressuring the Turks for months to allow us to use their lands. This way we would be able to get 15,000 soldiers from the 4th Infantry Division to into Iraq. We had promised to provide economic and military support, to help provide Turkey access to key International Monetary Fund (IMF) programs, and to continue our strong support for its accession to the EU. At one point it seemed like we were going to get the permission. Abdullah Gül's cabinet had approved our request. However, when the parliament held the final vote on the resolution on March 1, the resolution was not accepted with a slight difference. I was disappointed. In one of our most important requests to date, our NATO ally Turkey let down America.[74]

Paradigm Changes

Diplomacy crises with the U.S. during Erdoğan's time as party chairman in the period he was banned from politics, led to a serious paradigm change in Turkey's Middle East policy. Turkey now entered a new era in which it could take matters into its own hands. Erdoğan showed his attitude on Turkey taking a more active role in the region in the following years. It would not be wrong to say that the fracture between Turkey and the U.S. on March 1, 2003, continued after FETÖ's July 15 coup attempt. In this context, Erdoğan's changed political tone and new paradigm for diplomacy took shape along regional parameters. A practical reflection of this was Turkey building closer ties the Iraqi Kurdish regime, which was strengthening its regional power under Masoud Barzani. Turkey entering political and economic cooperation beyond

[74] George W. Bush, *Decision Points,* Broadway, 2011, p. 321.

recognizing the Barzani administration can be considered a critical move in terms of balances in the region.[75] In this context, homologizing Erdoğan's regional policy to Özal's would be correct. In the following period, Turkey having Barzani's support in operations it launched against PKK elements it considered a regional risk, disturbed U.S. Central Command (CENTCOM). In the following years, CENTCOM joined a strategic military alliance with the PKK's regional franchise in Syria, the Democratic Union Party (PYD) and its People's Protection Units (YPG) militia, in the north of the country and chose to give a direct message to Turkey. It seems the critical voices rising against CENTCOM from U.S. Congress as well as Turkey[76] would, however, push the U.S. administration to determine a new regional policy in the near future.

2007: Critical Threshold in Politics

The most critical threshold in the AK Party's political adventure that began in 2002 has been the developments that took place until 2007. The year 2007 had two elections scheduled, one for president and parliamentary elections. The atmosphere ahead of the presidential election was blurry. Erdoğan's outburst targeting CHP Chairman Deniz Baykal in which he said: "Don't run for presidency. Don't you dare",[77] further activated the people who participated in the Republic Rallies. Erdoğan's presidential candidacy was considered to be a strong possibility. As the presidential candidacy of party chairs is common practice in Turkish political tradition, expectations remained the same. The likelihood of a hija-

---

[75] Gökhan Atılgan, Cenk Saraçoğlu, and Ateş Uslu, *Osmanlı'dan Günümüze Türkiye'de Siyasal Hayat*, Yordam Kitap, Istanbul, 2015, p. 902.

[76] http://www.washingtontimes.com/news/2015/jan/28/inside-the-ring-gen-james-mattis-criticizes-obama-/

[77] Grand National Assembly of Turkey CHP Group Meeting, Minutes, May 4, 2007.

bi woman becoming first lady in Çankaya Palace increased the restlessness of secular and Kemalist circles. On December 24, 2006, former the Chief Public Prosecutor of the Supreme Court of Appeals, Sabih Kanadoğlu, made a comment that was debated in depth. He said that the presidential election could not take place in the event the number of deputies present in Parliament does not reach 367. This is a critical argument that can be used against Erdoğan in politics. Calculations were made to be over 367. The CHP decided to protest the Parliament session by not participate in the vote.

As the discussions continued, Erdoğan announced on April 24, 2007 that Foreign Minister and Kayseri Deputy Abdullah Gül, who he called "my brother", as the presidential candidate. However, in a speech he made at the War Academies Command ahead of the election, President Ahmet Necdet Sezer riled up debates in politics by saying: "Turkey is a political regime; never since the establishment of the Republic has it encountered such danger",[78] which prepared the psychological grounds for the deep forces that see themselves as the key element of the state. The first round of voting in the presidential election was held in Parliament on April 27, 2007. AK Party candidate Gül received 357 votes and was not elected in the first round. The military, which received the signal from Sezer, broke its silence in the evening, and a statement published on the website of the General Staff, would go in the history of Turkish coups as the "e-memorandum". The statement, supposedly written personally by Chief of General Staff General Yaşar Büyükanıt,[79] almost openly threatened the government to withdraw Gül as a candidate. Büyükanıt, who gave a statement in 2015 to the Public Prosecutor of An-

---

[78] Erdoğan, *Siyasî Hafıza / Eski Türkiye'den Yeni Türkiye'ye (1996-2016)*, p. 94.
[79] Aydın, and Taşkın, *1960'tan Günümüze Türkiye Tarihi*, p. 477.

kara, refute allegations, saying: "As claimed by certain groups, it was in no way a memorandum directed at the executive body or a bid aimed at our constitutional order under the guarantee of our Constitution."[80]

The TSK e-memorandum contains striking statements:

The problem recently standing out in the presidential election process is focused on the discussion of secularism. This is followed by the Turkish Armed Forces with concern. It should not be forgotten that the Turkish Armed Forces is a party in these discussion and the absolute advocate of secularism. Furthermore, the Turkish Armed Forces is absolutely against the ongoing discussions and negative comments and, where necessary, it will openly and clearly demonstrate its attitude and behavior. Nobody has a doubt about it.

In summary, everybody who stands against the "How happy is he who says I am a Turk!" understanding of Great Leader Atatürk, the founder of our Republic, is an enemy of the Republic of Turkey and will remain so. The Turkish Armed Forces maintains its unwavering determination in relation to perfectly fulfilling the clear duty assigned to it by law to protect these qualities, and its devotion and faith in this determination is absolute.[81]

The AK Party was not unresponsive to the TSK's e-memorandum. While government spokesman Cemil Çiçek clearly said in a press conference that the government does not recognize the memorandum, he said that the chiefs of General Staff are bureaucrats who have responsibilities to the presidency.[82] The AK Party's brave stance against the military al-

[80] http://www.trthaber.com/haber/turkiye/buyukanitin-27-nisan-e-muhtirasi-na-iliskin-ifadesi-222976.html
[81] http://www.hurriyet.com.tr/genelkurmaydan-cok-sert-aciklama-6420961
[82] http://www.dailymotion.com/video/xvhrbx_cemil-cicek-ten-27-nisan-e-muhtirasina-cevap_news

so gained praise from the left. In the following days, the Constitutional Court cancelled the application made by the CHP to cancel the presidential election. The court decision was no different from Sabih Kanadoğlu's orientation. The decision was made to cancel the elections. This time, on May 1, 2007, the AK Party and Erdoğan faced the Supreme Court's arbitrary decision. As a result of Erdoğan's foresighted policy, the AK Party decided to hold early elections on July 22, 2007. The process was extremely critical in terms of both the AK Party and Erdoğan's political future. That the AK Party won the elections and increased its vote share by 12 percent is no surprise. However, there was confusion about the kind of strategy to follow regarding presidential candidates.

Road to the Closure Case

Erdoğan did not want the still-budding AK Party to encounter an operation similar to the other National Outlook-based parties. Hence, Erdoğan's general attitude was to stand tall and not be stubborn against the military and tutelage groups. Thus, changing the presidential candidate, determining a new figure who would not create compliance problems in the transition phase was opened to debate behind closed door. Erdoğan was in favor of a smooth transition. This was also what his pragmatist political identity necessitated. The person of interest circulating in lobbies was National Defense Minister Vecdi Gönül, who was known to have good relations with the military. Claims related to Gönül's presidential candidacy would happen was in WikiLeaks documents that surfaced years later.[83] Abdullah Gül, however, did not want to withdraw his candidacy. Bülent Arınç was also in favor of Gül

---

[83] http://www.aljazeera.com.tr/portre/portre-vecdi-gonul

continuing his candidacy. Erdoğan was worried that Gül's insistence to stay on would push Turkey and the AK Party into a traumatic turn. Gül and Arınç's pressure produced results and the AK Party again presented Gül as candidate.[84] Following the 367 crisis, Erdoğan made an unexpected move and dealt a major blow to Kemalist tutelage with a radical reform that would eventually carry Turkey to an executive presidential government system in 2019.[85] The constitutional change that proposed the president be elected by the people was accepted with 69 percent of the vote in a referendum held on October 21, 2007. The AK Party responded to the Constitutional Court's arbitrary decision led by the CHP in relation to the quorum in the presidential election with a system reform. Thus, the nearly century-old paradigm of the Republic took an entirely different form with Erdoğan's reformist outbursts.

The regime change concerns of the anxious elites took on an Erdoğanophobic character with the changes in the fundamental paradigms of the founding ideology and concerns regarding Gül's presidential candidacy for the second time were justified. Turkey's old diseases returned during the deadlocked period of political struggles to overcome and, upon the complaint of the Chief Public Prosecutor's Office of the Supreme Court of Appeals on March 14, 2008, a case was filed with the Constitutional Court, demanding the permanent closure of the AK Party.[86]

---

[84] The AK Party passed the minimum number of 367 votes required for the presidential election with the support of the MHP. Kayseri Deputy Abdullah Gül was elected the Republic of Turkey's 11th president with 339 votes in the third round of voting held in the Parliamentary General Assembly. (August 28, 2007); Erdoğan, *Siyasî Hafıza / Eski Türkiye'den Yeni Türkiye'ye (1996-2016)*, p. 100.

[85] Çınar, *Vesayetçi Demokrasiden "Millî" Demokrasiye*, p. 111.

[86] "The Constitutional Court announced its decision on the closure case filed by the Chief Public Prosecutor of the Supreme Court of Appeals on the grounds that the AKP was the center of acts in violation of secularism. The Supreme Court dec-

The Dolmabahçe Meeting and Afterward

An important meeting that should not be overlooked took place in 2007. Erdoğan accepted Chief of General Staff General Yaşar Büyükanıt in his Dolmabahçe Office on May 4, 2007. He made no statement on the content of the meeting. It is not difficult to guess that the TSK's anti-democratic attitude toward the government was laid on the table in the meeting held after the e-memorandum. However, about one month after the meeting, on June 12, 2007, a new agenda took politics captive. Although it is hard to figure out at first glance, the concrete data that was revealed in later years, would lead to comments and observations that the content of the Dolmabahçe meeting was more critical than previously thought.[87]

The Istanbul Police Department responded to a tip-off and raided a makeshift house in Ümraniye. The 27 hand grenades and explosives seized in the makeshift home being registered in the TSK's inventory was a confusing find. The ammunition found in the following months in different provinces also being registered in the TSK's inventory further increased concerns.[88] On April 29, 2009, then Chief of General Staff General İlker Başbuğ, who was later arrested on accusations of running a terrorist organization, said that there was suspicion of a set-

---

reed that the AKP remain active, but its treasury support be reduced by half. The decision of the Constitutional Court on the case filed demanding the closure of the AKP was announced by Chief Judge Haşim Kılıç. Kılıç reminded that the case was filed upon the demand for its permanent closure in accordance with Political Parties Law No. 2008, article 101/b in the sixth paragraph of the Constitution Article 69, on the grounds that the AKP has become the center of acts in violation of secularism, and that with this case, the banning of 61 people from politics. Kılıç announced that as a result of negotiations, the Constitutional Court decided against the closure of the AKP." July 30, 2008;http://www.milliyet.com.tr/karar--font-color-red-bugun-mu--font--aciklanacak--siyaset-972729/

[87] http://www.haberturk.com/gundem/haber/1398471-basbakan-basdanisma-ni-abdulkadir-ozkan-feto-dolmabahcede-bitecekti

[88] http://www.cumhuriyet.com.tr/haber/diger/57056/Beykoz_daki_kazida_silah-lar_bulundu__.html

up in the process and contended: "Weapons are the military's honor. These weapons do not belong to the TSK."[89] The name of the TSK, which submitted the e-memorandum not long before, being involved in the process clarified the picture. The top story in *Taraf*, "AKP ve Güven'i Bitirme Planı" (Plan to End AKP and Trust), hurled Turkey toward a dangerous course to the Ergenekon and Balyoz (Sledgehammer) investigations and trials. Years later it would be understood that the manipulations in this critical course were operations conducted by the Parallel State Structure. Erdoğan, who saw the big game with Başbuğ's imprisonment, took a clear stance against the Ergenekon process, which he advocated at the time, and said: "I find the likenings and ascriptions made in relation to İlker Pasha wrong. In other words, I find approaches such as that he is an organization member absolutely vile. I certainly believe that ascribing, likening such to a man who served as chief of General Staff in the Turkish Armed Forces to be wrong and unjust."[90] Thus, Erdoğan went on record once more as the political leader who managed to overcome another major obstacle thanks to his pragmatism.

What Changed in 2007?

Erdoğan's political ideology is formed around the Turkish right wing's national will tradition, saying that the people's common mind, the collective conscious, would not make a mistake, and giving the national will a metaphysical meaning beyond the democratic differences and conflicts.[91] Thanks to his national will-based political discourse, the e-memoran-

---

[89] http://www.ntv.com.tr/turkiye/basbug-poyrazkoy-silahlari-tskya-ait-degil,nkbvmfx2-k6NUCDnYOL2kg
[90] http://www.sabah.com.tr/gundem/2012/08/06/basbugdan-erdogana-tesekkur
[91] Bora, *Cereyanlar, Türkiye'de Siyasî İdeolojiler*, p. 479.

dum in 2007, which was a new manifestation of the elites-nation conflict, was overturned with determination. Erdoğan, who did not backtrack in the face of the e-memorandum, the closure case, the Republic Rallies that were preparations for social insurrection, the presidential election, the Council of State's raid, the Zirve Publishing House attack, the illegal organizations that wanted to create an unstable environment, which he encountered during the same period, only strengthened his stance in favor of democracy. Erdoğan came out stronger in the 2007 elections and largely succeeded in keeping the military outside of politics with the changes he made in the military's echelons of command. The differentiation in Erdoğan's political discourse in the face of the secular-Kemalist cliques that continued to easily use the psychological instruments of February 28 in 2007 was not surprising. Erdoğan was stuck somewhere in between the military and the movement and struggled to survive between the two big threats in internal politics. As a result, Turkey was dragged into the psychological atmosphere of interim periods and relations with the EU lost significant momentum due to the West's lack of sincerity. Turkey's EU membership constantly being postponed, despite the country fulfilling the EU's adjustment laws to the letter, led Erdoğan to accuse the EU of being a Christian club. Similar problems encountered in Cyprus led Erdoğan to identify the Copenhagen criteria as the Ankara criteria. Although Erdoğan's Ankara criteria outburst came across as Turkey's claim of self-confidence, it was also subjected to criticism that it was a kind of diplomatic introvertedness.

When all these negative conditions are taken into consideration, the differentiation in Erdoğan's political discourse can be seen more clearly. However, it should be noted that the setbacks were not the only factors affecting Erdoğan's politics. The political success he achieved in the 2007 election turned him into the most important political figure in the history of the Republic. The self-confident outbursts he made, continuing on the path with the power of the national will, gaining the support of almost one out of every two people, was interpreted as the end of the transition period phase and the start of the return to the basics. However, trying to explain the change with Erdoğan's pragmatist political style alone is neither a correct analysis nor adequate. Therefore, the problematic areas of the period need to be determined correctly. The West's changed political attitude and Israel's occupying state practices in the Middle East had started to escalate once again. The U.S.' shift in its policies on the region and the internal dynamics of an out-of-control Turkey stood out as major problems that Erdoğan and the AK Party were expected to solve then. Analyzing Erdoğan's change in 2007 from this perspective yields the correct result.

The Kurdish Question and the Reconciliation Process

In 2005, Erdoğan made a critical move that would go into Turkish political history. He rolled up his sleeves to produce a permanent solution to the Kurdish question, which is almost as old as the Republic. Erdoğan's new attitude signaled a new paradigm outside the established state reflexes. Taking into consideration that the existence of Kurds was totally ignored with bans, let alone the state producing a solution,[92] the kind of mines that fill the field Erdoğan was trying to step through could be seen a lot clearer. Erdoğan was determined. A prime

---

[92] Metin Heper, "Devlet Kürtleri ne asimile etti, ne inkâr etti sadece bilinçli olarak göz ardı etti", *Hürriyet* newspaper, October 12, 2008; http://www.hurriyet.com.tr/devlet-kurtleri-ne-asimile-etti-ne-ink-r-etti-sadece-bilincli-olarak-goz-ardi-etti-10094707

minister taking concrete steps to solve one of Turkey's chronic problems for the first time since Turgut Özal disturbed certain groups. Erdoğan used the "Kurdish question" as a phrase for the first time in a meeting he attended and gave a new definition to the problem. The statements he made, having internalized the Kurdish question as his own problem, was extremely unorthodox. Although similar discourses have become very common in everyday politics now, the stance Erdoğan took on the unstable political ground of 2005 is significant:

> Every problem does not necessarily need to be named because the problems belong to us all. But if you must name them, the Kurdish question is not part of a nation, but the problem of all. It is my problem, too. Problems do not have divided addresses. Whether they are Turkish, Kurdish, Circassian, Abkhazian, or Laz, all problems are the common problem of the citizens of the Republic of Turkey. This is because the sun makes everybody warm, because the rain is mercy for all, because everybody, we all are a member of the same land, this is what it means to be a nation.

> Therefore, I tell those who ask what will happen to the Kurdish question that as the prime minister of this country, that problem is my problem before anyone else's. If they were to ask me about another matter of this country, I would tell them that matter is also my matter before anybody else's. We are a big state and, as a nation, we are going to solve every problem within the scope of the fundamental principles of the Republic, the Constitutional order we inherited from the founders of this country with more democracy, more citizenship laws, with greater prosperity, and this is the understanding with which we solve them and will solve them.[93]

Erdoğan continued his approach for a resolution to the problem in following years, despite the obstacles. In a speech

---

[93] Recep Tayyip Erdoğan's August 12, 2005, Diyarbakır speech.

he made in Parliament in 2010, he once again determined the agenda with the outburst, "As prime minister, I am defending the Kurdish question and I will continue to defend it."[94] Erdoğan was sincere in his position. He considered the resolution of the Kurdish question a critical threshold for the new Turkey to reach its goals. Erdoğan saw the ethnic nationalist discourse starting to rise in the Middle East with the Arab Spring as a serious threat to Turkey's perpetuity, and he took action to eliminate the obstacles standing in the way of democratization. He eliminated the obstacles that stood in the way of speaking Kurdish. This paved the way for Kurdish publicity. Universities were permitted to establish Kurdish language departments. Military operations were minimized, allowing the terrorist organizations in Turkey to leave the country. Despite the objections from the opposition, an environment of de-confliction was formed. The Kurds, thus, achieve the greatest political support they never before received throughout the history of the Republic under Erdoğan's rule. Erdoğan explained the point reached:

> You couldn't speak Kurdish on the streets, let alone be there Kurdish television broadcasts, newspaper or magazine publications. This country has witnessed people imprisoned for singing in Kurdish. Late Ahmet Kaya experienced so much trouble and was attacked by the media for saying that he was going to make a Kurdish album. My brothers and sisters, Ahmet Kaya, who was forced to leave Turkey, passed away yearning for his home country. Even dreaming of Kurdish education was not possible. We are the ones who solved all of these problems. The Diyanet said they would abolish the recently published a Kurdish translation of the Quran with the title Qur'an-ı Piroz Kurdi.[95]

---

[94] Grand National Assembly of Turkey speech, December 27, 2010.
[95] Mayıs 2, 2015 Batman speech.

However, in the following months, to the exploitative attitude of the other side in the Kurdish question, Erdoğan said, "It will be resolved even if it costs my life." The presence of a hand trying to sabotage the process through KCK operations that was realized late and turned the road that was set off on with hope of peace into a minefield. Speaking at an AK Party meeting in Muş in 2011, Erdoğan's political discourse evolved when he said, "There is no Kurdish problem in this country, there is a terrorism problem, there is a PKK problem."[96]

Trench Strategy, Revolutionary People's War!

On August 8, 2015, the PKK terrorist organization, which seemed to want to stage something like a rehearsal for a kind of civil war by carrying terrorist attacks to city centers, started to implement its revolutionary people's war with a trench strategy that turned Diyarbakır, Mardin, Hakkari, Cizre, and Silopi into fiery brimstone.

The ammunition was later found to have been stored in the cities with FETÖ members working in the region during the reconciliation process turning a blind eye. In the ensuing violence, 249 soldiers and security personnel died. Hence, all the efforts made to solve the Kurdish question, for which progress could be achieved only by paying a great price, was replaced by an irreparable new process. The point reached in the process affected Erdoğan's political discourse, as well. In a program he attended in Balıkesir in 2015, Erdoğan, the architect of the reconciliation process, said: "Now everything is about the Kurdish question. What Kurdish question are you talking about? There is no longer such a thing.

---

[96] http://www.haberturk.com/gundem/haber/626064-bu-ulkede-artik-kurt-soru-nu-yoktur.

What are you lacking? Did you vote for a prime minister? Are there ministers from among you? Yes. Do you have a presence in the TSK? Yes. What do you want, what more do you want?"[97] And just as Turkey was so close to reaching a solution to another gangrenous problem, it had to shelve it.

An important detail needs to be taken note of here. The definition of "one people" that Erdoğan embedded into Rabia, a term he added to the literature following the bloody coup in Egypt, is actually the manifestation of a homogenous description of a nation. It is not an approach that ignores Kurdish identity, as claimed. It is actually the definition of a supra-cultural identity that rejects ethnicity-based nationalist discourse, like Mustafa Kemal Atatürk emphasize in his statement, "How happy is he who says I am a Turk." With this discourse, which rejects ethnic nationalism in its entirety, Erdoğan described the demands concerning ethnic identities as a millennium-old game played by those wanting to wipe out the nation, which he likened to a great sycamore tree, as divisiveness, separatism, ethnic nationalism, racist nationalism, and religious nationalism.[98] As a result, Erdoğan thought ethnic differences could be dissolved through the common religious connection. At this point, he disassociated himself from the nationalism politics of the founding ideology and Atatürk, who thought that differences could be blended with a cultural revolution by moving away from what is religious. In saying that there was no longer a Kurdish problem, Erdoğan chose to evaluate the matter independently from an ethno-political definition.

---

[97] http://www.cumhuriyet.com.tr/haber/siyaset/231433/Erdogan_agiz_degistirdi__Ne_Kurt_sorunu_ya_.html

[98] Ülkü Doğanay, Halise Karaaslan Şanlı, and İnan Özdemir Taştan, *Seçimlik Demokrasi: Recep Tayyip Erdoğan, Kemal Kılıçdaroğlu, Devlet Bahçeli ve Selahattin Demirtaş'in Demokrasi Söylemi*, İmge Kitabevi, Istanbul, 2017, p. 142.

A Kurdish politician who found the discussion of the problem in the restricted context of ethnic nationalism dangerous was Ahmet Türk. Türk said that the discussions need to be taken out of the restricted context of nationalism, otherwise Kurds would not be able to establish their future correctly.[99] Although the HDP aimed to become a party for all Turkey in the 2014 presidential election in efforts to this end, the hesitant political discourse that was unable to escape the PKK's control did not allow Kurdish politics to find a social ground in the country's west.

Habur Crisis

Having given so much detail in relation to the reconciliation process, other important details must also be remembered. Perhaps the most critical road accident in the reconciliation process took place in Habur, on October 20, 2009. Thirty-four PKK members, who come from the Qandil and Mahmour camps upon PKK leader Abdullah Öcalan's call, entered Turkey through the Habur border gate. In the incident that took place as a noteworthy stage of the PKK strategy of laying down its arms and surrendering, the PKK members were almost welcomed with a ceremony. Those who arrived being tried by the mobile court and released escalated debates.[100] In addition to claims that there was no Turkish flag hanging in the court room, the welcoming footage appearing on television led to security forces, the judge, and prosecutors being accused of betrayal. Accusa-

---

[99] Namık Kemal Dinç, *Onlar Gittiler Biz Barışı Yitirdik*, İletişim Yayınları, Istanbul, 2016, p. 67.

[100] Of the 34 people tried, 29 were released by the prosecutor's office and five by the Silopi Criminal Court of Peace. See, http://blog.milliyet.com.tr/habur-da-kurulan-gecici-mahkeme-salonundan-turk-bayragi-ve-ataturk-portresi-niye-kaldirildi-/Blog/?BlogNo=241248

tions that the government gave legal assurance to the musical welcoming ceremony became the political opportunity the MHP was after all along to win back the nationalist vote that had shifted to the AK Party. The government was accused of implementing Öcalan's plan. Erdoğan responded to criticism and, protecting the process despite its political risks, said:

> Is it possible to have no hope in the face of the scene witnessed at the Habur border gate? This is a hope. Something is happening in Turkey, good, beautiful things are happening. There are hopeful developments. Thirty-four people crossed the border and were released within our laws. I would like to state that I consider this to be an extremely positive and delightful development. Some media groups are making statements implying that this process is controlled from İmralı Island. One would ask, wasn't he there for the last 11 or 12 years? Why wasn't such a step made? This is currently a step that has been taken as a requirement of a democratic initiation process, a project of brotherhood.[101]

Erdoğan also warned the DTP – later to become the HDP – which exploited the process: "Those wanting to turn this beautiful picture into a political show again, please behave responsibly." However, the development MHP Chairman Devlet Bahçeli called "dishonor",[102] in the long term, caused great injury to the national unity and brotherhood project that was launched to solve the Kurdish question. Hence, these incidents were the most traumatic road accident in the reconciliation process. However, one important detail surfaced years later when Hakim Asabil Yırtıcı, who interrogated the PKK

---

[101] *Radikal* newspaper, October 21, 2009.
[102] Devlet Bahçeli, Grand National Assembly of Turkey MHP Group Speech, February 16, 2010; https://www.dunya.com/gundem/mhp039den-hukumete-habur-tepkisi-haberi-105911.

members at Habur, was arrested after the July 15 coup attempt as a FETÖ member.[103]

Did We Drive Peace Away?

As a close follower of the AK Party's Kurdish policy, journalist Halime Kökçe is one of those who still maintain hope for the reconciliation despite all the negative incidents that happened. Kökçe summarized the process that started in 2005 and the point it has reached as follows:

> The political will took serious risks with the policies implemented under the reconciliation process, the discourse formed and in matters the country's west needed to be convinced about, and frankly, it managed to bring the matter to a certain point. However, at the end of the process, the government and President Erdoğan came to the point of saying, "There is no Kurdish question, there is the problem of my Kurdish citizens." Lifting the bans related to speaking Kurdish, the state allowing Kurdish broadcasts, opening of TRT Kurdi, Kurdish being taught at schools as an elective subject, Kurdish language and literature departments being opened in universities under the name of living languages, doing publicity in Kurdish and making one's defense in Kurdish becoming possible. The democratization steps taken since the AK Party came to power in 2002, had improved the general state of Kurds. There was no more need after this to give the definition of the Kurdish question. Kurdish citizens may well have certain problems like all the other citizens, but it would not be right to associate these with an ethnic belonging. This was the state and government's new approach to the matter. These were steps that

---

[103] http://t24.com.tr/haber/haburda-pkklilar-icin-kurulan-mahkemenin-hakimi-fetoden-tutuklu,369619.

could not even be dreamed of when compared to the times Kurdish was confined to homes.

However, this new approach was not received very well among the Kurds who are close to the PKK. The AK Party was criticized for moving in a pro-security direction and becoming like the MHP. Back in the days when the PKK members who were involved in violence entered the country through Habur on the condition of laying down arms, Turkey entered a new period in which it was targeted by the PKK, Daesh and FETÖ triangle, and it witnessed the July 15 coup attack. During this timeframe, dreams about the reconciliation process were shattered. ... Almost all studies conducted in Turkey show that Turks and Kurds, unlike in the other countries they live, are close-knit and, despite the PKK's violence, the state's attitude at one time that made ambiguous the distinction between the terrorist organization and the Kurdish people, this deep-seated relationship remains unshaken. Perhaps this is the strongest capital we possess. At the end of the day, we are going to solve this problem here, together, and perhaps, even if the time comes when we have no democratic deficiencies, all economic imbalances are eliminated, we will still be discussing this topic in one aspect. Ethno-political problems are never solved entirely. However, the theory that nationalisms formed and were produced before nations had gained significance is the strongest ideology to date. Once it spreads through the system, it is not easy to overcome.

We see today that despite the intense, bloody violence that followed the reconciliation process and the physical and psychological destruction it led to, there is still hope for peace. We frightened peace, but we haven't driven it away.[104]

---

[104] Halime Kökçe, *AK Parti ve Kürtler*, Kopernik Kitap, Istanbul, 2017, pp 14-19.

Chronology of the Reconciliation Process

With the failure of the process, Erdoğan was again targeted.[105] He was also targeted by figures who at one time served in important positions in the AK Party.[106] Those criticizing Erdoğan somehow did not see those who turned the streets into a bloodbath on October 5-6, and the PKK's actions and discourse that undermined the process. The European Union's collective political stance supportive of terrorism also led to Erdoğanophobic outbursts. With the impact of HDP politicians carrying out systematic operations in the West, Erdoğan was accused both in Turkey and abroad as "sacrificing [the reconciliation process] for his political ambitions."[107] However, realpolitik is much different than what is claimed. Just as making an analysis without taking into account the exploitations that led the process to failure, this would not be a just stance, either. Therefore, it is necessary to closely examine how the process was abused from 2012 onward:

• December 16, 2012: MİT Undersecretary Hakan Fidan visits İmralı Island Prison to meet with Öcalan.

• December 29, 2012: Prime Minister Erdoğan announces live on TRT that they had a meeting at İmralı Prison.

• January 3, 2013: The first BDP delegation, consisting of Ayla Akat, Altan Tan, and Ahmet Türk, visits İmralı.

• January 8, 2013: Sakine Cansız, Fidan Doğan, and Leylâ Söylemez are murdered in the attack on a PKK office in Paris.

[105] Hakan Aksay, "Erdoğan'ın savaşına hayır, barış süreci korunmalıdır" July 29, 2015; http://t24.com.tr/yazarlar/hakan-aksay/erdoganin-savasina-hayir-baris-sureci-korunmalidir,12387.
[106] https://www.haberler.com/dengir-mir-mehmet-firat-ak-parti-bogulma-emareleri-6604089-haberi/.
[107] http://www.haberturk.com/gundem/haber/1182321-kilicdaroglundan-erdogana-elestiri-sen-bu-yemini-niye-ettin.

• January 10, 2013: On the plane back from Africa, Erdoğan evaluates the demand for a law to be passed in Parliament for withdrawal: "What can we guarantee them. Certain operations were conducted in previous outbursts. We will not allow such acts in outbursts they make by dropping their weapons."

• January 17, 2013: The funeral ceremony held in Diyarbakır for the three female PKK member is attended by hundreds of thousands of people and calls are made for peace.

• February 24, 2013: The PKK's urban militia, the Patriotic Revolutionary Youth Movement (YDG-H) announces its establishment.

• February 28, 2013: The minutes of the meeting between the BDP delegation and Öcalan on February 23, 2013 in İmralı Prison are published in *Milliyet* with the signature of a journalist with close ties to the HDP. In the minutes, it is revealed that businessman Osman Kavala sent a letter to Öcalan that said, "Do not support the presidential system." Two people working at the BDP headquarters in question are fired in relation to the leaking of the minutes.

•March 21, 2013: Öcalan's letter is read out during the Nowruz celebrations in Diyarbakır: "We have reached the point of silencing weapons and communicating through ideas. I repeat again, we are at the stage of withdrawing our armed elements beyond the border. This is not giving up on the fight, but the start of a much different fight."

• April 4, 2013: The 63-member Wisemen Committee is determined and they start to go around Turkey.

• April 15, 2013: The fifth BDP delegation visits İmralı.

• April 18, 2013: The military's authority to conduct operations is bound to governors with a protocol signed between the Interior Ministry and the General Staff and a regulation made to the Provincial Administration Law.

• April 20, 2013: MHP Chairman Bahçeli starts rallies against the reconciliation process. CHP Chairman Kılıçdaroğlu accuses the government of leaving the initiative for the reconciliation process to the PKK.

• April 25, 2013: Murat Karayılan announces at a Qandil press conference broadcast live and attended by hundreds of journalists that the PKK will withdraw as of May 8, without any pre-condition.

• April 30, 2013: The number of people released in the KCK cases reaches 200.

• May 7, 2013: BDP Co-Chair Selahattin Demirtaş: "The withdrawal officially starts tomorrow. We estimate it will last three to four months. The government has also taken certain administrative measures concerning withdrawal."

• May 8, 2013: The Parliamentary Investigation Commission that was established in Parliament to seek ways for social peace and to evaluate the reconciliation process holds its first conference. The CHP and MHP provide no members for the commission.

• May 29, 2013: The Gezi Park protests start in Istanbul. From the first day there are voices asking where the Kurds are.

• June 7, 2013: Demirtaş, who meets with Öcalan on İmralı Island, says: "Abdullah Öcalan salutes the Gezi Park insurgents. He made a call to watch out for provocation, he said, 'The Ergenekon group should not be given an opportunity.'"

• June 26, 2013: Erdoğan meets with members of the Wisemen Committee who present their report at Dolmabahçe Palace. Some members do not attend the meeting due to the Gezi protests. In response to the question, "The PKK has been drawn abroad and the first stage is complete. Now the government is expected to take steps," Erdoğan says, "Only 15 percent of the organization has withdrawn."

• July 2, 2013: In June, the PKK calls for action on fortified gendarmerie stations. The construction of fortified gendarmerie stations is actually not a new matter. At the time the PKK stated its withdraw outside the borders, 114 stations were completed. Demonstrator Medeni Yıldırım dies in demonstrations in Lice, Diyarbakır, in protest of the fortified gendarmerie station and road operations.

• July 5, 2013: Cemil Bayık and Bese Hozat become the KCK co-chairs.

• July 10, 2013: The YDG-H starts to establish public order units in cities and broadcasts oath-taking ceremonies over Twitter. Hijackings and vehicle arson start.

• July 31, 2013: Cemil Bayık speaks on BBC Turkish: "If the government takes no step until September 1, we are going to stop the withdrawal and those who have withdrawn will also return."[108]

• August 11, 2013: The first association with Kurdistan in its name is established.

• August 12, 2013: PYD Co-Chair Salih Muslim comes to Turkey.

• August 19, 2013: Cemil Bayık says, "If the process collapses, it could lead to a greater war."[109]

---

[108] http://www.haberturk.com/yazarlar/nihal-bengisu-karaca/1117505-neden-buzdolabinda
[109] http://www.adanapost.com/cemil-bayik-buyuk-savas-olur-32654h.htm

• September 9, 2013: KCK announces that it has halted the withdrawal.

• September 30, 2013: The government announces its democratization package. Kurdish is allowed in private schools. The oath is lifted. The BDP and DTK say, "The mountain has brought forth a mouse."[110]

• October 29, 2013: Cemil Bayık requests a third party for the first time in negotiations.[111]

• November 16, 2013: Erdoğan holds a rally in Diyarbakır with Iraqi Kurdistan Regional Government President Masoud Barzani and Şiwan Perwer. In the rally, Erdoğan says: "We will see those in the mountains come down, prisons empty, [the population of] 76 million become one, come together to form the great Turkey, become the new Turkey. Have no doubt."[112]

• December 3, 2013: Cemil Bayık: "If it goes like this, of course there will be war in Turkey. We gave them until spring. If they accept these conditions by spring, if they take a step in the direction of negotiation, they will advance on the path to solution. Otherwise, it is no longer possible for us to continue business like this."[113]

• December 6, 2013: Two protesters die in the incidents that erupt because of the PKK cemetery in Yüksekova.

• December 17, 2013: The Gülen Movement severs ties with the AK Party, showing the closing down of prep schools

---

[110] http://www.radikal.com.tr/politika/paketten-yasam-tarzi-cikti-1153298/
[111] http://www.iktibasdergisi.com/catismasizlik-nasil-sona-erdi/
[112] http://www.cumhuriyet.com.tr/haber/turkiye/9947/Erdogan__Cezaevlerinin_bosaldigini_gorecegiz_.html
[113] www.milliyet.com.tr/kandil-den-tehdit-gibi-aciklama/gundem/detay/1802013/default.htm

as grounds for the move, and presses the button for the December 17 and December 25 judicial coup to start.

• January 11, 2014: Öcalan meets with the İmralı delegation and calls the

December 17 and December 25 attempt a coup: "Those who want to turn the country into a disaster area once again with a coup should know that we are not going to carry wood to this fire. We will stand against every coup attempt from now on as we have until now."[114]

• January 17, 2014: Photographs of Öcalan taken with HDP members at İmralı are shared via the media.

• January 21, 2014: The PYD declares democratic autonomy in Rojava. News that the AK Party is backing al-Nusra Front spread fast in PKK media.

• March 15, 2014: The KCK announces it has ended the process once again: "The AKP government is no longer the addressee of the democratization process launched by leader Apo, for whose success our movements have also exerted great efforts."[115]

• March 17, 2014: Murat Karayılan: "As long as Öcalan is in prison, the PKK will not lay down its arms. Provided that no step is taken until a couple weeks after the election, everybody needs to know that the process is over."[116]

• March 21, 2014: Öcalan's letter is read out on Nowruz in Diyarbakır: "We were not afraid when resisting, we will not be afraid when making peace either." Öcalan maintains

---

[114] http://www.radikal.com.tr/turkiye/ocalan-bu-atese-benzin-tasimayaca-giz-1170417/
[115] http://www.bbc.com/turkce/haberler/2014/03/140315_kck_akp
[116] http://www.karar.com/gundem-haberleri/pkk-ve-hdp-cozum-surecini-boy-le-bitirdi

his post-December 17 stance: "The burning question in front of us awaiting an answer is whether we will continue on our path with repetitive coups or a full and radical democracy."[117]

• March 30, 2014: Local elections are held. The AK Party, which is claimed to have lost blood in the December 17 and December 25 processes, shows that it has maintained its power with 45 percent of the vote.

• April 26, 2014: Adjustments are made to the MİT law, adding: "MİT members can meet with the detainees and convicts held in penitentiary institutions while carrying out their duty, they can arrange meetings, contact all organizations threatening national security, including terrorist groups, as required by duty, with prior notice."

• June 1, 2014: The HDP delegation visits İmralı. Öcalan: "The most important reality is that the process is at a new stage."[118]

• June 4, 2014: Mothers in Diyarbakır whose children have joined the PKK start a sit-in in front of the municipality building, saying they want their children back. The municipality intervenes. Demirtaş says, "They are receiving money from MİT."[119]

• June 5-7, 2014: Two people are killed in the incidents that start during the fortified gendarmerie station protests in Lice.

• June 6, 2014: The AK Party organizes a reconciliation workshop in Diyarbakır. The reconciliation process is revived.

[117] http://rusencakir.com/Ocalan-tamam-degil-devam-dedi/2592
[118] http://www.sabah.com.tr/gundem/2014/06/02/en-onemli-realite-surecin-ye-ni-asamaya-gelmesi
[119] http://www.sde.org.tr/userfiles/file/SD_EYLUL2015_SAYI70_BASKI.pdf

• June 9, 2014: A PKK member lowers the flag in the Diyarbakır 2nd Air Force Command's yard. Öcalan calls it a provocation and instructs the PKK to start investigations.[120]

• July 10, 2014: Parliament accepts the draft Law on Ending Terrorism and Strengthening Social Integration, which provides the ground for the reconciliation process.

• July 11, 2014: The last two detainees in Diyarbakır in the KCK main case are also released, leaving no detainee defendants.

• August 5, 2014: Öcalan during the HDP's visit to İmralı: "A 30-year war is on the verge of conclusion with a major democratic negotiation."[121]

• August 19, 2014: A statue of PKK member Mahsuni Korkmaz is erected in Lice. The court rules for its destruction. One person is killed in the incidents that break out.

• September 3, 2014: MİT Undersecretary Hakan Fidan goes to İmralı Island and reaches an agreement with Öcalan on the road map for the reconciliation process. HDP members Önder and Buldan take the road map to Qandil.

• September 10, 2014: Prime Minister Ahmet Davutoğlu, who meets with HDP politicians, guarantees that the process will be expedited if the PKK guarantees that will put an end to its illegal activities in Turkey such as hijackings and setting up courts.

• September 15, 2014: Daesh surrounds Kobani, Syria. The PKK's media increases propaganda that Turkey backs Daesh with a new photograph and so-called documents they produce daily.

---

[120] http://www.hurriyet.com.tr/2-hava-kuvvetleri-komutanligindaki-bayragi-in-dirdiler-26575475.
[121] http://www.bbc.com/turkce/haberler/2014/08/140816_ocalan.

• September 20, 2014: Upon Daesh's siege of Kobani, more than 100,000 Kurdish residents of the city seek refuge in Turkey. The 49 Mosul Consulate General employees who are held hostage on the same day by Daesh are later brought to Turkey.

• October 2, 2014: The Syria resolution passes Parliament.

• October 3, 2014: The PKK attacks the police station in Pülümür, Tunceli.

• October 6-8, 2014: The KCK and HDP call the people to resist for Kobani. Those who respond to the calls and take to the streets attack HÜDA-PAR and AK Party supporters' associations and shops. Fifty-two people are killed in the clashes. Öcalan makes the call that puts an end to the demonstrations. Öcalan: "If Kobani falls, the reconciliation process will be over."[122]

• October 11, 2014: Saying that the resolution passing in Parliament is a declaration of war, Cemil Bayık announces that all the units they withdrew will be sent back.

• October 13, 2014: PKK members are noticed as they pass through to the base area in Tunceli. Clashes ensue.

• October 20, 2014: The U.S. airdrops weapons and ammunition to YPG forces in Kobani.

• October 21, 2014: During the HDP's visit to İmralı, Öcalan says a new stage was reached on October 15, and that concrete steps will be taken.

• October 25, 2014: Three ranking soldiers in civilian clothes are killed in the middle of the street in Yüksekova.

• October 29, 2014: Aysel Tuğluk says: "The AK Party is no longer a partner in the reconciliation process," and calls the "secular forces" to duty.

---

[122] http://www.diken.com.tr/ocalan-kobani-duserse-cozum-sureci-biter/

• October 30, 2014: First Sergeant Necdet Aydoğdu, 24, is martyred in Diyarbakır as a result of an armed attack by two masked people while shopping at a local bazaar with his wife.

• November 4, 2014: An HDP administrator is heavily wounded in an attack on HDP headquarters.

• November 24, 2014: KCK administrator Sabri Ok: "Laying down weapons is not on our agenda."[123]

• December 18, 2014: Speaking to German *Die Welt*, Cemil Bayık says: "Daesh's real caliph is not Baghdadi. It is Erdoğan."[124]

• December 20, 2014: Cemil Bayık: "Laying down arms means death."[125]

• December 27, 2014: The fight that breaks out between YDG-H and HÜDA-PAR members in Cizre turns into a clash. This would give rise to the risk of Hezbollah-PKK clashes restarting.

•January 23, 2015: The HDP delegation starts to shuttle back and forth between İmralı and Qandil. The government wants Öcalan to make a final call to the armed fight in order to return to the reconciliation process. Öcalan writes a statement that asks for the government to steps to be taken in every area from women's rights to environmental problems. Qandil insists on these steps being the precondition for it to lay down its arms. The government objects to the 10 articles containing a general democratization program being the precondition, as it sees it as the PKK's excuse to avoid giving up their weapons.

---

[123] http://www.milliyet.com.tr/pkk-icindeki-derin-ayrilik-gundem-2100900/
[124] //haber.sol.org.tr/turkiye/cemil-bayik-isidin-gercek-halifesi-el-bagdadi-degil-erdogan-104569
[125] Fadime Özkan, "PKK-HDP muhataplıktan nasıl düştü?" *Star*, November 11, 2015; http://www.star.com.tr/yazar/pkkhdp-muhatapliktan-nasil-dustu-yazi-1068893/.

• February 9, 2015: The discussion on the Homeland Security Package in Parliament is postponed for a second time.

• February 15, 2015: The HDP's İmralı and Qandil contacts increase. Qandil says that the Homeland Security Package will harm the process.

• February 22, 2015: The Tomb of Süleyman Shah is moved with Operation Shah Euphrates to the PYD-held village of Eshme, Syria.

• February 17, 2015: HPD Co-Chair Selahattin Demirtaş: "For Öcalan to make a call, the government must first do its 10-article homework. If they don't announce it, we will."[126]

• February 25, 2015: Demirtaş lists on CNN Türk the 10 articles he says Öcalan brought forward as the precondition to make the call to lay down arms and says, "Öcalan made a conditional call to lay down arms."[127]

• February 28, 2015: Qandil and İmralı reach an agreement over the call Öcalan would make to the PKK for the disarmament congress. The 10 articles, including a vast democratization program, are not stipulated to drop arms and, to guarantee that these articles will be put into effect, a decision is made to have them read out in a meeting with the government present. Öcalan's disarmament congress assembly call to the PKK is read out in the meeting at Dolmabahçe Palace by HDP Deputy Sırrı Süreyya Önder, who is from among the İmralı delegation, with Deputy Prime Minister Yalçın Akdoğan, Interior Minister Efkan Ala, AK Party Group Deputy Chairman Mahir Ünal, former MİT vice president who carried out the meetings with Öcalan, and

---

[126] http://m.turkiyegazetesi.com.tr/yazarlar/yildiray-ogur/587467.aspx
[127] http://www.mynet.com/haber/guncel/rakamlarla-7-yilda-teror-ve-cozum-sureci-2425443-1

Public Security Undersecretary Muhammed Dervişoğlu in attendance.

• February 28, 2015: HDP Co-Chair Demirtaş is the first to react to the historic announcement 20 minutes later on a live broadcast. Demirtaş points to the Homeland Security Package and says: "The government cannot claim that it is making progress in democratization while it insists on the package. This draft is not a bill that will bring peace. We are not striving to move away from peace, we want peace very much. The government does not come close to peace or promise the slightest hope with the policies it pursues."[128]

• February 28, 2015: PKK administrator Mustafa Karasu makes a statement the same day: "Will the AKP government negotiate the 10 articles brought forward by the leadership and solve the problem or not? The answer to this question is very important. Approaches such as the PKK will drop arms before this problem is solved, and that the PKK is going to hold its congress and decide to drop its weapons, are demagogy, they are deception and twist the problem."[129]

• March 11, 2015: Cemil Bayık and Bese Hozat speak to Banu Güven on IMC TV: "Statements that the PKK will drop arms are election propaganda. The dropping of arms can only be decided at a congress Öcalan attends in person. In other words, this decision will not be announced before Öcalan is released. The congress gathering, the congress making decisions like they say is unthinkable before these steps are taken, before our movement, the people, Turkey's democracy forces are given assurance."[130]

---

[128] http://www.diken.com.tr/demirtastan-cozum-aciklamasina-ic-guvenlik-paketi-uyarisi-demokratiklesme-bu-paketle-olmaz/
[129] http://odatv.com/sorun-cozulmeden-pkk-silah-birakacak-demek-demagojidir-aldatmaktir--2802151200.html
[130] http://www.star.com.tr/acik-gorus/catismasizlik-nasil-sona-erdi-haber-1050354/

• March 17, 2015: HDP Co-Chair Demirtaş decides to enter the HDP in the elections as a party and takes to the platform in his party's parliamentary group session for a three-sentence speech referring to Erdoğan: "We will not allow you to become president. We will not allow you to become president. We will not allow you to become president."

• March 18, 2015: The media announces the people claimed to be on the Watch Committee.

• March 20, 2015: President Erdoğan says that he is not positive about the Watch Committee: "I have been reading it in newspapers. I really don't have any clue about such a matter. And I say this very clearly, I am not positive about it. This is not right. Such operations are carried out through intelligence organizations."

• March 21, 2015: In his letter read out on Nowruz in Diyarbakır, Öcalan calls on the PKK to hold a disarmament congress with a new precondition: "In addition to agreement in principles, as required by the declaration, I see it as historical and necessary to hold a congress to stop the armed struggle that has been carried out by the PKK against the Republic of Turkey for nearly 40 years, and to set the political and societal strategies and tactics that are suitable for the spirit of this new period. I hope that we can come to a principal agreement in the shortest possible time, and through the Truth and Reconciliation Commission formed of members of Parliament and the Monitoring Council, successfully realize this congress."[131]

• April 11, 2015: Four soldiers are wounded in a PKK attack in Ağrı.

131 http://dirilispostasi.com/a-1851-ocalan-tarihi-mektuptan-cikardi-mi.html

• May 5, 2015: KCK Co-Chair Bese Hozat: "We currently have no agenda such as assembling the congress because
this process did not work and no step was taken. The dialogue process also ended, let alone negotiations. There has
been no meeting with our leadership for a month. The delegation does not visit our leadership. The PKK was going to
gather the congress based on the steps to be taken by the state.
We have taken the congress off our agenda. The PKK will not
hold such a congress before the Kurdish problem is solved. It
can never assemble such a congress before Kurdish identity is
recognized, before changing the Constitution based on this,
and before accepting the status of Kurds. Öcalan needs to be
officially accepted as a side."[132]

• June 7, 2015: Following an aggressive election campaign,
the HDP passes the 10% electoral threshold with 13 percent of
the vote, winning 80 seats in Parliament. The AK Party, remaining at 41 percent, loses its ability to come to power alone.

• June 12, 2015: The KCK is not late to respond to Demirtaş's statements after the election that the PKK could drop its
arms upon Öcalan's call: "We need to make clear the matter of
the PKK ending its armed struggle against Turkey and the will
in this regard belongs entirely to us. Everybody should know
that the HDP is not the PKK's legal party. Hence, just as the
HDP cannot make such a call, even Abdullah Öcalan cannot
make such a call in his current condition from İmralı. Waiting
for the HDP and Öcalan to make a call to drop arms and to make
such impositions is insisting on the lack of a solution, and this is
unacceptable to our movement. Our attitude is neither disobe-
dience to Öcalan nor to stop the HDP from doing politics."[133]

[132] http://www.sozcu.com.tr/2015/gunun-icinden/pkkdan-silah-birakma-sartla-
ri-823658/
[133] http://www.radikal.com.tr/turkiye/kck-silah-birakma-iradesi-bize-ait-1378056/

• June 26, 2015: President Erdoğan speaks on the PYD's attempts to establish a state in northern Syria and Turkey's discussions on military intervention: "I am calling out to the whole world. Whatever the cost, we will never allow the establishment of a state either in the north or the south of Syria."[134]

• June 29, 2015: Karayılan: "I will say it openly, if they intervene in Rojava, we will interfere in them, then all of Turkey will turn into a battlefield. Turkish authorities must not forget our people's insurrection on October 6-8. It is known very well that only our leader Apo, who did not see the atmosphere in which it developed befitting, could stop the great rebellion of our people. It is clear that this people will not allow such an intervention. In brief, the decision for such an intervention would be a strategic decision for Turkey, and the start of a new era for the Kurdish people. We are not going to beg anybody in this regard. It's up to them. If they do, of course, as the Kurdish people, there will be things that we will do too."[135]

• July 11, 2015: The KCK declares the cease-fire over, giving dams as the reason: "The meticulous attitude of our freedom movement has been abused. The dams and the vehicles used in building the dams are going to be targeted by our guerilla forces. Every detention is now going to be a reason for the guerilla to retaliate. Our freedom movement will no longer accept the cease-fire to be exploited. It will also take its position against the policies that have left the Kurdish problem without a solution."

• July 14, 2015: KCK Co-Chair Bese Hozat writes an article titled "Yeni Süreç: Devrimci Halk Savaşıdır" (New Era:

---

[134] http://www.hurriyet.com.tr/bedeli-ne-olursa-olsun-engel-olacagiz-29394009
[135] http://www.radikal.com.tr/turkiye/karayilan-rojavaya-mudahale-olursa-sa-vas-cikar-1387653/

The Revolutionary People's War) for *Özgür Gündem* in which she calls for a "revolutionary people's war".

• July 20, 2015: Thirty-three people are killed in a Daesh suicide bombing while members of the Federation of Socialist Youth Associations (SGDF) gathered in Suruç to go to Kobani are making a statement.

• July 20, 2015: Specialist Corporal Müsellim Ünal is killed in a clash with the PKK and in Adıyaman.

• July 20, 2015: KCK Co-Chair Cemil Bayık calls on the people to arm and prepare tunnels and shelters: "Our people should also develop their legitimate defense organization and conscious. They should develop their legitimate defense as a people, not only on the basis of growing military forces. All our people should have guns and train themselves and become organized on this basis. Underground systems, tunnels, a local system should be developed in villages, cities, and neighborhoods against any kind of attack by Daesh and colonial powers."[136]

• July 22, 2015: Police officers Feyyaz Yumulak and Okan Acar, who are on duty in Ceylanpınar, Şanlıurfa, are killed in the early hours while asleep. A Fırat News Agency story reports: "On July 22, a pro-Apo defense team conducted a punishment act against two police officers who were in cooperation with Daesh gangs at about 6 a.m. today in retaliation for the Suruç massacre."[137]

• July 22, 2015: Kalem-Der member Ethem Türkben is killed in Adana in front of his expectant wife and three children based on claims that he is a Daesh member.

---

[136] http://www.aksam.com.tr/guncel/cemil-bayik-silahlanin-tunel-kazin/haber-424316
[137] https://firatnews.com/kurdistan/hpg-2-polisi-apocu-fedai-timi-cezalandirdi-51114

• July 23, 2015: A police team that follows up on a traffic accident report in Diyarbakır is ambushed. Police officer Tansu Aydın is killed in the attack and another officer is injured.

• July 23, 2015: Daesh militants on the Syria side of the border open fire on the Dağ Hudut Gendarmerie Station in Elbeyli, Kilis. Noncommissioned Officer Yalçın Nane is killed in the attack.

• July 24, 2015: TSK jets set out on an air operation on Daesh in northern Syria and PKK targets in northern Iraq in the first military operation on the PKK in the last three years.

The reconciliation process Erdoğan kick started despite the political risks he was taking, being exploited by the PKK, was a concerning outcome for the future. Following the end of the process, Turkey was obliged to fight not only the PKK and its derivatives, but also other terrorist organizations like Daesh and FETÖ, which have international intelligence connections. At the end of the day, it should no longer be as easy as it was in the past to say anything new about the future of the Kurdish issue. The form the present question will take in the future is unknown, yet the U.S. establishing a new strategic alliance that would gain legitimacy for terrorist groups in northern Syria through the YPG and PYD, KRG President Barzani's decision to hold a independence referendum in Iraqi Kurdistan, shows that the Kurdish issue will in following years continue to maintain its position on the agenda as a national problem rather than a regional one.

Changing Balances and the "One Minute" Outburst

As time progresses, balances change in foreign policy just as in internal policy. The crisis that took place in January 2009 in Davos, Switzerland, was the manifestation of a great reaction formed over time. Erdoğan, who spoke at a panel on Gaza, displayed an unforgettable reaction to Israeli President Shimon Peres's tone that completely disregarded diplomatic ethics. Erdoğan was also irritated by the prejudiced attitude and interventions from moderator David Ignatius and left Davos with an unexpected reaction. This incident, which was given as breaking news by foreign news agencies, was broadcasted by Agence France-Presse (AFP): "Turkish Prime Minister Tayyip Erdoğan abandons panel as lightning following a fiery discussion on Gaza with Israeli President Shimon Peres."[138] Relations between Turkey and Israel reached a breaking point following this dispute, which is known in Turkey as the "one minute" incident.[139] Erdoğan's reaction, saying "one minute", was welcomed in Turkey. This eventually led to the nationalist and conservative sections of society consolidating more around Erdoğan and AK Party. The pleasure from Erdoğan's brave reaction was not only limited to Turkey, either. In the eyes of Islamic countries, Erdoğan now became an important political phenomenon who taught a lesson to Israel. While Lebanon's *As-Safir* published the developments, it published: "From Erdoğan to Peres: You know very well how to murder."[140] Erdoğan, kept a harsh stance against Peres, gained a reputation in the Arab world as the first political leader to have stood up against and challenged Israel.

However, many years later, Erdoğan's "one minute" outburst received criticism. Professor Nevzat Yalçıntaş, who was a figure involved during the stages of the formation of AK

---

[138] http://www.radikal.com.tr/dunya/dunya-basini-davos-sokunu-boyle-duyur-du-919321/

[139] http://www.ntv.com.tr/dunya/davostaki-moderator-kendini-savundu,cS0iQ-b3yHU-QPZsk7N2I0w

[140] *As-Safir*, January 30, 2009.

Party, claimed that the Davos incident was staged and used accusatory language against Erdoğan. Yalçıntaş eventually gave an interview to *Bugün*, which was later shutdown due to its links to FETO, in which he said: "The leader, who represented Turkey in Davos, used cutting but true words against another individual at the same table. He should have considered the possible reactions while he was abandoning that platform with such tumult. I suspect that his advisors staged this. This is the impression I got, because these types of things only happen in movies. Surely he can use language that has weight in actual politics. You cannot expect the closure of a committed offence yet; you must wait for the response of your addressee. Then, you respond and the meeting continues. However, dramatizing only takes place on movie sets. We eventually saw its results, too. The advisors and ministers all tired Mr. Tayyip out. They took every single matter before him and requested him to make the final decisions. Today Mr. Tayyip is not the same Mr. Tayyip as yesterday!"[141]

A response to the claims from Yalçıntaş, who was also a prominent supporter of the separatist movement led by Abdüllatif Şener following his split from AK Party, came from Cüneyd Zapsu, who was the organizer of the Gaza Panel, a prominent advisor to the World Economic Forum, a founding member of the AK Party, and an advisor to the Erdoğan while he was prime minister. Zapsu said "the incident was too real to be staged". He further denied Yalçıntaş's claims:

> We had been actively involved in the organization of the Gaza Panel at the Davos Summit. We were informed just a short period before the panel began that the moderator had changed. When we found out that the moderator was to be David Igna-

---

[141] *Bugün*, July 20, 2014.

tius, we informed the Economic Forum administration of our concerns that he would not be impartial on the issue of Israel, but it was too late. Following Peres' fiery speech, our Prime Minister took his turn and made a historic speech. In addition to the moderator's prejudice, inexperience and disrespect, Mr. Erdoğan chose to abandon the panel. The fact that the whole process, including the preparations and the actual incident, took place right before us, I would like to state as the individual most involved within the whole program, that the accusations that it was staged is not just wrong, but also clearly sinister. Whoever wants more details is more than welcome to approach me.[142]

The tensions with Israel were not limited only with the "one minute" incident. On May 31, 2010 the Freedom for Gaza flotilla, which included the Mavi Marmara, carrying many foreign activists on board, set sail from Istanbul with the aim of breaking the blockade on Gaza. Israeli commandos raided it in international waters killing 10 people. This incident, which caused unrest in the international community, is considered to be Israel's gravest response to Turkey following the "one minute" incident.[143]

Turkey's response to this incident was harsh as it suspended the continuous trade, military, and political relations the countries had shared since 1948. Turkey considered Israel's actions to be piracy and called it state terrorism. Israel was then considered to be the most problematic in terms of its regional politics. The report by the Palmer Commission, which was formed by the United Nations, legitimized Israel the actions in a blow to the conscience. Many years later, Erdoğan took the dais at the U.N. General Assembly and said: "The

---

[142] Exclusive interview with Cüneyd Zapsu.
[143] Dr. A. Oğuz Çelikkol, *One Minute'ten Mavi Marmara'ya Türkiye-İsrail Çatışması,(The Turkey-Israel Conflict From One Minute to Mavi Marmara)* Doğan Kitap, Istanbul, 2014.

world is bigger than five,"[144] causing an unusual political discourse in diplomacy. This change pointed to a new era in the history of Turkey's foreign policy. This process, which has been called a transition from a soft power to a hard power,[145] attracted much criticism from liberal sectors, yet the general population considered Erdoğan's change exhilarating.

The Mavi Marmara crisis experienced by Turkey, which wanted to distance itself from opening a new problematic front in diplomacy, forced the regional paradigm to be reconsidered once again. It is for this reason that the rebellious social movements of the Arab Spring pivot and Turkey's changing and developing political choices should be analyzed from a perspective of axial dislocation. This new state was not a policy that could have been continued from the aspect of Israel. It was for this reason that then President Barack Obama undertook a role as negotiator to mend relations. On March 22 2013, Israeli Prime Minister Netanyahu, who perceived the suspension of bilateral relations as an open threat to Israel's security, apologized to Erdoğan over the telephone three years later[146] and accepted to pay compensation to all the families who lost a family member in the raid.

A point needs to be emphasized here. Erdoğan's unexpected outburst at Davos inadvertently played into the hands of those who wanted to see hatred of and opposition against Erdoğan in the West. In 2009, it journalist Aslı Aydıntaşbaş accused Erdoğan of authoritarianism. She wrote a column for

---

[144] http://www.aljazeera.com.tr/haber/erdogan-dunya-5ten-buyuktur
[145] Oran, *Türk Dış Politikası: Kurtuluş Savaşından Bugüne, Olgular, Belgeler, Yorumlar,* Vol. 3, p. 8.
[146] http://www.haaretz.com/israel-news/netanyahu-phones-erdogan-to-apologize-for-deaths-of-turkish-citizens-on-gaza-flotilla.premium-1.511394

Forbes titled "Erdoğan's Davos Outburst Is Nothing New",[147] in which she paints Erdoğan as a Middle Easterner who cannot control his feelings and has temper tantrums:

> But for us Turks, watching Erdoğan "lose it" at the World Economic Forum's meeting in Davos, Switzerland, was nothing new. It was, rather, an Erdoğan classic–charismatic yet boorish; ardent but intimidating.[148]

Aydıntaşbaş's column eventually was the signal flare of anti-Erdoğanism that will increase in the years to come.

The Arab Spring Begins and Ends

The street rallies that began in Tunisia in December 2010, and almost spread throughout the rest of the Arab world acquired the name the Arab Spring.[149] Just like almost every international development, the Arab Spring cannot solely be explained with a single reason or factor. In fact, it will not be right to say that the reasons for the Arab Spring were national or international issues, as the developments in the Middle East, which has had its system occupied by the international system for more than 100 years, cannot be explained independently from international dynamics along with the inter-

---

[147] Aslı Aydıntaşbaş, "Erdoğan's Davos Outburst Is Nothing New," *Forbes*, January, 2009; https://www.forbes.com/2009/01/30/erdogan-turkey-davos-opinions-contributors_0130_asli_aydintasbas.html

[148] https://www.forbes.com/2009/01/30/erdogan-turkey-davos-opinions-contributors_0130_asli_aydintasbas.html

[149] The Arab people's movements that were initiated by the people of Arab countries in December 2010 and affected North African and Middle Eastern countries. The movement was an act of rebellion against the regimes, administrations, and governments with calls for changes, revisions, revolutions, insurrections, uprisings, and many similar other things. The actual incident that sparked all of these events will be explained in more detail later, but the first tinder spark was when a young Tunisian university student, Muhammed Buazizi, was slapped by council police for working as a pedlar and had his belongings confiscated. See, http://www.tuicakademi.org/arap-bahari-ve-nedenleri/

nal dynamics of other regional countries and actors.[150] The youth who had organized themselves through social media unfurled the red flag against oppressive government systems. Although their demands for freedom were met with bloody responses, the Arab Spring is clear proof that the Middle East will never be the same again. It is unfortunate that the incidents that took place without bringing about democratic regimes, eventually turned into unrealistic hopes and dreams, postponed for another spring.

There is no doubt that the Arab Spring initially had set off a great process within the countries themselves as well as in the Middle East and the international system. The toppling of the dictators in Tunisia, Egypt, and Libya and the appointment of new leaders in their place was, in and of itself, a great sign of change. Although there may be uncertainties surrounding the next step in this process and how it will be reflected in other countries or even the possible type of governance styles, it is crucial to accept that the Arab Spring initially brought a new state and era for the people as well as for the region and global politics.[151]

At this stage, it is beneficial to explore how Erdoğan's political stance settled throughout the duration of the Arab Spring. The incidents that began in Tunisia and spread to other regional countries, enflaming the Middle East, was a phase of transformation that should be analyzed in detail. The AK Party's Middle East policy, which it has been implementing ever since its first years in office, played a distinctive role in the region throughout the Arab Spring. During his role as foreign policy advisor, Ahmet Davutoğlu's strategic

---

[150] Ramazan Gözen, "Türkiye ve Arap Baharı: Değişimi Açıklamak ve Anlamak," *Adam Akademi*, 2011/2, pp. 1-25.

[151] Gözen, "Türkiye ve Arap Baharı: Değişimi Açıklamak ve Anlamak," 2011/2, pp. 1-25.

thesis known as "zero problems with neighbors", which emphasized Turkey's historical and geopolitical depth, was perceived as the main reason for the AK Party's diplomatic failures.[152] On the other hand, historian Kemal Karpat considers Davutoğlu's "zero problems" principle as having a similarity to Atatürk's concept of "Peace at home, peace in the world", and further says that Turkey, for the first time, was acting in accordance with historical, cultural, and geographical realities.[153] However, Turkey's political discourse built on the Davutoğlu's strategic depth thesis, eventually reached an uncontrollable point when the events in Syria evolved into civil war, leaving Turkey with zero neighbors instead of zero problems. Just two months into the conflicts, a hawkish policy and the suspension of all diplomatic relations with Syria eventually caused Turkey to keep its distance from the topic of the future of Syria. Although the AK Party's Syria policy had initially received tremendous criticism, it is a striking detail that today the international public has also taken up its position in close proximity of Turkey's own stance.

The Egyptian Coup and Anti-Muslim Brotherhood Sentiment

Erdoğan clarified his idea of Turkey undertaking an active role in every event win the Middle East in reference to the legacy of being a country of leadership as well as having brotherly relations with the people of the region.[154] It is for this reason that he could not remain indifferent to the developments taking place in the Middle East. The prohibition of the Muslim Brotherhood in Egypt on the claims of it partaking in terror-

---

[152] Nuri Yeşilyurt, Atay Akdevelioğlu, "AKP Döneminde Türkiye'nin Ortadoğu Politikası," *AKP Kitabı: Bir Dönüşümün Bilançosu*, Phoenix Publishing, Ankara, 2013, p. 382.

[153] Karpat, *Kısa Türkiye Tarihi: 1800-2012*, p. 286.

[154] Türk, *Muktedir, Türk Sağ Geleneği ve Recep Tayyip Erdoğan*, p. 335.

ist activities, and the toppling of the country's first democratically elected president, Mohammed Morsi, on July 3, 2013,
in a bloody coup[155] forced Erdoğan to become embedded in
a critical conflict with a Saudi Arabia-centered Arab world.
Erdoğan criticized the Western world for its silence and also
spoke out against the stance of the Muslim world. Erdoğan's
style further toughened, targeting global politics for its praise
of the parties involved in the coup, and said: "There has never
been an oppressor throughout history to have prospered with
oppression. Egypt's putschist leaders need to understand that
even the most powerful pharaohs in this world were mor-
tal beings. In fact, they would know this better than anyone
else. Sooner or later, a Moses will come along and make you
pay for your oppression."[156] Following the tragic events taking place in Egypt, Erdoğan increased the power of his reactions and said: "Those, who do not have the honor of calling
a coup an actual coup have their hands drenched in the blood
of all those innocent children who have been slaughtered."[157]

Erdoğan reacted by placing the events in Egypt on an axis of justice and oppression. It is for this reason that he did
not see any difference between Abdel-Fattah el-Sissi in Egypt
and Bashar Assad in Syria. However, the fact that the West
and the Muslim world kept silent on the matter did not bode
well. Erdoğan considered the West's glorification of the coup

---

[155] A military coup took place in Egypt on July 3, 2013, when the Chief of Staff of the
Egyptian military Abdel-Fattah el-Sissi warned the government and protestors to
reach a form of negotiation within the next 48 hours, and as a result of the failure
to do so, toppled the government. While the first democratically elected president,
Mohammed Morsi, was arrested following the coup, all activities of the Muslim
Brotherhood throughout the country were suspended. As a result of the violence
against Morsi supporters, hundreds of people were slaughtered. Rabia Square, where the protestors gathered thoughout the protests, becomes a symbol of resistence.

[156] Recep Tayyip Erdoğan, "Bir Musa Çıkar Zulmün Hesabını Sorar," http://aa.com.
tr/tr/politika/bir-musa-cikar-zulmun-hesabini-sorar/225638, August 15, 2013.

[157] Recep Tayyip Erdoğan, "Mısır'da İnsanlık Hedef Alınmıştır," http://www.enson-
haber.com/erdoganin-turkmenistan-ziyareti-oncesi-aciklama-2013-08-15.html.

in Egypt as a possible attitude the West would display if Turkey were to ever suffer a coup in the future. He would end up correct in this observation, too. The fact that the Western world had defined the failed coup on July 15 2016 as theater,[158] and that Western leaders did not visit Turkey afterward was a crucial result that justifies Erdoğan's foresight. The fact that even the opposition in Turkey had spoken of the July 15 failed coup as "a controlled coup"[159] without any evidence, thus, accusing Erdoğan and the government of perpetrating it, is quite striking and thought provoking.

Erdoganophobia in the West

Anti-Erdoğanism, which has gained such crucial momentum in the West, cannot be solely interpreted as an opposition to Erdoğan's hardening political discourse. As Edward W. Said laid forth, the West acts with anti-Islamic codes in relation to the Muslim communities that it considers "the other", and forms a consensus accordingly. In accordance with the historical foundations of the West, the East is the "other" and Islam is a religion that belongs to the East. It is for this reason that the targeting of Erdoğan by Western politics and media and equating him with authoritarianism is directly related to Edward Said's concept of orientalism.[160]

The fact that Turkey surfaced as a new actor during a period of time when the European Union is on the verge of disintegration, and to gravitate toward projects that fortifies its status, has been a critical step to destroy the paradigm of the

---

[158] "Muslim cleric Gulen: Coup bid in Turkey could have been staged," http://www.reuters.com/article/us-turkey-security-gulen-remarks-idUSKCN0ZW11D.

[159] Kemal Kılıçdaroğlu, "15 Temmuz Kontrollü Darbe Girişimidir," March 3, 2017; http://www.bbc.com/turkce/haberler-turkiye-39478777

[160] Edward W. Said, *Orientalism: Western Conceptions of the Orient,* Metis Publishing, Istanbul, 1995.

West's efforts this past century. Putting aside periodic mistakes, it is generally accepted that the regional reputation of Turkey in the past 15 years has reached a peak. It is also clear that political Islam, which is considered a political success by the "other", harbors a great threat to the West. The politics of fear,[161] in which the West, at a macro level, has produced on an Islamophobic foundation, is crucial in terms of realizing it with anti-Erdoganism following the July 15 coup attempt. In fact, this situation is taken to a whole other level with a statement from French Professor Philippe Moreau Defarges, who said, "The only choice for Turkey is for Erdoğan to be murdered."[162] This clearly illustrates how extreme the problem is in the Western mind. Another example is when retired U.S. Army Lieutenant Colonel Ralph Peters, a Fox News analyst, wrote a column following the failed coup, titled "Turkey's last hope dies".[163] This once again shows how the phobic politics of the West has transformed into a hate crime. In his article, Peters continuously juxtaposes themes of darkness and light. In his opinion, Islam is a dark religion and its people are dark, and the Muslim world is generally immersed in darkness. "But the difference between ISIS, Al Qaeda and the Muslim Brotherhood isn't one of purpose, but merely of manners: Muslim Brothers wash the blood off their hands before they sit down to dinner with their dupes."[164]

At this stage it is appropriate to evaluate how the Western media unites on being anti-Erdoğan in reference to Said's book, *Covering Islam,* in which he explores the orientalist

---

[161] http://www.takvim.com.tr/guncel/2017/05/01/yuzu-maskeli-teroristlerden-er-dogana-olum-tehdidi
[162] https://tr.sputniknews.com/avrupa/201704241028201391-erdogan-oldur-mek-kaliyor-fransiz-siyaset-bilimci-sorusturma/
[163] http://www.foxnews.com/opinion/2016/07/16/turkeys-last-hope-dies.html
[164] Halil Berktay, *Tarihçi Gözüyle Siyaset (Politics From A Historian Perspective)*, Kopernik Kitap, Istanbul, 2017, p. 28.

codes of the Western media and their Islamophobic codes in presenting Islam and Muslims. In *Covering Islam*, Said claims that the Western media has a tendency to evaluate social and political events taking place in Middle Eastern societies on an Islamophobic foundation:

> The deliberately created associations between Islam and fundamentalism ensure that the average reader comes to see Islam and fundamentalism as essentially the same thing. Given the tendency to reduce Islam to a handful of rules, stereotypes, and generalizations about the faith, its founder, and all of its people, then the reinforcement of every negative fact associated with Islam – its violence, primitiveness, atavism, threatening qualities – is perpetuated.

> Yet there is a consensus on "Islam" as a kind of scapegoat for everything we do not happen to like about the world's new political, social and economic patterns. For the right, Islam represents barbarism; for the left, medieval theocracy; for the center, a kind of distasteful exoticism. In all camps, however, there is agreement that even though little enough is known about the Islamic world, there is not much to be approved of there.[165]

The Western media's wholesale approach of defining the people who flooded the streets following Erdoğan's call against the coup attempt on July 15, as flocks, Islamists, and forces loyal to Erdoğan, should be analyzed as the continuation of the orientalist tradition with the West positioning Middle Eastern nations as barbaric.[166]

Said's determinations and Oliver Roy's thesis in his book, *The Failure of Political Islam*, allows us to make a general in-

---

[165] Filiz Barın Akman, *15 Temmuz Darbe Girişimi Batı Medyası Söylem Analizi Neo-Emperyalizm, İslamofobi ve Oryantalizm*, Kadim Publishing, Ankara, 2017, pp 79-81.

[166] Akman, *15 Temmuz Darbe Girişimi Batı Medyası Söylem Analizi Neo-Emperyalizm, İslamofobi ve Oryantalizm*, p. 80.

ference of just how the Western mind's orientalist paradigm forming the foundations of the adversity between the West and East at the end of the second millennium, has evolved into dimensions of hatred. The fact that political movements similar to those of Hassan al-Banna and Mawdudi have not been successful are compelling developments that inevitably strengthens the West's conceptualizations. As a result, political failures in these regions were perceived as a means to conveniently penetrate them. In the early 2000s, however, a new political model surfaced in Turkey that completely discombobulated the Western paradigm of political Islam. This political discourse, which blossomed with a Muslim, conservative, and liberal democrat identity, was initially welcomed with appreciation. However, without delay, it was seen as a serious threat that could be perceived as a precedent for similar political movements within the Muslim world. The most critical point at this stage is how this political style had been perceived as a deviation from Western ideas following the Davos incident.

Is the World Bigger than Five?

With his brave stand in the international arena, Erdoğan undertook the role of being the representative of oppressed nations. Erdoğan attained popularity, particularly in the Muslim world, and positioned himself as a protector of the oppressed. Thus, Erdoğan transformed into a political phenomenon challenging the established system. His conscientiousness in relation to the Syrian refugee crisis has reaped admiration the world over. Despite the fact that this issue has become polemic in domestic public opinion, Erdoğan criticizes the inhumane attitude of the West concerning Syrian refugees at every turn. Alev Alatlı interprets Erdoğan's conscientious outburst as the bravest stance of the last century around the world. Alatlı likens Erdoğan's mantra of "the world is bigger than five", as a challenge against the established order, to George Orwell's attitude against the status quo. Alatlı took the stage at the Presidential Culture and Arts Awards Ceremony in December 2014, and supported Erdoğan, saying: "If Orwell were alive today, he would stand up and applaud you. Indeed, Daniel Defoe would stand up and applaud you." Alatlı's speech drew the attention of anti-Erdoğan crowds among artists.[167] Alatlı praised Erdoğan with the following:

> The world is bigger than five. It is also bigger than the cartels of international media and the tactless worlds of the various strategists. Mr. President, history will uphold you for your decision of opening your doors to 1.5 million Syrian refugees. You said that the world is bigger than five, and as a result you have defeated all the oligarchs. Today, if George Orwell were alive he would stand up and applaud you. Indeed, Daniel Defoe would stand up and applaud you. Your most sincere friends are among the artists and men of literature.[168]

While Alatlı regards the changes in Turkey as a renaissance, she also believes Erdoğan's existence in politics to be a great fortune. Alatlı once explained: "He appeals to the general community in a world where oligarchy rules, and yet it is always expected for words that do not reflect the mentality of the general public to arouse anger and also be suffered." In regard to the failures surrounding us, Alatlı once said:

> And today, whether individuals have personally given their blessings or not in regard to a disagreement, once the laws au-

---

[167] Adnan İsmailoğulları, "Paçozlaşan Türkiye'nin Edebiyat Ödülü Alev Alatlı'ya," *Yeniçağ*, December 6, 2014.

[168] http://www.sabah.com.tr/gundem/2014/12/03/alev-alatli-konustu-erdogan-gozyaslarini-tutamadi

thenticate and make a ruling on who is right, one cannot suggest any form of conscience to the winning party. One cannot ask them to waive their acquisitions for the sake of the public interest or to take a step back in the name of humanity. However, what really matters is whether one had given their blessings following a disagreement and forgiven them. It should have been about writing off each other's debts. Forgiving each other should have been nobler than winning a court case.

Because every given legal right is not an honest earning, drawing a border between Suruç and Kobani may seem the legal right earned by the victors of World War I, but it is not rightfully theirs. Likewise, it may be legally permissible for you to purchase your brother's house that is on fire sale, but it is not truly an honest thing to do.

However, giving up one's legal rights in today's society, self-sacrifice from personal gains, and voluntary devotion for the good of the public are all considered a form of ineptness if not stupidity. A contractor who has a license for construction is legally innocent while he rapes the horizons of the city. An oil company that legally purchases all the rights for a new and cheaper energy in order to prevent its entry into the market is also legally innocent of any crime. A food producer that adds carcinogenic additives to bread dough in order to make it expire at a later date is also innocent as long as the date is printed on the package. A columnist who can cause a bunch of defiant youngsters to flood the streets with a single strike of his pen while he sits and watches the events from the comfort of his home is also be considered innocent of any crime.

I believe the greatest project of the 21st century would be to coincide what is conscientiously right with what is legally right.[169]

---

[169] Recep Koçak, "Alev Alatlı'nın Söyledikleri," *Milat*, December 15, 2014.

SECTION THREE
THE MATHEMATICS OF POLITICS

THE PERCEPTION OF POLITICS

Erdoğan's political strategy is set on the foundations of authenticity and sincerity. False pretenses and creating a different image through the media are the main factors from which Erdoğan generally abstains. He meticulously protects the fine line between authenticity and exaggeration and comes to the forefront as a political figure who avoids false sentimentalities.[1] One of his most characteristic features, his keeping his word, is effective in his friendly communications with the people. Breaking his fasts in slums, which he had made a habit of while he was Istanbul mayor, and continuing his out of the blue house visits during his terms as prime minister, clearly illustrate how Erdoğan's political strategy is settled on a populist foundation. Although Erdoğan embraces all of Turkey in his speeches, but from time to time, can use marginalizing language that may be seen as a drift of his political strategy, the truth is that it is only efforts to consolidate votes. Erdoğan's harsh rhetoric and blunt discourse in the meetings he has been attending gains social recognition in time. Tanıl Bora interprets this attitude of Erdoğan's with Necip Fazıl's teaching of "standing erect against the non-be-

[1] Yalçın Akdoğan, *Lider, Siyasî Liderlik ve Erdoğan*, Turkuaz Kitap, Istanbul, 2017, p. 89.

lievers."[2] However, Bora fails to understand that the changes in Erdoğan's political discourse are a reaction developed against the hatred of Erdoğan, which has become systematic. Although Erdoğan's embracing discourse, which he has developed within a political system, could be perceived as the product of forming a common consciousness, he cannot escape apprehensive elites' accusations of him making intervention into people's lifestyles. He challenges all while answering this criticism: "No one's lifestyle in Turkey is under any form of systematic threat. We will never allow this. We have never allowed this to happen during the 14 years we have been in office. If there is anyone who claims the opposite, they have the obligation to prove it with physical evidence."[3]

Erdoğan continued his embracing attitude until 2011, with short interruptions along the way. He said the following at the AK Party congress in 2009:

> If there are any individuals who have expectations that are different from this party and this movement, who have goals that have nothing to do with serving this nation and this country, they should part ways with us. Those who have lost their excitement, enthusiasm, their love of serving, should step aside. Those who feel tired should take a break. For the past seven years, we have appeared before our nation in honestly and with our heads held high, and from this day onward we will continue to be with and embrace them. We have suffered great pains. We have come as the last hope of the poor. We have always stood by those in need, we have always taken the fronts in our struggles against poverty, and from this day onward, we will continue on this path. We will continue to be the voice and breath of

---

[2] Bora, *Cereyanlar*, p. 503.
[3] http://tr.euronews.com/2017/01/04/erdogan-turkiye-de-hic-kimsenin-ha-yat-tarzi-tehdit-altinda-degildir.

the poverty-stricken, the waif, the needy, the oppressed and the marginalized. For the past seven years, we have tried to reach our citizens, to heal the homes of the poor, to warm the hands of the cold, to rekindle the burned-out furnaces, to give a hand to the fallen, and we will never lose this spirit. Never forget this, and remind all: the burden of my brothers laboring from Dilovası to Kadıköy is upon our shoulders. The rights of the Gazi suburb in Istanbul, Kuşcağız in Ankara, Benu Sen in Diyarbakır, are upon our shoulders. The rights of young girls who have trouble holding their pens due to the lack of heaters in their homes are upon our shoulders. The rights of the elderly in need of a bowl of hot soup are upon our shoulders. The rights of the orphans are upon our shoulders. No matter how heavy the burden upon our shoulders, we will continue to dash about and take care of all troubles.[4]

Erdoğan developed a new political language within the framework of "Turkishness". This style, which became more visible during the democratization process, is the effort of producing a mutual consciousness without discriminating between religion, language, or race. Erdoğan's assuring discourse has led to a social softening, even on the riskiest topics.[5] The fact that the criticism made by the Nationalist People's Party (MHP) during the reconciliation process was not successful in transforming into a social reaction among the AK Party base can only be explained by Erdoğan's assuring political stand. This rare situation in the history of Turkish politics surfaces as a result of Erdoğan establishing a form of empathy politics with his voters. While Erdoğan establishes a connection with the oppressed within the community, he also challenges the status quo. On the topic of the Dersim mas-

4   Recep Tayyip Erdoğan, AK Party Ordinary Grand Congress speech, October 3, 2009.
5   Akdoğan, Lider, Siyasi Liderlik ve Erdoğan, p. 90.

sacre, he destroyed all the rooted reflexes of the state, as he said: "If there is a need to make an apology on behalf of the state, then I will apologize."[6] Erdoğan gathered many prominent figures from the entertainment world at his office at Dolmabahçe Palace on April 17, 2010, and said:

> As the government, just as Alev Alatlı put it, we say it is time to stop crying, and go back to square one. Elif Şafak says you cannot force a person who is constantly in mourning to love rainbows. One, who constantly stares at black and grey, will be dazzled by colors. We want to illustrate that this country is not just black and white, but that it is also as colorful and exhilarating as a rainbow. We want to prove to Hilmi Yavuz, who says that sorrow is most fitting to us, that joy, happiness and peace will also be most suitable for this nation. We listen to Bejan Matur, who says whatever has been experienced, whether it is the Kurds or Turks who have suffered, we can only cure one another's wounds by understanding each other. And also lend an ear to Haydar Ergülen, who shouts out, oh mother, will you be able to endure it all even if you had a heart of stone? We yell just like Ayşe Kulin, who says we are the children of the same land. And just like Murat Menteş, we say, do not fear, count me in. And now we are expanding this and saying count us in. Just like İskender Pala, we say love is to forgive for the sake of the days to come. Just like Muhsin Kızılkaya, who expresses the languages that have become intertwined with one another, that we, too, want to take concrete steps in ensuring that those ethnic and religious groups that have become intertwined with one another, that have become siblings, to once again live together as a family. We are working so that all the pains written in Yılmaz Karakoyunlu's novel Salkım Hanım'in Taneleri [Mrs. Salkım's Diamonds] will never be relived again.[7]

---

[6] http://www.milliyet.com.tr/erdogan-dersim-icin-ozur-diledi-siyaset-1466430/
[7] http://www.hurriyet.com.tr/erdoganin-yazarlarla-bulusmasinda-yaptigi-konus-ma-14448731

Erdoğan opens his arms to all sectors of society without discriminating between ideas and faiths and attempts to listen with complete attention to all who have something to say. However, his path has now diverged from many of the figures he referenced in his speech. On this point, there is a crucial and critical problem that surfaces in the political positioning of the elite intellectuals in Turkey. That many of the figures who Erdoğan referenced in his speech support Western politics, which uses anti-Erdoğanism as a political strategy, is clearly a characteristic problem of Turkish intellectuals. Ever since the withdrawal of the Ottomans from the stage of history and the establishment of the Republican system, the intellectual typology, which has continuously changed sides, which sees no problem in switching sides from time to time, and which claims to have done this in the name of patriotism, continues its existence as the foundational problem of the life of Turkish intellectuals today.

While Erdoğan uses a balanced style in his social messages, he is elaborate in using a style to keep polemics alive when criticizing the opposition. The most serious breaking point that led to Erdoğan's change in political discourse took place in May of 2013 with the Gezi upheavals in Istanbul. The restlessness that started at Gezi Park in Taksim isolates Erdoğan from his traditional codes of discourse. It is for this reason that the great change in Erdoğan's political discourse post-Gezi protests should be analyzed from a sociological perspective taking into account manipulation. This new situation with discriminating, marginalizing, and polarizing tones led to criticism of Erdoğan and caused the foundation for him to become more isolated in global politics. This eventually led to many questions about whether the global wisdom's long-term plan for Turkey, was initiated through FETÖ during this period.

Gezi Begins and Ends

The Gezi upheaval has been liked as the Turkey version of the social upheaval of the Arab Spring t in the Middle East and North Africa through the guidance of foreign agencies. The Artillery Barracks planned to replace Gezi Park was shown as the reason for the rallies. The protestors who set up camp in Gezi Park stood their ground in declaring the park a zone of rebellion despite the many warnings from the police. HDP Deputy Sırrı Süreyya Önder's images of challenging the heavy construction vehicles have been committed to memory for many. Those images, so to speak, became the first signs that the protests would shortly deteriorate beyond recovery. This restlessness displeased Erdoğan, as it took place during a time in which Turkey was in great need of social consensus. This upheaval in which intelligence-guided criminal organizations were involved, and led by artists who chanted: "This is not about a few trees, don't you get it?" justified Erdoğan's concerns. However, Erdoğan's stern tone from the very beginning, which was presented as ignoring the social problems, further whetted the appetite of those who wanted to intervene in the political discourse in the country. While Erdoğan has said the Gezi incidents were an operation against the growing and developing Turkey by the "interest rate lobby", he called the protestors as marauders. The call to cancel the third airport, third bridge, and other major investment projects, which was submitted as part of the list of demands from the Gezi Park Committee in the form of social negotiations,[8] was actual proof that the upheaval was not about trees. Erdoğan evaluating the Gezi incidents as follows:

---

[8] http://www.haber7.com/ic-politika/haber/1035100-gezi-parki-temsilcileri-nin-hukumetten-7-talebi

Just as I have previously said earlier, our police force has successfully overcome a very crucial and critical democracy test. It is fair to say that our police force has made history. Only our police would have been able to pursue a struggle with the utmost composure and to maintain their stance without food and water for 48 hours. We are a government that has zero tolerance for torture. We are a government that has paved the way for change and democratized police intervention and arrest and interrogation rules. If our police make a mistake, we will come clean and honestly say it and do what is necessary. However, no one has the right, whether they are a members of Parliament or not, to insult our police officers.

However, a critical problem surfaced at this stage. Whereas Erdoğan said the police force showed heroic traits, they were accused of using unnecessary force, which eventually led to the interpretation that Turkey has a serious intelligence problem. That is to say, many years later, the same FETÖ-linked police officers who were accused of using excessive force and burning protestor tents, which was the breaking point of the Gezi protests, surfaced once again with their attempt to topple the government in the December 17 and December 25 judicial coup attempt.

The political discourse of Turkey's opposition parties, which cannot produce values, also transformed into a social reaction during the Gezi events. The secondary target of the different factions that united with the purpose of protesting the government is now the opposition parties. While the efforts of the opposition in transforming the Gezi upheavals for their own benefits yielded no results, the image of "the liberated zone" formed in Taksim disturbed the government. In the following days, images of armed criminal organizations clashing in the streets were broadcast. Foreign journalists, who had reserved their places in Taksim many days earlier, broadcasted these clashes taking place in the center of Istanbul to the whole world. These images led to interpretations of the events as the beginning of a "Democracy Spring" in Turkey. At this point, the Istanbul 6th Administrative Court granted issued a stay for the Artillery Barracks project. Erdoğan called the *cacerolazo* protests in the streets "ridiculous". On the other hand, what Erdoğan said while he was in Tunisia was very crucial, as he said he would make sacrifices for democratic requests. However, upon his return to Turkey, he preferred to continue his grim tone and insisted on the police acting. Yet, Erdoğan's opinions on some police personnel after December 17 and December 25 evolved on a completely different course.[9]

The Gezi upheavals were most critical breaking point that Erdoğan experienced with the Gülen Movement in politics. The dispute that it ignited was the most incarnate state of the AK Party-Gülen Movement conflict. Fetullah Gülen accused the government of bullying while criticizing the events:

> The only thing we will achieve when we react against the fierce minorities without any plan is to waste carbon dioxide. We will be doing nothing but bullying the other. The whole problem needs to be dealt with from its roots. What is our problem? How can we solve this, how can we fix it? That is how we need to deal with the problem, that is how we will be following the path of the prophet. ... Instead what we are doing is in order to suppress a single problem, we are causing 50 more injustices and committing 50 more oppressions. We are causing oppression and injustice. We are fuelling hatred and anger. We are causing unresolvable problems. ... Now if you stand up and say, "This is what it is...

---

[9]   Türk, *Muktedir, Türk Sağ Geleneği ve Recep Tayyip Erdoğan*, p. 252.

there is no issue in seeking rights!" then you will be ignoring the innocent people and innocent requests. First of all, we have always neglected them. They are the generation that has resulted from our own neglect. Secondly, they must have some reasonable demands. In all honesty, they have a right to say, "It is a park, the trees should not be uprooted, let people enjoy their walks and their park!" They may claim a call for the ecosystem and that you are murdering the environment![10]

AK Party-Gülen Movement Conflict

The milestones that led to the AK Party and Erdoğan's separation from Fetullah Gülen are the most crucial to understand, as Gülen was able to form good relations with political figures in Turkish politics throughout many decades with the exception of the leader of the National Outlook movement, Necmettin Erbakan. Otherwise, it is impossible understand the reasons for the political fragility Turkey has been experiencing in these past years, evolving relations with the West, and Erdoğan's changing political discourse.

In the 1970s, Gülen took on a leading role with an American-controlled Islamization project.[11] The conception of a Turkish-Islamic synthesis, which became a government policy with the 1980 coup, prepared the foundations for individuals in the Gülen Movement to lay hold of crucial units such as security, intelligence, and the military. In the 1990s, the number of bureaucrats who were members of the Gülen Movement – known as *Cemaat* in Turkish – increased at a level that

---

[10] "Fetullah Gülen'den Gezi Parkı Açıklaması," *Habertürk*, June 6, 2013, See also, http://www.haberturk.com/gundem/haber/850438-fethullah-gulenden-gezi-parki-aciklamasi.

[11] For more information, see, Özkan, *Modern Zamanların Hasan Sabbah'ı: Fetullah Gülen*.

clearly posed a danger.[12] Necip Hablemitoğlu, an academic at the time, voiced his concerns regarding the cadres held by Gülenists. However, due to his wholesale approach that also targeted all Islamic factions in Turkey, his concerns were interpreted as an ideological attack and ignored. Yet, Hablemitoğlu's evaluations were correct, and by the early 2000s, most of the Gülenist infiltration of the cadres in public offices was complete, save for except for the Justice Ministry. When the AK Party came to power in 2002, it inclined to work in alliance with the existing cadres. Turkey's political circumstances, the traumatic years the AK Party cadres experienced before, and the aggressiveness of the fraught secular figures all constrained Erdoğan to take imperturbable steps.

At this point, it is crucial to stress that both Erdoğan and Gülen are ontologically from different worlds. One is a political leader with a background in political Islam who defines himself as a conservative democrat arising from the National Outlook tradition while the other is a leader of an organization who "has links to intelligence and perceives all paths as legitimate and permissible"[13] in order to achieve his own agenda. In these circumstances, the ongoing relations with both Erdoğan and Gülen continued with pragmatism. Gülen, who gave an interview to the German channel ZDF following the July 15 coup attempt, said the following in regard to the ontological differences he had with Erdoğan following a meeting he had in the U.S. in 2000:

> It isn't true that I have had close relations with him. He once visited me when he was the mayor, and I also visited him once. I do not even remember whether he offered me any tea. I believe I have only met with him twice in my life. That is all there is to

[12] Necip Hablemitoğlu, *Köstebek,* Pozitif Publishing, Istanbul, 2016, p. 176.
[13] Selim Çoraklı, *Darbelerin Efendisi Hoca,* Eftalya Publishing, Istanbul, 2016, p. 34.

it. He visited me once during his work in forming his party. As I perceived him to be a sincere Muslim, I explained my thoughts to him. After he left, apparently he told a mutual acquaintance in the lifts that these people need to be dealt with initially. In other words, he clearly expressed his intolerance to other alternatives. ... I do not recall him ever mentioning my name. Therefore, I believe it is quite clear whether there was any form of close relations with him through these incidents.[14]

This confession told firsthand is a crucial detail that invalidates the criticism such as that Erdoğan was the one who nurtured and carried the Gülen Movement within the state. The fact that Erdoğan knocked on Gülen's door with a very broad political thought while forming the AK Party despite the fact that Erbakan, the leader of National Outlook, had always kept his distance from Gülen is evidence of the relations to continue solely on a political level.

The fact that following July 15, the opposition kept harping on Erdoğan's statement concerning the Gülen Movement in which he said, "We gave them everything they wanted," regarding the transitions of private teaching institutions, is in fact in reference to all official references of both national and overseas educational activities of the organization, which has always promoted itself as being an educational and charitable movement. Upon his return from Russia, where he attended a High Level Cooperation Council in November 2013, in reference to the discussions about the private teaching institutions, Erdoğan said to journalists:

The allegations that steps taken against the movement were based on bad blood are complete slander and lies. What have the

---

[14] https://www.youtube.com/watch?v=BVuXf8yWS60, https://www.youtube.com/watch?v=TBOZSguvIqA.

prominent figures of the movement ever brought forward up until today that was ever refused by Tayyip Erdoğan? We have done as much as we could for them, whether it is in relation to opening universities or many other activities. I have never refused any request from them. God is my witness.[15]

Erdoğan saying that they gave Gülenists everything they wanted would be distorted ad nauseam. Thus, a perception of being caught red-handed was put forth concerning previous relationship between the AK Party and the Gülen Movement. However, Erdoğan's statement is quite transparent, as he clearly referenced the support shown to its educational institutions during his time in office. He once again clarified the issue and made the following statement at a program he attended in Trabzon following the December 17 and December 25 operations:

Shame on him, as he said the following about me the other day: "This tall man has stabbed us in the back." And how exactly did we do that? They came to me to establish 17 universities and I consented. Was this backstabbing? What kind of a conscience do you have? You requested land for schools and we provided it. They invited us to international circles and we referred our statesmen to attend these programs. They organized Olympiads and we provided all forms of support. What kind of ingratitude is this? What was it that you desired and could not attain? The truth is clear: they wanted something else. You know how we reformed the private tutoring institutions. This bothered them. I advise you to remove your children from these institutions. They are demanding too much money and then they force you to go to other courses. Enough is enough. They are like leeches. Then again, leeches are more virtuous. Leeches draw bad blood. These people have sucked good blood.[16]

---

[15] *Star*, November 23, 2013.
[16] Recep Tayyip Erdoğan, Trabzon speech, March 24, 2014.

It should not to be forgotten that the schools in the Turkic republics[17] were established on solid foundations with the reference of the state during the terms of Özal and Demirel, and then the schools in Africa and the Balkans were established later during Erdoğan's time in power. Erdoğan largely refused the political and cadre requests from the Gülen Movement, and this later would be the breaking point of relations between Gülen and Erdoğan.

2004 National Security Council Decision

The years that were considered the alliance of AK Party and Gülen Movement were in fact an indication of the state preparing for a severe operation against Gülen and his organization. The report submitted to Erdoğan during the 2004 National Security Council described the threat of the high numbers of offices and positions held by Gülen's followers within the government. The report was signed by President Ahmet Necdet Sezer as well as Prime Minister Erdoğan, Abdullah Gül, Cemil Çiçek, Abdülkadir Aksu, and Vecdi Gönül on the government's side and the Chief of General Staff General Hilmi Özkök, Navy Commander Admiral Özden Örnek, Air Force Commander General İbrahim Fırtına, Army Commander General Aytaç Yalman, and Gendarmerie Forces Commander General Şener Eruygur. Many years later, all of these commanders who signed this report would be tried by FETÖ-linked judges and sentenced to aggravated life imprisonment for their supposed role in the fabricated Ergenekon and Balyoz coups attempts. The report presented to Erdoğan inevitably causes great unease within the movement.

---

17 http://fgulen.com/tr/turk-basininda-fethullah-gulen/fethullah-gulen-hakkinda-dizi-yazilar-dosyalar/fethullah-gulen-web-sitesi-ozel-dosyalar/9897-merhum-turgut-ozal

Gülen became extremely bothered by how the military convinced Erdoğan, whose relations have always been formal and based on pragmatism. Following the increasing momentum in the conflict between the movement and the AK Party, *Taraf* printed an article in 2013 with the headline "Decision to End Gülen Made at 2004 National Security Council"[18] eventually led to interpretations of both sides having taken off their gloves.[19]

On August 25, 2004 the National Security Council prepared a report, titled "The Precautions to be Implemented against the Activities of Fetullah Gülen Organization", which was given to the government as an advisory decision to prepare an action plan against the Gülen Movement. The National Security Council's report said: "For the purposes of preventing activities of Fetullah Gülen's organization and the Nur Movement, legislative regulations ensuring severe sanctions must be implemented and an action plan prepared." The report eventually caused panic within the movement and Gülen did not waste any time in giving the green light from Pennsylvania to manipulate the process.

Alper Görmüş, a journalist at *Taraf*, evaluated the National Security Council the decision in an article:

> The question is this: If there is any truth to the decision to liquidate all movement members from within the government was made a long time before the head of intelligence, Hakan Fidan, was called for a statement, then when was this decision made exactly? Or since when did the falling out between the state and the movement begin? I have personally been hearing all the talk about how the state has become uncomfortable with the exis-

---

[18] *Taraf* Nnwspaper, November 28, 2013.
[19] http://odatv.com/guleni-bitirme-plani-2004-mgkda-alindi-2811131200.html.

tence of the movement within its units and will make a move soon since 2006. However, I was not aware of the decision made at the 2004 National Security Council in relation to the monitoring of the Gülen Movement. And yet, it was.[20]

This being the case, all attention turned to the statements from the state. The deputy prime minister of the time, Bülent Arınç said, "It was only advice and was not applied."[21] However, the tangible steps taken by the state in regard to the National Security Council decision were eventually disclosed in the following years in news reports.[22] According to the details in the newspaper reports, the state relentlessly pursued all the necessary reporting since 2006. As of 2007, the difficulties endured by AK Party in politics, the attack on the State Council, the exposed coup diaries of Özden Örnek, the Democracy Rallies, the e-memorandum, the party closure case, the artillery found in the woods, and the phobic attitude of the media, military, and prominent figures against Erdoğan all become a hindrance in taking steps against Gülen and his organization, and thus, Gülen's manipulation strategy succeeded in overtaking Turkey's daily agenda once again.

A final point is that Gülen had also implemented a similar strategy in 2007 with the critical Dolmabahçe meetings and the incidents that took place right after the December 17 and December 25 judicial coup attempt. It is not a mere coincidence that the Ergenekon and Balyoz investigations and trials, which reshaped the whole structure of the Turkish Armed Forces, took place almost one month after Erdoğan's meeting

---

[20] Alper Görmüş, "MGK 2004'te Cemaati Takip Kararı Alıyor" *Taraf*, November 28, 2013.

[21] http://www.hurriyet.com.tr/guleni-bitirme-iddiasina-ak-partiden-art-arda-a-ciklamalar-25228969

[22] http://www.radikal.com.tr/turkiye/hukumet-mgknin-2004teki-cemaat-ey-lem-planini-uygulamis-1163747/

with Chief of General Staff General Büyükanıt. While on the other hand it is quite evident that all of the operations were portrayed as an ordinary cat and mouse game following December 17 and December 25, they were actually plots to reshape the politics.

The Paradigm Difference

The major foundational point that politically disconnects Gülen and Erdoğan are their political paradigm differences. Erdoğan's Middle Eastern policies, his teaching a humanitarian lesson to Israel, his mantra that the world is bigger than five, his political style, and the peace and brotherhood processes initiated within the internal dynamics of Turkey was a challenge to all the power holders Gülen considered to be the authorities.[23] According to Gülen, every single undertaking initiated without getting permissions from the authorities was doomed to fail. As such, Erdoğan's defiant attitude against the authorities had no place within Gülen's philosophy. What is most essential for Gülen is obedience and commitment. Gülen was uneasy with Erdoğan's eventual escalation as a political figure who he knew could not be controlled. Erdoğan solely takes his political references from the national will and eventually came to realize the dimensions of Gülen's political aspirations with the MİT crisis on February 7, 2012. The MİT crisis was not only an assault against Erdoğan and head of intelligence Hakan Fidan, it was one of the greatest blows to the reconciliation process that Turkey considered move for national unity and brotherhood. Turkey experienced a similar blow with the MİT trucks scandal in relation to which Can Dündar printed the national security se-

---

[23] Özkan, *Modern Zamanların Hasan Sabbah'i: Fetullah Gülen*, p. 93.

crets in *Cumhuriyet*, hiding behind his press credentials.[24] Erdoğan challenged them by say that it was himself who had sent Fidan to Oslo:

> It is I who sent the head of the National Intelligence Organization. If it is I who sent him, then you can question me. Why would you try to take him in for questioning? I want complete transparency here. I do not find the method of the judiciary in this case acceptable, and it is because of this that I have made this statement. I will do the same again if necessary.[25]

With the passing of time, the disintegration between Erdoğan and Gülen deepened and led to conflicts, and Turkey eventually became the target of the unthinkable assaults of an intelligence-guided professional organization that had "infiltrated the capillaries of the state"[26] over the past 50 years. After Gülen's probing with the December 17 and December 25 judiciary coup, his role was decrypted regarding the July 15, 2016 coup attempt in which 249 people were killed and thousands more were injured. His role was revealed when many repentant commissioned officers confessed and the fugitive Adil Öksüz, a prominent figure in the movement, was arrested at Akıncı Air Base but later mysteriously released.[27] These incidents are crucial in terms of paving the way for and providing the opportunity for the state to cleanse its body from this disease.

The Trial of Political Islam: Statist Discourse

Erdoğan has always been known as a vehement leader whose political life had always been struggle-oriented against the

---

[24] http://aa.com.tr/tr/gunun-basliklari/berberoglu-dundarla-goruserek-mit-tirla-ri-goruntulerini-verdi/841743
[25] Recep Tayyip Erdoğan, Channel 7, September 26, 2012, İskele Sancak TV show.
[26] Özkan, *Modern Zamanların Hasan Sabbah'ı: Fetullah Gülen*, p. 46.
[27] Kemal Gümüş, *İşgalin Yapı Taşları*, Kopernik Kitap, Istanbul, 2017, p. 345.

status quo. He was criticized for adopting a statist discourse following the social incidents endured in 2013. The political tradition that Erdoğan owes his own background to equates statist discourse with the status quo and opposes it.[28] However, the objection here was not against the state's own implementation, but against the state's founding ideological stand against religion and the marginalization, discrimination, and disregard of the religious as the state's ideological definition. This approach, which has been developed by center-right politics as a reflex against a despotic state, has existed ever since the Democrat Party aspired to end the state's tutelage of society.[29] Erdoğan has continued his existence as a political leader, who places importance on the coalescence of the state and the nation, just as Özal had done before. With his insight of serving the state,[30] Erdoğan has shown that apart from the democratization of Turkey, he can also implement crucial steps to ensure the social coalescence without any ideological impositions.[31] This approach, which has provided a crucial foundation for the AK Party to attain social legitimacy, is perceived in the West as a struggle to save democracy from the implementations of an authoritarian state against the center. However, Erdoğan's conception of his definition of Turkish identity based on a single state, single country, single flag, single nation, has eventually led to the interpretation of the political doctrine that Kemalism has internalized.[32] At

---

[28] Etyen Mahçupyan, *Yüzyıllk Parantez*, (Interview: Şener Boztaş and Mehmet Âkif Memmi), Profil Publishing, Istanbul, 2014, p. 207.

[29] Mustafa Şen, "Türk-İslâmcılığının Neoliberalizmle Kutsal İttifakı", Dipnot Publishing, Istanbul 2006, p. 36.

[30] Some English academic journals have mentioned the AK Party's most differentiating feature to be that of having a "state of service" understanding. See, *The Emergence of a New Turkey: Democracy and the AK Parti*, H. Yavuz (ed.), Salt Lake City: University of Utah Press, 2006.

[31] "AK Parti ve Muhafazakâr Demokrasi", http://www.akparti.org.tr/muhafazakar.doc

[32] Yasemin Çongar, "Erdoğan, gönül ve şerlerin en kötüsü," *Taraf*, October 12, 2008.

this point, one should to take a closer look at Erdoğan's new definition of nationalism. Following the incidents in Egypt, Erdoğan's new nationalism definition of the "Turkish Rabia" is an effort to form a citizenship identity independent from ethnic identity, and in this sense, it also coincides with the nationalism conception of Mustafa Kemal Atatürk. Although this has drawn protests from Islamists, Erdoğan's recent political analysis, which equates love of the homeland with loyalty to the state, portrays the state as a holy instrument. Thus, with Erdoğan, the statist discourse evolves into a new identity inspired by Ibn Haldun's concept of social solidarity, or *asabiyya*.[33]

In this regard, Erdoğan addressed the youth at a meeting in Ankara:

> We have four main topics. We will never allow anyone to undertake an assault on them. We have come to power as a single nation with a single flag. And we will continue our path in this way. A single homeland – a single, 780-million-square-kilometer homeland. It is unacceptable to accept any form of disintegration within this land. The fourth is a single state. We will never accept a state within a state. We have a duty of loyalty to our flag and our martyrs. Each and every one of you needs to have faith and confidence in yourself. You will never bow down before any other state or civilization. You will never feel like a second-class citizen. I sincerely request that you look at one another with tolerance. Racism has never been able to take hold in our land. We have never believed the superiority of one over another. You will all adopt the same perception of loving the creature because of the creator. We have put our trust in all of

[33] İbn Haldun, *Mukaddime*, Dergâh Publishing, Trans. Professor Süleyman Uludağ, Istanbul 2017. "According to Ibn Haldun, the unity of a political society is ensured by *asabiyya* – in other words, the solidarity of the community. Erdoğan's attempts to form unifying politics surfaces as a result of a mutual ideal."

you. We have complete faith that you will never disappoint this glorious nation.[34]

Erdoğan has always highlighted his adversarial identity throughout his political life and he fortified his stand of prioritizing the state, particularly after the failed coup attempt. In truth, this new stance Erdoğan has begun to show has been interpreted as a the state and nation coalescing with center-right politics, which has been indisputably accepted by right-wing voters as a derivative of the understanding of serving the nation so that the state may survive.[35]

The Changing Definition of Conservatism

Erdoğan is a conservative politician with traditional codes. With this, following his National Outlook background, he consciously placed himself as a conservative democrat. The fact that political Islam has endured a Kafkaesque[36] metamorphosis vis-à-vis conservative democracy has been interpreted as conservatism being integrated with Islamism.[37] If conservatism is considered a historical perspective and a form of cultural orientation, then this definition paves the way to establish links with the past, future, culture, and wisdom and can be considered to be directly in connection with Erdoğan's aim of raising a religious generation, increasing the number of religious schools, and building his grand mosque at Çamlıca. However, while Erdoğan is criticized for legitimatiz-

---

[34] Recep Tayyip Erdoğan, "Okullara Bir Milyon Tablet Dağıttık," http://www.radikal.com.tr/turkiye/erdogan-cocuklari-santajcilardan-koruyoruz-1177243/

[35] In his famous novel *Osmanak*, Tarık Buğra uses this political statement in reference to Sheikh Edebali in the context of the centre-right's unity of the state and nation. See, Tarık Buğra, *Osmanak*, Ötüken Neşriyat, Istanbul 2017.

[36] This is used to explain Franz Kafka's unique imaginative style. Kafka uses this style as he transforms a known fact into a completely different truth.

[37] Hasan Aksakal, *Türk Muhafazakârlığı*, Alfa Publishing, Istanbul, 2017, p. 21.

ing conservatism at a religious foundation, the conservatism that has surfaced in Turkey in recent years has become independent from the classic terminology and the target of accusations such as that it is a new ideology becoming regionalized. In reference to the changing definition of conservatism, Hasan Aksakal says the following:

> It has come to such a point that daily incidents are spoken of by reference to the characters of Ahmet Hamdi Tanpınar's novels and religious festivals celebrated with a reference to a poem by Yahya Kemal Beyatlı. Politicians have come to such a stage where they unnecessarily recite from Necip Fazıl and Mehmet Akif and hold their places at Rumi's Shab-e 'Arus [Night of Union] celebrations that have been turned into a complete tourist attraction. ... During these past years, while the books of the Ministry of National Education have been censoring Steinbeck, Pir Sultan Abdal, and Yunus Emre, the environment has been filled with courses on marbling and reed flute. While the major classics such as Hamlet, Faust and Les Miserable are being removed from theater stages, discussions have reached a point of whether Shakespeare was a Muslim or not. ... Soccer matches being played with the Mehter team, tribune groups referencing the year 1453, and sports clubs being named Ottoman sports or Halide Edip Adıvar have all led to conservatism being turned into a bad caricature.[38]

The erosion of the perception of conservatism and religiosity during the AK Party's time in power cannot simply be explained as a degeneration stemming from daily politics. The fact that worldliness has increased along with religiosity becoming a tool for pomposity is most probably one of the most crucial traps that AK Party has come to face. Erdoğan

---

[38] Aksakal, *Türk Muhafazakârlığı*, p. 14.

is quite well aware of the changing and transforming social structure. It is for this reason that he articulates the raising of a true and healthy religious youth every chance he gets. He approaches religiosity from a perspective of freedom and modernity and answers his critics:

> I would like to address those who have been writing their columns during this past week. Would you like for the youth to become drug addicts? Would you like this generation to be rebellious to their elders? Would you like them to become a generation who is torn from the national and spiritual values, who have no destination and ideology? We cannot come to an agreement with you on this issue. Gentlemen, first give some thought as to how a modern and religious generation can be raised. A religious generation is one that is respectful of freedoms and different thoughts. They are also respectful of other faiths. We are a generation that has been taught to respect. Up until today, we have been able to illustrate how respect is shown and we will continue to do so.[39]

Erdoğan draws an ideal moral frame in regard to lifestyles as a result of his own conservatism.[40] It is for this reason that raising a religious generation is vital to him. In fact, Erdoğan's hope for a religious generation is that virtuous individuals make a virtuous society. However, this attitude is perceived as an intervention to secular lifestyle. His opinions on having at least three children, abortion, mixed-gender state dormitories, and venue-based alcohol regulations trouble secular society. Erdoğan delivered a speech at the opening of a new hospital and ignited the wick of a great discussion when he said abortion is murder. This eventually led many to voice

---

[39] Recep Tayyip Erdoğan, "Bu gençliğin tinerci olmasını mı istiyorsunuz?" February 6, 2012; http://www.milliyet.com.tr/erdogan-bu-gencligin-tinerci-olmasi-ni-mi-istiyorsunuz--siyaset-1498747/

[40] Türk, *Muktedir, Türk Sağ Geleneği ve Recep Tayyip Erdoğan*, p. 320.

their opinions with comments such as that abortion is a right, it is a woman's choice, and no one can intervene with a woman's body. If this is the case, then we should give our blessings to those who want to commit suicide. Why do we intervene with a suicidal individual who is about to jump from a bridge? Should one be able to use this right? This is complete nonsense.[41] Tanıl Bora interprets Erdoğan's anti-abortion stance within the conservatism tradition in that "women are perceived as the nation's biological production as well as women having to carry the responsibility of cultural production."[42] However, some other similar deliveries Erdoğan has mas are a result of his mastery in changing the daily agenda. He spoke about mixed-gender housing and successfully changed the daily agenda once again:

> Although we have numerous times said that we do not interfere with anyone's personal lifestyle choices, we are continuously faced with accusations of having intervened in people's lifestyles. I served as a mayor for four and a half years. I faced the same type of accusations back then, too. At the end of it, I was not imprisoned because of those accusations, but because of merely reciting a poem. Why? They told me that I had muddied the waters. And now, I have been governing Turkey for the past 11 years. If you take a close look, you will still see how they are trying to come up with similar accusations. During these 11 years of the AK Party being in power, whose lifestyle have we ever intervened in? Have we ever intervened in anyone's choice of lifestyle? If there has been any part of this society that has been victimized by such oppression, it has always been conser-

[41] Recep Tayyip Erdoğan, "Kürtaj yasağını çıkartacağız", May 29, 2012; http://www.radikal.com.tr/politika/erdogan-kurtaj-yasasini-cikartacagiz-1089484/

[42] Tanıl Bora, "Analar, Bacılar, Orospular: Türk Milliyetçi-Muhafazakâr Söyleminde Kadın", *Şerif Mardin'e Armağan*, comp. A. Öncü, and O. Tekelioğlu, İletişim Yayınları, Istanbul, 2009, p. 244.

vatives. They have been oppressed in education, health, justice and the police forces. It is simply because those times have come to an end that some people are trying to intervene. We should always be aware of one fact as a conservative democratic party in responsibility, all of the children of parents in this country are consigned to our security.

We have never allowed girls and boys to live in the same state dormitories together and we will never do so. Some newspapers have written about this. They can write whatever they want. One cannot justify this in the educational psychology of any country. We are involved with this issue and will continue to ensure the existence of single-gender housings at our state dormitories. In some locations, there are some problems concerning insufficient lodging and, therefore, students live in private housing. Our police forces have been receiving complaints regarding these residences. Our governorships are intervening. Why does this make some people uncomfortable? We cannot ignore complaints such as these just because some journalists maliciously write about these issues in their columns.[43]

It can be said that this strategy from Erdoğan in which he discusses issues that he believes will cause an uproar in society serve in inclining society toward conservatism by discussing factors that may affect the peace and continuity of society.[44]

Kasımpaşa Character: Sincerity and Authenticity

Erdoğan's admirers appreciate his youthful stance, his identity of brave dissident that defies the system, and the source of his protest spirit that he has had since his youth that have all

---

[43] http://www.hurriyet.com.tr/basbakan-erdogandan-onemli-aciklama-lar-25048293.
[44] Türk, *Muktedir, Türk Sağ Geleneği ve Recep Tayyip Erdoğan*, p. 329.

come from his Kasımpaşa character. Politics is not the usual vehicle for appreciation of these characteristics. Although his Kasımpaşa character is used positively in places, it is generally an image that is used to describe Erdoğan's quick temper and hotheadedness. However, the social reading of his Kasımpaşa character is that of his sincerity and authenticity. Erdoğan once said, "Kasımpaşa character is clear – it is the name of being a brave man."[45] As a leader, Erdoğan's Kasımpaşa character distinguishes him as his most distinctive feature. He is separated from his competitors for being a genuine, sincere, and patient leader.[46]

We were often confronted with his lively outbursts while he was prime minister. On a visit to Kars in 2011, he called a sculpture made to symbolize peace between Armenia and Turkey a monstrosity, giving that as the reason to remove it, and his instruction to demolish the sculpture caused a great debate. Erdoğan said:

> I will emphasize one thing: they have put a monstrosity there, right next to Hasan Harakani's tomb. They have erected something strange. Of course, it is unthinkable that this is the place where all the foundation work and that piece of art are. Our mayor will quickly perform his duties with regard to the matter. We expect this quickly. God willing, we will see it in our first developments. By expropriating that environment, the municipality will bring a beautiful park to that area as well. [47]

Culture and Tourism Minister Ertuğrul Günay, trying to explain away Erdoğan's criticism, said that what was de-

---

[45] *Hürriyet* newspaper, February 15, 2000

[46] From an interview of late Erol Olçok: "He behaves the way he is, the way he is made. Consequently, he has no need for advertisers or image makers. His biggest image is himself." Interview with Erol Olçık: "Why Shouldn't We Reach 60 Percent Support," *CNBC-e Business*, P. 65, March 2012

[47] http://www.hurriyet.com.tr/gunaydan-insanlik-aniti-aciklamasi-16726377.

scribed as a monstrosity was not the sculpture, but a distorted structure in the city. His aim was to dissipate the reaction that occurred in the media. However, Erdoğan refuted his own minister two days later, saying that he was not referring to a shanty, but directly to the sculpture. Günay probably experienced the greatest trauma of his political career. Without reversing gear, Erdoğan said:

> Did you use the expression monstrosity for the sculpture or for the slums around? I used it for the sculpture. Those who evaluate the event there, those who come out on TV, have not come and seen the sculpture and the place. I am speaking in the capacity of a mayor. There are historical artifacts where the statue is. I'm not interested in the content of the statue. I know more or less what the statue is. You do not have to be a graduate of fine arts to use discretion for sculpture in any case. They ask a citizen who passes by about a folksong, 'Do you like it?' They do not ask if you graduated from the conservatory. Why was that friend [former AK Party mayor of Kars] not re-nominated as a candidate? Because that friend did not have the qualities we were looking for. The conservative democrat was not re-nominated because he did not suit our sensibilities.[48]

Erdoğan also exhibited a similar attitude while president. On February 28, 2015, the prime minister's meeting with HDP and government officials at his Dolmabahçe Office regarding the reconciliation process drew a reaction from Erdoğan, who reflected on the disturbances he heard on TV while returning from Ukraine. This unexpected issue created a shock to the government. Erdoğan would not spare his words appraising if the government did not approve of the policy on the line of presidential debates:

---

[48] http://www.milliyet.com.tr/basbakan-konustu-bakan-gunay-yikildi-siya-set-1338681/

There is no such thing as the president of the Republic discussing every situation at any moment with the government. I mean, it is not the right approach to exaggerate events like that. It could be the time we go to the presidential system that you would say that. It's not before the presidential system. They used their own savings there. Good luck means drop me. But I also have the right to say that I am uncomfortable with this situation. ... I do not find the meeting there correct either. I personally do not find it correct to present a picture at this meeting of a group that is now in Parliament side by side with the government's deputy prime minister. Earlier when it was needed, a friend negotiated with them and a statement was made. But, as it was at the meeting, two separate texts were declared by going to the media. It never happened. I do not find it right. When it comes to the 10-item text, there is no call for democracy in that text. How am I going to accept this text in the name of democracy? When we examine the text, most of the topics there are not even closely related to democracy or anything like that. There are still new demands that come up. Then there is a statement made by our deputy prime minister totally contrary to theirs. So there is nothing completely overlapping. Then what did they discuss? Could you call it a common declaration? Is there anything like that?[49]

Erdoğan's authenticity is not a very common behavior in the history of Turkish politics. The typification of the politician that Aziz Nesin brought to *Zübük*[50] (Egoist) is a gen-

---

[49] "Erdoğan slammed Dolmabahçe too" http://www.gazetevatan.com/erdogandolmabahce-ye-de-sert-cikti--752383-gundem/.

[50] Aziz Nesin, for the character he wrote in *Zübük*, a corrupt politician, says: "I now truly understand that zübük is not one but we all are zübüks. If we did not inherently carry the characteristics of zübük, if we, each of us, were not a zübük, such zübüks would not be sprouting from amongst us. The zübük inside each of us combine to form the zübüks who lead us. Actually, zübükness is within us. We create them from our own zübükness. And then when we see that our zübükness combined into one Zübük, we get angry with it." Azizs Nesin, *Zübük*, Nesin Publication, Istanbul 2005.

eral character that emerged as a reaction to the corruption in politics. Erdoğan's role as a political figure, which overthrows this typology, plays an important role in his social acceptance. Erdoğan's confidence in the sincerity and authenticity of society lies in the background of his emergence as the least wounded from the relentless struggle he has been engaging in against Fetullah Gülen, his organization, and Western politics. For this reason, the manliness, correctness, and sincerity of one from Kasımpaşa in the face of *Zübük*, which represents the lies and forgery in Turkish politics, still finds itself an important place.

The way that Erdoğan does politics, not fitting the resident patterns of Ankara, is seen as contrary to state traditions.[51] Media organizations highlight Erdoğan as an irritable and angry politician. With emphasis on fatigue, some want Erdoğan to be heaped with ridicule and sarcasm. The goal then was to create a perception of a sick prime minister who is ill tempered. Journalist Fatih Altaylı diagnosed Erdoğan in the summer trying to add a scientific air, saying Erdoğan's disease is chronic fatigue.[52] However, the media's perception operation has not worked against, and Erdoğan continues to maintain his place on the social trust index.

Codes of Discord Politics and Populism

Erdoğan stands out as a political leader who makes the best use of his words. Sometimes, when his style gets stronger while responding to satire from opposition parties, he usually succeeds in communicating correctly. For this reason, Er-

---

[51] "AKP's Koçak Is Fired," http://www.radikal.com.tr/politika/akpli-kocak-ihrac-edildi-784707/.

[52] Türk, *Able, Türkish Right Wing Tradition and Recep Tayyip Erdoğan,* P. 365.

doğan will be referred to as one of the rare politicians who can connect people with their personal characteristics and style in their exclusive style. Erdoğan is accepted as the leader farthest from elitism and the most successful in being a man of the people in Turkish political history, shouldering to the front of a funeral to get in front of the coffin for prayers, his references to the people in his speeches, and his fatherliness toward children, distributing toys.[53]

Erdoğan influences many voters thanks to the power of his oration. Thus, he has the opportunity to present his thoughts more clearly and meaningfully. Academic Ozan Örmeci describes Erdoğan's ability to influence the populace, which he arrives at with a generally critical approach, by connecting it to the power of discourse:

> At this point it should be emphasized that Erdoğan is a very good orator. As an observer who has been able to listen to him in person several times, I can say that Erdoğan's public talks have always been fascinating and that he has deeply influenced people with a loud and interesting tone and emphasis. The rhetoric lesson Erdoğan took at the imam-hatip high school and the fact that from an early age he has been a good debater and reciter of poetry have been influential in the development of this feature. [54]

Erdoğan is also a master at ensuring that his political rhetoric reaches society's ears. He generally gives important messages at the end of Friday and holiday prayers. The interviews he gives to the media on trips abroad mark the country's agenda. What Erdoğan said and where he said it is also important in terms of the power of the message. McLu-

[53] Mehmet Doğan, *An Assessment of Turkish Politicians From a Perspective of Charismatic Leadership,* Post-Graduate Thesis, Selçuk University, 2014, p. 86.

[54] Ozan Örmeci, "Recep Tayyip Erdoğan", http://ydemokrat.blogspot.com/search?q=tayyip

han's theory of the medium is the massage is a method that Erdoğan often uses in political communication. He is also a strong character in measuring probabilities and overcoming setbacks. For that reason, he does not cease to work toward his targets without giving up faith. According to Hussein Besli, faith in God is Erdoğan's trademark. For Erdoğan, faith in God is a psychodynamic that leads to challenge, self-restraint, dedication, taking all kinds of risks, and walking alone on the right course.[55] Erdoğan's power, in a sociological sense, is hidden when the people find themselves in it. For that reason, he is seen as the "other"[56] amid existing politicians.

For Erdoğan, success is firstly the will of God, then the work of the nation to be accomplished with love. According to Erdoğan, the success of the nation is promising to be a servant. For this reason, he shapes the politics of discourse at the center of the concepts of service and success. Accepting the constant service to God to serve the nation, Erdoğan said:

> We have come to be servants, not to be masters, of this nation, because we are children of a civilization who see public service as service to God. ... Brothers, here you are gathered in an hour. What love, what great love, what kind of love is this? Could this national happiness be greater than servitude? We always say not to be a master, but this nation has become a servant. My brothers and sisters have spoken to us before today, but we talked about our projects and talked about our applications. After that, we will continue to make the way with our projects.[57]

Even if Erdoğan's speeches are populist from time to time, he is not a political leader who uses populist rhetoric in the

---

[55] Besli-Özbay, *The Birth of a Leader Recep Tayyip Erdoğan,* p. 217.
[56] Nuran Yıldız, *The New Shape of Politics in Turkey: Leaders Appearances Media,* Phoenix Publications, Ankara 2002, p. 138.
[57] "Much-Awaited Announcement from President Erdoğan," http://www.milliyet.com.tr/son-dakika-cumhurbaskani-erdogan-siyaset-2433585/.

classical sense. He never resembles an elitist leader. He speaks the language of the people, addressing the people in the street. In this way, he brings the environment to the center through political speech and representation of the oppressed, despondent, and outspoken.[58] He criticizes the use of populism as a language of propaganda, having said:

> We need to listen to the voice of the nation and listen to their requests to listen. I also declared from the parliamentary dais that we will never tend toward populism as discourse or implement election economy. I believe that our nation will judge this attitude fairly, that populism will be well differentiated from the builders of the future of the country.[59]

Yalçın Akdoğan says that populist demands are changing due to Erdoğan's transformative power over society. In this respect, Erdoğan's transformative leadership is linked to the fact that the political culture produced by populism is grounded in reality and rationality.[60] It is useful to point out an important detail, which was true for for Demirel and Özal, as well, which is the common feature of coming from within the people, coping with the same problems, struggling, rising, and achieving success. This can easily be said for Erdoğan. However, the most distinctive difference that separates Erdoğan from his opponents is that he has won by colliding with regulations[61] and coming from the people, the position he found through his own efforts, which is different from the

---

[58] Akdoğan, *Leader, Political Leadership and Erdoğan,* p. 107.

[59] "Tough answer form Erdoğan: They are inconsiderate," http://www.hurriyet.com.tr/erdogan-sert-yanit-suursuzlar-5753501.

[60] Barış Yetkin, *Populism As a Political Communication Device: A Comparative Analysis of Turgut Özal's "From the Action," and Recep Tayyip Erdoğan's "State of the Nation,"* Post-Graduate Thesis, Akdeniz University, 2010, p. 85.

[61] Ece Ayhan, "Long Story Short, they hit us and we grew, brother"", http://www.gazetevatan.com/-velhasil-onlar-vurdu-biz-buyuduk-kardesim--300413-gundem/.

elites of the Republic who constitute other domesticated politicians who have come from the machinations of the state.[62]

Sociological Analysis of Opposition to Erdoğan

Today, both domestically and abroad, the hostility toward Erdoğan can be understood as a pathologically phobic political outlook, which can be called a counter-personality cult that has transformed into a fixation, in a sense, by articulating or deriving from the traditional anti-democratic mindset in Turkey.[63]

The system of the politics of fear,[64] which has been systematically promoted to a chosen politician, is not compatible with the tradition of democracy and often jumps out as a problem in modern classical political theories. In the past years, the efforts of opponents to group together in opposition to Erdoğan have been an important problem for the future in an environment where the opposition has focused on producing politics of horror rather than producing value politics concerning Turkey's future. It is inevitable that the sociological milieu that feeds on separation, helplessness, and despair will seriously damage Turkish democratization in the long run. At this point it would be suitable to evaluate "Erdoganophobia", which has gained momentum abroad with opposition to Erdoğan formed domestically in different parameters. Journalist Vedat Bilgin describes the phobic atmosphere that emerged in Turkey's anti-Erdoğan opposition for many years as "the shak-

[62] Ahmet İnsel, "Regularization of democracy and modern conservatism," *Birikim Journal*, p. 163-164, November-December, 2002, v. 22.

[63] Vedat Bilgin, "An analysis of a pathological mental mode: Social psychology of animosity toward Erdoğan," http://www.aksam.com.tr/yazarlar/patolojik-bir-halin-analizi-erdogan-dusmanliginin-sosyal-psikolojisi/haber-506163.

[64] Halis Çetin, *Politics of Fear and Fear of Politics*, İletişim Publishing, İstanbul 2012, p. 55.

ing of the ideological hegemony of the elites holding authority or of the groups under their political influence":

> Those who do not base their enmity of President Erdoğan on rational politics turn to attacks with a language of hostility and hate and smear campaigns. They excite and are satisfied by and find support from some groups or crowds and their slogans. And we have to realize that, from a social point of view, the spread of such a language from politics is destructive. Since it is unable to put forth critical politics vis-à-vis the ideas Erdoğan represents, this destruction creates a political approach acting with hopelessness and despair, which we can say is a pathological condition. What are the reasons for this pathological condition and from which sources are they fed? I want to focus on the socio-psychological dimension that precedes these questions.

Conservative political understanding had existed for a long time in a closed form in the Turkish social structure before it came to the political stage. Westernizing politics, which has continued with a bureaucratic, authoritarian approach in Turkey's anti-democratic political tradition, has led to the liquidation of all social traditions and institutions with the goal of launching a veritable war against the local culture and destroying it, which means to be exposed to some operations to resist this attitude of Western political elites who put their own people in some sort of colonialist politics. In this respect, the people had to wait for the opening of political participation for them. The Democratic Party and the parties from the same tradition have tried to practice politics against the statist cadre of the authoritarian Republic as representatives of civil society in the Turkish political structure. In this respect, the social ground on which the cadre of civil politics is nourished is the conservatives trying to protect the local against the Westernization operation. The attitude of those who act with hatred for President Erdoğan based on socio-psychological trauma rather than politics is related to this issue. As Erdoğan turned to reforms that dismantled the authoritarian state conception of anti-democratic politics, the ideological hegemony of the power groups of this old structure, the elites who had adopted its worldview, and the groups under their political influence, have been shaken and shattered. The reason for this pathological situation is the helplessness and weakness that they have experienced in democracy in response to this new politics and the representative object of hate, as it represents more than the loss of power of a ruling coterie produced by the tradition of Westernization over 100 years. Turkey's ruling elites, who have been in power for more than 100 years, have entered a socio-psychological crisis in response to the response they gave to the local cultures they destroyed.[65]

Despite the change in the electorate's sociology in Turkey, Erdoğan's ability to mobilize the masses, his reformist stance, political pragmatism for constant change, and scolding protests defying the status quo make him a target for the ruling elites who lost their ability to represent. These elites refer not only to everyday politics, but also to a small group that has the ability to direct a significant amount of time to the deep politics of the state. For this reason, it is not a coincidence that in his political life, Erdoğan has been made a sitting target in the form of a political figure for his attackers. In response to the rise of the social center, the political power of the party cadres forming the political center would collapse rapidly in terms of both ideological and institutional dominance and the entry into the liquidation process would form the basis of the

---

[65] Vedat Bilgin, "An analysis of a pathological mental mode: Social psychology of animosity toward Erdoğan," http://www.aksam.com.tr/yazarlar/patolojik-bir-halin-analizi-erdogan-dusmanliginin-sosyal-psikolojisi/haber-506163.

emergence of the opposition to Erdoğan in Turkey.[66] In other words, Erdoğan's goal for the "New Turkey" would come into being in defiance of the established elite group's paradigm. Erdoğan explained how they disturbed the worried elites who resists change in the 2014 presidential nomination publicity meeting:

> They said to us, 'you are only washers of corpses,' because we are studying at imam-hatip. They humiliated us because we pray, because we take our shoes off when we enter the house. The more we struggled, the more they increased their attacks. They jailed [us] and said we couldn't even be headmen. They did not think democracy, equality in the eyes of the state, to be equal fitting for us. We did not care how they described us and what others told us. We did not strive to be standard citizens. We stood upright without scowling! In the times when it was asked when will God's help come, we were those who said 'God's help is close, be patient'. They pushed [us] around; we were even more determined. We were strengthened with every blow. We did battle with headlines and grew. God was always our measure. We minded what the nation said. As Yunus said, 'I love the created because of the creator,' we said, too. We also liked those who didn't like us. We took service to those who did not vote. We didn't say Kurd, we didn't say Turk, we didn't say Jew, we didn't say Christian. This country is the country of those who do not vote for us just as much as it is for those who vote for us. This country is the country of those who do not like us just as much as it is for those who do like us.[67]

The concept emphasizing "us and them" frequently found in Erdoğan's discursive world is not used to describe other

66 Vedat Bilgin, "An analysis of a pathological mental mode: Social psychology of animosity toward Erdoğan," http://www.aksam.com.tr/yazarlar/patolojik-bir-halin-analizi-erdogan-dusmanliginin-sosyal-psikolojisi/haber-506163.
67 "Erdoğan I never forgot two bracelets," http://www.cumhuriyet.com.tr/haber/siyaset/88985/Erdogan__iki_bilezigi_hic_unutmadim.html.

political parties and opposition. Erdoğan, who sees himself as a "negro" Turkish citizen, sees "the other" as old, white-bearded White Turks[68] who represent the established status quo. It is an important indicator when Erdoğan emphasized white-black discrimination in response to the criticism of the iftar (fast-breaking meal) invitation to the Presidency of Religious Affairs and the religious community to the Presidential Palace Complex: "The issue here is that the Presidential Complex has become a national monetary asset. We are meeting with headmen here for the seventh time today. It has been seven months that we have been gathering with those close to martyrs, veterans, workers, and those from all walks of life. This is the main discomfort. This chafes them. Instead of coming together and embracing our nation, they welcomed White Turks. Because they call me a Negro Turk. I am proud to be a Negro Turk."[69]

Erdoğanophobia: The Impasse of Western Politics

It is necessary to analyze the depths of the ruptures Erdoğan has experienced with Western politics. The West depicts Erdoğan as a dictator[70] who will get rid of the Republic and democracy in the near future, whose political discourse hardens by the day, and who has a tendency toward authoritarianism and building in a one-man regime. The main target of Erdoğan's person is Turkey. After July 15, Erdoğan's attempt at civil reform to liquidate the FETÖ structures en-

---

[68] Fatih Altaylı, "Whitest Turk is as white as Michael Jackson," http://www.haberturk.com/polemik/haber/822746-en-beyaz-turk-michael-jackson-kadar-beyazdir.

[69] "Erdoğan: I'm proud of being a Black Turk," https://www.haberler.com/erdo-gan-saray-da-verilen-iftarla-ilgili-7447759

[70] Dexter Filkins, "Turkey's Vote Makes Erdoğan Effectively a Dictator" The New Yorker, 17.04.2017; http://www.newyorker.com/news/news-desk/turkeys-vote-makes-er-dogan-effectively-a-dictator.

trenched in the bureaucracy were not be accepted. The troubles experienced in the prosecution process were presented as an attempt of the opposition's silencing efforts, billing Erdoğan with a wholesaler approach. Because of this, the West has not supported Turkey's efforts to rebuild democracy, despite the hurdles, after the unsuccessful July 15 coup attempt. In fact, it would reach the stage in important Western capitals of trying to show Erdoğan as a war criminal through claims of politicians connected to Daesh and the unfurling of banners containing death threats directed at him.[71] Without a healthy analysis of this critical point, it will not be possible to correctly read the codes of unrelenting war that Western politics has engendered with Erdoğan.

It must be acknowledged that the West was a powerful force over Islamic societies in the previous century, militarily, politically, economically, and socially, and that the region is a powerful actor in the shaping of the distribution of incomes. It is an important detail that the two poles that persisted for centuries interacted – or in other words, the fact that the East-West struggle continued for the past few centuries in the psychological superiority of the West. The West considers both the present and the past as a mark of superiority mentally, politically, economically, and militarily. For this reason, the history and civilization of Islam in the Western paradigm are not explained according to their internal stature and it is regarded as an inverted image of Western history. If Islam is a religion of violence, it is explained that Christianity is a religion of peace and love. If Islam is oppressive and patrimonial, this is the result of Western,[72] liberal approaches. In

[71] "Death threat to Erdoğan from masked terrorists," http://www.haber7.com/dis-politika/haber/2320458-yuzu-maskeli-teroristlerden-erdogana-olum-tehdidi.
[72] İbrahim Kalın, *I, the Other and Beyond*, İnsan Publishing, Istanbul 2016, p. 317.

the article "Islamophobia and Limits of Multiculturalism"[73], İbrahim Kalın says that the West, surrounded by modernist, enlightened, and secular ideas, is not involved in Islam, and that it is also satisfied with multiculturalism.

Thus, American political scientist Samuel P. Huntington put the political paradigm that has deepened the East-West divide into circulation with his argument in *The Clash of Civilization and Remaking of World Order* in 1988. In 1992, the theory of another political scientist, Francis Fukuyama, in *The End of History and The Last Man*[74] was regarded as an absolute victory in the West's battle for supremacy. The proposal Huntington gives that there will be a great battle between Islamic and Western civilization in the coming century constitutes the basic philosophy of the liberation projects that have increased in the Middle East since the 1990s.[75] Thus, all Muslims pay for the terrorist attacks that have escalated in the Middle East. That Islam equals terrorism and Muslims equal terrorists in fueled by anti-Islam sentiment and Islamophobia. Huntington summarizes the perception of the Islamic world as follows: "I cannot say that all Muslims are terrorists, but all terrorists are from among Muslims."[76] The Gulf War, the invasion of Afghanistan, the Arab Spring, and even the embargo on Qatar, which began after September 11, are political developments in the Middle East as a reflection of this paradigm. In 1994, French political scientist Olivier Roy's *The Failure of Political Islam* emphasizes the political failures of the

---

[73] John L. Esposito, Ibrahim Kalin, *Islamophobia: The Challenge of Pluralism in the 21th Century*, Oxford University Press, Oxford 2011, p. 236.

[74] Francis Fukuyama, *The End of History and The Last Man,* Avon Books Inc, New York 1992.

[75] Samuel P. Huntington, *The Clash of Civilizations and the Remaking of World Order,* as translated by Cem Soydemir-Mehmet Turhan, compiled by Hande Şarman, Okyanus Publishing, Istanbul 2013.

[76] Hüseyin Koç, "From Political Islam to Islamophobia," http://fikircografyasi.com/makale/siyasal-İslâmdan-İslamofobiye.

Islamic world. It is not foreseen that political Islam, which has been criticized for an inability to stand up to modernity, will be successful because political Islam has lost its ability to be an alternative to oppressive Western modernization. In other words, it continues to spread and increase its influence, but it has lost its original impetus.[77] Islamist movements in Algeria, Tunisia, and Egypt are largely examples of Roy's argument. Actors who come from Islamist roots and practice politics must fail in the final analysis. A political figure that would otherwise be successful would inevitably turn into a liberator of regional politics waited on for a century. Today, the Muslim Brotherhood in Egypt is declared a terrorist organization[78] after being completely liquidated after the Sissi coup in a strategic move aimed at ignoring the political trends in the Islamic world. Unlike this picture, Erdoğan has been and is a successful political leader. In the Islamic world where democratization is realized on a minimum scale, in the country that gives reference to its cultural origins while providing a serious contribution for its integration with the West, in his speeches often referring to the Ottomans, in joining the generation of the religious to the party's program, and becoming more of a phenomenon in the Islamic world as days pass, he who turns conservative democracy into a political doctrine vis-à-vis Islamism in the last analysis is the figure of Erdoğan, who is perceived as a serious threat to the Western paradigm. Thus, the Western mind will find a way of getting rid of a political movement that is no longer capable of being tamed, in this case Erdoğan and the non-democratic elements he represents. Words and phrases such as authoritari-

---

[77] Tuğba Yürük, *The Transformation of Political Islam: The Ennahda Movement in Tunisia,* Post-Graduate Thesis, Ankara University, iv.

[78] "Muslim Brotherhood declared a terrorist group," http://www.bbc.com/turkce/haberler/2013/12/131225_musluman_kardesler.

an, dictator, and one-man rule are not merely a preferred bag of concepts by chance. On a global scale, while reshaping the Islamic world, it is part of a big plan put into practice in order to contribute to the West's share of the income. For this reason, Erdoğan, who before was not called a dictator when he hardened his discourse, is now put on the same level as extreme undemocratic figures such as Vladimir Putin, Kim Jung-un, and Hugo Chavez,[79] and passed into the literature as an authoritarian, indicating the dimensions of the opposition reaching the point of phobia. It is important at this point to correctly read Erdoğan's relations with the West in order to well enough understand Erdoğanophobia.

Is Erdoğan an Islamist?

Islamism is to make Islam dominant over life again in the 19th and 20th century as a whole, including faith, worship, ethics, philosophy, politics, law, and education. It is considered a movement that embodies all the predominantly activist and eclectic political, ideological, and scholarly studies conducted in the name of saving Muslims and the Islamic world from Western exploitation, oppressive and despotic rulers, slavery, imitation, and superstitions and to bring forth civilization to unite and improve people rationally.[80] Erdoğan, who, in the early 2000s, identified himself as a conservative democrat, is actually an actor who, according to this definition, can be considered to be a political Islamist. However, just as Islamism has no single definition, the National Outlook tradition is also dead set against the Islamism that is ori-

---

[79] Anna Borshchevskaya, "Is Erdogan A Russian Ally Or Putin's Puppet?", *Forbes*, January 2017; https://www.forbes.com/sites/annaborshchevskaya/2017/01/27/is-erdogan-a-russian-ally-or-putins-puppet/#54177fe01596.

[80] İsmail Kara, *Türkiye'de İslâmahk Düşüncesi*, Dergâh Yayınları, Istanbul 2011, Vol. 1, p. 176.

entalism defines. Although it is thought the Turkish under-standing of Islamism overlaps with the Ottoman tradition, is more tolerant compared to other interpretations of Islamism, and that it is an Islamic understanding more compatible with the globalization,[81] Erdoğan identifies himself as Muslim, not an Islamist. However, Erdoğan, who comes from a National Outlook background, is a political Islamist who has, from the West's angle, transformed.[82] Roy does not see Erdoğan as a political Islamist in the classic sense and, despite this, Er-doğan and the AK Party's political stance is interpreted based on "a strategy that assumes Islamism without assuming it."[83] Erdoğan will continue, in the eyes of the established elites in Western politics, to remain a huge question. It could be said that Erdoğan annotating Islamism by identifying himself as a Muslim politician is an objection aimed at the AK Party, as a homogenous political party, being as marginalized as Islamism "coding religion as a pragmatist political element."[84] However, in the final analysis, it needs to be accepted that Erdoğan's Islamist reflexes are a lot more developed than those who portray themselves as pure Islamists. The local and national terms he has introduced are seen as a concrete initiation for Islamists in the intellectual sense. The recent debate started on the basis of the purge of Islamists, brings to mind the question of whether it is a counterattack developed against the wide social acceptance of the AK Party. On his return from India, Erdoğan put an end to the Islamist debates, responding to a journalist's question with:

---

[81] Taşkın, *AKP Devri: Türkiye Siyaseti, İslâmcılık, Arap Baharı*, p. 136.

[82] Scott Peterson, In Turkey, "Erdoğan fans an Islamic nationalism to build Ottoman-style influence," 22.02.2017, *The Christian Science Monitor*, https://www.csmonitor.com/World/Middle-East/2017/0222/In-Turkey-Erdogan-fans-an-Islamic-nationalism-to-build-Ottoman-style-influence

[83] Tanıl Bora, "Reel İslâmcılık", *Birikim*, July 2017, issue: 339, p. 72.

[84] Mustafa Öztürk, "Dünü ve bugünü itibariyle İslâmcılığın kısa hikâyesi," *Sebilürreşad*, issue: 1017, June 2017, pp 5-7.

It is said that those who are Islamists are thrown out, those who are not are brought in. It is wrong anyway to make a distinction between being an Islamist or not in the operations of a political party. We are not looking for students for the [dervish] lodge. What is essential for a political party is to be people who are honest, principled, who love their country and people, who will abide by the party's principles. This is what needs to be done. But some have completely gone off the rails. They have come to the point of considering those who embrace their own rights, who remain within the frame they have determined as right and the people outside that box as wrong. Yet, nobody has such a right. They also don't have such a right or authority – neither do I. None of us have the measure of the eternal world. Nobody should try and put this on the scale. It is going to be pretty harsh, but nobody should play God.[85]

Writer Abdurrahman Arslan says, "Islamism expresses Muslim's behavior and attitude in the face of a modern or foreign situation. In this case, whether they accept it or not, all Muslims are Islamists."[86] Professor İsmail Kara defines Islamism as:

Islamism, born into the special conditions of the 19th century as a modern-day political movement, contained reactance, at least in terms of it gaining conceptual presence. Does this state of reflex fix the position of Islamism, Islamist politics as opposition? What would Islam say about this? Isn't this in itself against the suggestion of Islamism? Describing Islamism solely as an oppo-

---

[85] "Cumhurbaşkanı Erdoğan, 'İslâmcılık tartışması'na nokta koydu: Tekkeye mürit aramıyoruz," *Habertürk* newspaper, 03.05.2017; http://www.haberturk.com/gundem/haber/1481700-cumhurbaskani-erdogan-İslâmcilik-tartismasina-nokta-koydu-tekkeye-murit-aramiyoruz

[86] Abdurrahman Arslan, "Bütün Müslümanlar İslâmcıdır," Interview: Nil Gülsüm, *Milat,* August 13, 2012; http://m.milatgazetesi.com/butun-muslumanlar-İslâmcidir-haber-32419

sition and uprising movement is wrong or at least incomplete. Islamism is also the movement of harmony and reconciliation.[87]

Professor Burhanettin Duran confirms that despite Erdoğan and the AK Party not being the representatives of political Islam, the external perception of them is that they are Islamists. Duran explains the reason behind Erdoğan's reputation weakening in the eyes of the West:

> Ever since the establishment of the party, he never identified himself as Islamist. He preferred to say conservative democrat and use the term civilization. In the recent period, he added to these being national-local. However, the AK Party also could not escape being associated with Islam in every critical stage of its 16-year political life. And, the AK Party was labeled as the agenda of different intentions and actors, like a blind person would describe an elephant. In reality, Islamism is a term used loudly by the opposition to describe the party from the outside as negative and its supporters use in a low voice to describe it as positive.

At a time when Western media was leaning toward the AK Party, between 2002 and 2013, the AK Party and Erdoğan were moderate Islamists. He wanted integration with the West and was a reformist actor who united Islam and democracy. Following the "one minute" outburst in 2009 in Davos and the Mavi Marmara raid, Israel as well as the Gülen Movement (later known as FETÖ) started to use the term radical Islamist to identify Erdoğan. For Kemalists and the CHP, ever since the start, the AK Party, similar to the National Outlook, had a hidden agenda to establish an Islamic state. The common characterization related to Erdoğan in Western media post-Gezi inci-

---

87 İsmail Kara, "Her Müslüman İslâmcıdır ifadesi teşvik kokuyor," Interview: Fadime Özkan, *Star* newspaper, August 13, 2012; http://t24.com.tr/haber/prof-kara-her-musluman-İslâmci-degildir,210796

dents, was first as an Islamist authoritarian, and later as an Islamist fascist, dictator. In the eyes of its supporters, the AK Party is Islamist as an actor that shows an interest in the problems of the Muslim world that observed the affairs of the ummah. Erdoğan is a leader who is able to join the feelings of the oppressed Muslims from Syria to Somalia and to Arakan. He was an opponent that criticized the unjust world order under the control of the Western world.[88]

As a result, although accusing Erdoğan using terms such as radical Islamist and authoritarian, his prominent Muslim personality alongside his conservative democrat identity explain these attacks as reactions to his discourse policy, which has harshened in the face of political problems. It is clear that the process reached this point as a result of serious planning. It is now a lot clearer that FETÖ leader Fetullah Gülen turning Erdoğan into the target of systematic propaganda since 2013[89] was all part of a global plan that included attempts such as deepening the conflict with the government.

---

[88] Burhanettin Duran, "AK Parti, Erdoğan ve İslâmcıların tasfiyesi," *Sabah*, April 29, 2017; http://www.sabah.com.tr/yazarlar/duran/2017/04/29/akpartierdoganve-İslâmcilarintasfiyesi

[89] Fetullah Gülen, "Eğitime darbe plânı," www.herkul.org/herkul-nagme/391-nag-me-egitime-darbe-plani

CONCLUSION

ERDOĞANOPHOBIA

Fear in Politics, Politics of Fear

Phrases such as fear in politics or politics of fear are nothing new. The politics of fear is almost as old as the history of humanity. The term Islamophobia,[1] which has entered the literature in modern times, is defined as an irrational fear, derived from the Greek word "phobia".[2] It generally includes hate speech and is used more to express cultural and political opposition, rather than social opposition. It would not be wrong to make the observation that anti-Turkish sentiment and Erdoğan hate, which have gradually gained speed in the West, especially since 2010, are today turned into a systematic fear taking a phobic form in Islamophobia. Conceptualizing this newly emerged situation with "Erdoğanophobia" allows a better understanding of the subject.

Xenophobia in the West evolving, especially in recent years, to a fascistic political discourse, helps pave the way for other phobic movements. The perception operations targeting Erdoğan having come into effect after 2011 is a significant and interesting detail. *The Times* magazine accusing Erdoğan in 2011

---

[1] The term Islamophobia was first used in 1992 by orientalist Etienne Dinet. See, Etienne Dinet, "L'Orient vu de l'Occident", Paul Guethner, Rue Jacob, Paris, 1922.
[2] Hilâl Barın, *Tedirgin Nefret: İslamofobi ve DAEŞ*, Tezkire Yayınları, Istanbul, 2016, p. 49.

of founding a dictatorial regime[3] at a time Turkish political maturity was at its peak and economic stability was gaining praise, was the starting point of the operation. The same magazine increasing its accusations of Erdoğan to him bringing dictatorship in 2013, while including Fetullah Gülen and Abdullah Öcalan on the list of the "100 Most Influential People of the Year",[4] is one of the most important signs to confirm this analysis. An article in *The Economist*, "Democrat or Sultan?" as the cover story published in the aftermath of the 2013 Gezi Park upheavals, the call to not vote for Erdoğan right before the November 1, 2015 elections, and publishing eight articles about Erdoğan's "new sultanate" in 2016, show how systematically Western media's plan to finish off Erdoğan is being carried out. *The Economist*'s comment on the April 16, 2017 referendum is even more striking:

> Turkey is being dragged to dictatorship. ... Having a powerful president it not a bad thing, but Turkey's new constitution is going too far. The country may be left subject to a 21st century sultan who is restricted very little by Parliament. ... Turkey will continue to play an important role after April 16. If Erdoğan loses, Turkey will be an ally with a difficult future ahead of it. But if he wins, he will be able to rule the country like an elected dictator.[5]

Anti-Erdoğanism proceeds in Western media on the grounds of anti-Islamism. In his article, "Turkey's elected dictator",[6] *The Huffington Post* writer Professor Alon Ben-Meir relates the Turkish people's support for Erdoğan to his manipulating the masses using his "inexplicably strange" influence and most fundamentally to the people's poverty and Islamic tendencies.

---

[3] Refik Erduran, "Erdoğanofobi," *Sabah*, June 21, 2011; http://www.sabah.com.tr/yazarlar/refik_erduran/2011/06/21/erdoganofobi.

[4] http://time100.time.com/2013/04/18/time-100/

[5] "Economist: Türkiye diktatörlüğe sürükleniyor," April 12, 2017, http://www.bbc.com/turkce/haberler-turkiye-39582101

[6] Alon Ben-Meir, "Turkey's Elected Dictator," *The Huffington Post*, July 29, 2016; http://www.huffingtonpost.com/alon-benmeir/turkeys-elected-dictator_b_11093160.html

Thus, he depicts those who support Erdoğan as ignorant people who have no clue about democracy. In reference to the West losing its power over Turkey, Ben-Meir calls the U.S. and EU to intervene vis-à-vis Erdoğan:

> Even before the failed military coup, Turkey's President Erdogan governed like a dictator who had the last word on all state matters. The botched coup was nothing but, as he put it, "a gift from God" to purge what is left of Turkey's democracy and cleanse the army and judiciary in order to ensure the total subordination of all institutions to his whims.

> For Erdogan, being elected was akin to being granted a license to trample and dismantle all democratic tenets to consolidate his powers and promote his Islamic agenda.

> [T]he US and the EU must use this occasion to put Erdogan on notice that history has shown time and again that totalitarian regimes come to a bitter end, and that he too will not be spared his day in court.[7]

It is now quite visible that Western media is attempting a clear operation against Erdoğan and, consequently, Turkey, to gain psychological superiority. It is a sure fact that one of the primary factors behind this process evolving against Turkey is the disinformation operations carried out by the Gülenist Terror Group (FETÖ) diaspora that has become institutionalized abroad for many years. Erdoğan's proposition for a world citizenship under equal conditions and equal terms, challenging the Western paradigm, is an extremely critical move that led to his fall out with Western politics. Etyen Mahçupyan analyzes this situation as follows:

> Turkey now demands to be considered at the world level, in the

---

[7] Akman, *15 Temmuz Darbe Girişimi Batı Medyası Söylem Analizi Neo-Emperyalizm, İslamofobi ve Oryantalizm,* p. 140.

same class as the other big countries, to be an equal, to be respected. This feeling is taking shape in the conservative mind as a principled stance and political expectation.[8]

In the final analysis, Erdoğan and the political line he represents has indispensable significance for the security of both the region and Islamic communities, despite the setbacks experiences from time to time. It needs to be accepted that under AK Party rule, Turkey has now turned into a value beyond being merely Turkey, and Erdoğan, beyond being an important milestone in Turkish politics, is a matchless political actor who has rolled up his sleeves to represent oppressed nations. Thus, with his rights and wrongs, good and bad, with the political mistakes he makes from time to time, but ultimately with the pragmatist and rationalist understanding he represents, he is the second-greatest statesman the country has seen who has made the biggest contribution to New Turkey's democratization journey.

Even though he differs from the paradigm of the Republic's founding ideology, Erdoğan is a political leader with authentic and national patriotism that cannot be debated, and whose entire cause, care, and, hope are for the betterment of Turkey and all of humanity. Stopping the disease of Erdoğanophobia, which the West uses and is determined to use as a sort of psychological tool of war, before it reaches the extent of threatening not only Turkey's peace and calm, but that of the entire region, is mandatory for the sake of world peace. Hence, the political duty in Turkey and abroad where conscience is still intact is to rapidly realize a new future that will make common sense prevail for the good of the world.

---

[8] Etyen Mahçupyan, "AK Parti ve Yeni Milliyetçilik," *Akşam*, February 24, 2014.

BIBLIOGRAPHY

Akdoğan, Yalçın. *Modern Türkiye'de Siyasî Düşünce İslâmahk*, İletişim Yayınları, Istanbul, 2004.

—. "Adalet ve Kalkınma Partisi", *Modern Türkiye'de Siyasî Düşünce İslâmahk*, Vol. 6, İletişim Yayınları, İstanbul 2014.

—. *AK Parti ve Muhafazakâr Demokrasi*, Alfa Yayınları, Istanbul, 2004.

—. *Lider, Siyasî Liderlik ve Erdoğan*, Turkuaz Kitap, Istanbul, 2017.

Akgül, Ahmet. *Erbakan Devrimi*, Togan Yayıncılık, Ankara, 2011.

Akman, Filiz Barın. *15 Temmuz Darbe Girişimi Batı Medyası Söylem Analizi Neo-Emperyalizm, İslamofobi ve Oryantalizm*, Kadim Yayınları, Ankara, 2017.

Akman, Nuriye. *Zaman*, March 24, 2004.

Aksakal, Hasan. *Türk Muhafazakârlığı*, Alfa Yayınları, Istanbul 2017.

Aksay, Hakan. "Erdoğan'ın savaşına hayır, Barış süreci korunmalıdır," July 29, 2015; http://t24.com.tr/yazarlar/hakan-aksay/erdoganin-savasina-hayir-baris-sureci-korunmalidir,12387.

Akyol, Taha. "Belediye Görüntüleri," *Milliyet,* December 28, 1993.

Alatlı, Alev. *Haberlerin Ağında İslâm,* Babil Yayınları, Istanbul, 2000.

Al-Rasheed Madawi, and Marat Shterin. *Dying For Faith: Religiously Motivated Violence in the Contemporary World,* I.B.Tauris, New York, 2009.

Arslan, Abdurrahman. "Bütün Müslümanlar İslâmcıdır," Söyleşi: Nil Gülsüm, *Milat* newspaper, August 13, 2012; http://m.milatgazetesi.com/butun-muslumanlar-İslâmcidir-haber-32419.

Atılgan, Gökhan, Cenk Saraçoğlu, and Uslu Ateş. *Osmanlı'dan*

Günümüze Türkiye'de Siyasal Hayat, Yordam Kitap, Istanbul, 2015.

Aydın, Suavi, and Yüksel Taşkın. *1960'tan Günümüze Türkiye Tarihi*, İletişim Yayınları, Istanbul, 2015.

Aydıntaşbaş, Aslı. "Erdoğan's Davos Outburst Is Nothing New," *Forbes*, January 2009; https://www.forbes.com/2009/01/30/erdogan-turkey-davos-opinions-contributors_0130_asli_aydintasbas.html.

Ayvazoğlu, Beşir. *Sîretler ve Sûretler*, Ötüken Neşriyat, Istanbul, 1999.

Bahçeli, Devlet. MHP Group speech, February 16, 2010.

Bal, İhsan. *Militan Demokrasi, Habertürk*, April 16, 2012.

Balcı, Bayram. *Orta Asya'da İslâm Misyonerleri / Fethullah Gülen Okulları, İletişim Yaynlan*, Istanbul, 2005.

Barın, Hilâl. *Tedirgin Nefret: İslamofobi ve DAEŞ*, Tezkire Yayınları, Istanbul, 2016.

Ben-Meir, Alon. "Turkey's Elected Dictator," *The Huffington Post*, July 29, 2016; http://www.huffingtonpost.com/alon-benmeir/turkeys-elected-dictator_b_11093160.html.

Berktay, Halil. *Tarihçi Gözüyle Siyaset*, Kopernik Kitap, Istanbul, 2017.

Besli, Hüseyin, and, Ömer Özbay. *Bir Liderin Doğuşu Recep Tayyip Erdoğan*, YTY, Istanbul, 2014.

Bilâ, Fikret. "Senin Ne İşin Var Suriye'de," *Milliyet* newspaper, February 6, 2016.

Bilgin, Vedat. "Patalojik bir halin analizi: Erdoğan düşmanlığının sosyal psikolojisi," http://www.aksam.com.tr/yazarlar/patolojik-bir-halin-analizi-erdogan-dusmanliginin-sosyal-psikolojisi/haber-506163.

Birand, Mehmet Ali, and Reyhan Yıldız. *Son Darbe 28 Şubat*, Doğan Kitap, Istanbul 2012.

Bora, Tanıl. *Cereyanlar, Türkiye'de Siyasî İdeolojiler*, İletişim Yayınları, Istanbul, 2017.

—. "Reel İslâmcılık", *Birikim* Dergisi, July 2017, p. 339.

—. "Analar, Bacılar, Orospular: Türk Milliyetçi-Muhafazakâr Söyleminde Kadın," *Şerif Mardin'e Armağan,* A. Öncü and O. Tekelioğlu (eds.), İletişim Yayınları, Istanbul, 2009.

Borshchevskaya, Anna. "Is Erdogan A Russian Ally Or Putin's Puppet?" *Forbes,* January 2017; https://www.forbes.com/sites/annaborshchevskaya/2017/01/27/is-erdogan-a-russian-ally-or-putins-puppet/#54177fe01596.

Buğra, Tarık. *Osmancık,* Ötüken Neşriyat, Istanbul, 2017.

Bush, George W. *Decision Points,* Broadway, 2011.

Coşkun, Ahmet Hakan. "Bağışla Bizi Erbakan Hocam," *Hürriyet,* September 26, 2013.

Çağaptay, Soner. *The New Sultan, Erdoğan and The Crisis of Modern Turkey,* I.B.Tauris, London, 2017.

Çakır, Ruşen. "Fazilet Kongresi: Demokrasi Virüsü FP'ye de Sızdı." *Birikim,* pp 134-135, June-July 2000; birikimdergisi.com/birikim-yazi/3956/fazilet-kongresi-demokrasi-virusu-fp-ye-de-sizdi#.WMEeLDvxhp8.

—. "Necmettin Erbakan: Adaletin Bu Mu Düzen?" *Homopolitikus: Lider Biyografilerindeki Türkiye,* drl. S. Öngider, Aykırı Yayıncılık, Istanbul, 2001.

—. "Pragmatizmin Sınırları," June 15, 2017; http://medyascope.tv/2017/03/15/erdoganin-pragmatizminin-sinirlari/.

Çalmuk, Fehmi. "Necmettin Erbakan," *Modern Türkiye'de Siyasî Düşünce: İslâmahk,* İletişim Yayınları, Vol. 6, Istanbul, 2014.

Çandar, Cengiz, *Mezopotamya Ekspresi / Bir Tarih Yolculuğu,* İletişim Yayınları, Istanbul, 2012.

Çelikkol, A. Oğuz. *One Minute'ten Mavi Marmara'ya Türkiye-İsrail Çatışması,* Doğan Kitap, Istanbul, 2014.

Çetin, Halis. *Korku Siyaseti ve Siyaset Korkusu,* İletişim Yayınları, Istanbul, 2012.

Çınar, Menderes. *Vesayetçi Demokrasiden "Milli" Demokrasiye*, Birikim Yayınları, Istanbul, 2015.

Çiğdem, Ahmet. *Geleceği Eskitmek AKP ve Türkiye*, İletişim Yayınları, Istanbul, 2014.

—. *D'nin Hâlleri: Din, Darbe, Demokrasi*, İletişim Yayınları, Istanbul, 2009.

Çongar, Yasemin. "Erdoğan, gönül ve şerlerin en kötüsü," *Taraf*, October 12, 2008.

Çoraklı, Selim. *Darbelerin Efendisi Hocia*, Eftalya Yayınları, Istanbul, 2016.

Dinç, Namık Kemal. *Onlar Gittiler Biz Barışı Yitirdik*, İletişim Yayınları, Istanbul, 2016.

Dinet, Etienne. "L'Orient vu de l'Occident," Paul Guethner, Rue Jacob, Paris 1922.

Doğanay, Ülkü, Halise Karaaslan Şanlı, and İnan Özdemir Taştan. *Seçimlik Demokrasi: Recep Tayyip Erdoğan, Kemal Kılıçdaroğlu, Devlet Bahçeli ve Selâhattin Demirtaş'in Demokrasi Söylemi*, İmge Kitabevi, Istanbul, 2017.

Doğan, Mehmet. *Karizmatik Liderlik Bağlamında Türk Siyasetçilerinin Değerlendirilmesi*, Yüksek Lisans Tezi, Selçuk Üniversitesi, 2014.

Duran, Burhanettin. "AKP and Foreign Policy as an Agent of Transformation," *Sabah*, April 29, 2017.

—. "AK Parti, Erdoğan ve İslâmcıların tasfiyesi," *Sabah*, April 29, 2017.

Erbakan, Necmettin. "İşbirlikçiler ve AKP'nin Ekonomik Yıkımı," *Millî Kurtuluş Konferansları (National Independence Conferences)*, esam.org.tr/Doayrinti.aspx?DosyaID=61, 28 Haziran 2007.

—. "Medeniyet Davamız," *Davam*, MGV Yayınları, Ankara, 2013.

—. "Yaratılış ve İnsan," *Davam*, MGV Yayınları, Ankara, 2014.

—. "Türkiye'nin Meseleleri ve Çözümleri," *Erbakan Külliyatı*, Vol. 2, comp. M. M. Uzun, MGV Yayınları, Ankara, 2013.

—. "Kahramanmaraş Refah'la Bütünleşmiş," June 28, 1993, *Erbakan*

Külliyat, Vol. 5, comp. M. M. Uzun, MGV Yayınları, Ankara, 2013.

—. "Basın Toplantısı" (Press Conference), May 14, 2003, *Erbakan Külliyat*, Vol. 4, comp. M. M. Uzun, MGV Yayınları, Ankara, 2013.

—. "Millî Görüş, Ekonomik Kalkınma ve Herkese Refahı Nasıl Sağlayacak?" Millî Kurtuluş Konferansları 2, *Erbakan Külliyat*, Vol. 2, comp. M. M. Uzun, MGV Yayınları, Ankara, 2013, p. 383.

Erdoğan, Recep Tayyip. *"Bizde İslâma olmaz, Müslüman olur."*, hurriyet.com.tr/basbakandan-turban-cikisi-8024104.

—. "Millî Görüş Gömleğini 28 Şubatta Çıkardık," *Akşam*, August 14, 2003.

—. "Bir Musa Çıkar Zulmün Hesabını Sorar," http://aa.com.tr/tr/politika/bir-musa-cikar-zulmun-hesabini-sorar/225638, August 15, 2013.

—. AK Party Ordinary Grand Congress speech, October 3, 2009; http://www.milliyet.com.tr/erdogan-dersim-icin-ozur-diledi-siyaset-1466430/

—. "Mısır'da İnsanlık Hedef Alınmıştır," http://www.ensonhaber.com/erdoganin-turkmenistan-ziyareti-oncesi-aciklama-2013-08-15.html.

—. Kanal 7, September 26, 2012 İskele Sancak TV program.

—. "Okullara Bir Milyon Tablet Dağıttık," http://www.radikal.com.tr/turkiye/erdogan-cocuklari-santajcilardan-koruyoruz-1177243/.

—. "Bu gençliğin tinerci olmasını mı istiyorsunuz?" June 2, 2012; http://www.milliyet.com.tr/erdogan-bu-gencligin-tinerci-olmasini-mi-istiyorsunuz--siyaset-1498747/.

—. "Kürtaj yasağını çıkartacağız," May 29, 2012; http://www.radikal.com.tr/politika/erdogan-kurtaj-yasasini-cikartacagiz-1089484/

—. "Cumhurbaşkanı Erdoğan, 'İslâmcılık tartışması'na nokta koydu: Tekkeye mürit aramıyoruz", *Habertürk*, May 3, 2017; http://www.haberturk.com/gundem/haber/1481700-cumhurbaskani-erdogan-İslâmcilik-tartismasina-nokta-koydu-tekkeye-murit-aramiyoruz.

—. "Erdoğan: Zenci Türk olmaktan gurur duyuyorum," https://www.haberler.com/erdogan-saray-da-verilen-iftarla-ilgili-7447759-haberi/.

—. "Erdoğan, Dolmabahçe'ye de sert çıktı," http://www.gazetevatan.com/erdogan-dolmabahce-ye-de-sert-cikti--752383-gundem/.

—. Speech, Trabzon, March 24, 2014.

—. Speech, Diyarbakır, August 12, 2005.

—. Speech Grand National Asssembly of Turkey, December 27, 2010.

—. Speech Batman May 2, 2015.

—. Speech, Grand National Asssembly of Turkey AK Party Group, January 13 2009.

—. "My Country is Your Faithful Ally and Friend," *The Wall Street Journal,* March 31, 2003.

Erdoğan, Mehmet. *Siyasî Hafıza / Eski Türkiye'den Yeni Türkiye'ye (1996-2016),* Kopernik Kitap, Istanbul, 2017.

Erduran, Refik. "Erdoğanofobi," *Sabah,* June 21, 2011; http://www.sabah.com.tr/yazarlar/refik_erduran/2011/06/21/erdoganofobi.

Esposito, John L., and İbrahim Kalın. *Islamophobia: The Challenge of Pluralism in the 21st Century,* Oxford University Press, Oxford, 2011.

Filkins, Dexter. "Turkey's Vote Makes Erdoğan Effectively a Dictator," *New Yorker,* April 17, 2017.

Fukuyama, Francis. *The End of History and The Last Man,* Avon Books Inc, New York, 1992.

Fuller, Graham. "Freedom and Security: Necessary Conditions for

Moderation," *American Journal of Islamic Social Sciences*, 22/3 (Summer 2005).

—. "Turkey's Strategic Model: Myths and Realities," *Washington Quarterly*, Vol. 27, No. 3, Washington 2004.

Gözden, Ramazan. "Türkiye ve Arap Baharı: Değişimi Açıklamak ve Anlamak," *Adam Akademi*, 2011/2: 1-25.

Göle, Nilüfer. *Modern Mahrem, Medeniyet ve Örtünme*, Metis Kitap, Istanbul 1991.

Görmüş, Alper. "MGK 2004'te Cemaati Takip Kararı Alıyor," *Taraf*, November 28, 2013.

Gümüşçü, Şebnem, and Deniz Sert. *The Power of the Devout Bourgeoisie: The Case of the Justice and Development Party in Turkey*, Middle Eastern Studies, Vol. 45, No. 6, 2009, http://www.jstor.org/stable/40647179.

Gümüş, Kemal. *İşgalin Yapı Taşları*, Kopernik Kitap, Istanbul, 2017.

Güngör, Nasuhi. *Yenilikçi Hareket*, Elips Kitap, Istanbul, 2005.

Gürel, Burak. "İslâmcılık: Uluslararası Bir Ufuk Taraması," *Neoliberalizm, İslâma Sermayenin Yükselişi ve AKP*, Neşe Balkan, Erol Balkan, and Ahmet Öncü (eds.), Yordam Kitap, Istanbul, 2013.

Heblemitoğlu, Necip. *Köstebek*, Pozitif Yayıncılık, Istanbul, 2016.

Heper, Metin. "Devlet Kürtleri ne asimile etti, ne inkâr etti sadece bilinçli olarak göz ardı etti," *Hürriyet*, October 12, 2008.

Huntington, Samuel P. *Medeniyetler Çatışması ve Dünya Düzeninin Yeniden Kurulması*, trans. Cem Soydemir, Mehmet Turhan, comp. Hande Şarman, Okyanus Yayınları, Istanbul, 2013.

Ibn Haldun. *Mukaddime*, Dergâh Yayınları, trans. Professor Süleyman Uludağ, Istanbul, 2017.

İnsel, Ahmet. "Olağanlaşan demokrasi ve modern muhafazakârlık," *Birikim Dergisi*, Issue: 163-164, (November-December, 2002).

İsmailoğulları, Adnan. "Paçozlaşan Türkiye'nin Edebiyat Ödülü Alev Alatlı'ya," *Yeniçağ*, December 6, 2014.

Kahraman, Hasan Bülent. *AKP ve Türk Sağı*, (Söyleşi: Recep Yener), Agora Kitaplığı, Istanbul, 2009.

Koç, Hüseyin. "Siyasal İslâm'dan İslamofobi'ye", http://fikircografyasi.com/makale/siyasal-İslâmdan-İslamofobiye.

Kalın, İbrahim. *Ben, Öteki ve Ötesi,* İnsan Yayınları, Istanbul, 2016.

Kara, İsmail. *Türkiye'de İslâmahk Düşüncesi,* Dergâh Yayınları, Istanbul, 2011.

—. "Her Müslüman İslâmcıdır ifadesi teşvik kokuyor," Söyleşi: Fadime Özkan, *Star,* August 13, 2012; http://t24.com.tr/haber/prof-kara-her-musluman-İslâmci-degildir,210796.

Karpat, Kemal H. *Osmanh'dan Günümüze Elitler ve Din,* Timaş Yayınları, Istanbul, 2015.

—. *Kısa Türkiye Tarihi 1800-2012,* Timaş Yayınları, Istanbul, 2016.

Keyman, E. Fuat. *Türkiye'nin Yeniden İnşası, Modernleşme, Demokratikleşme, Kimlik,* Bilgi Üniversitesi Yayınları, Istanbul, 2013.

KILIÇDAROĞLU, Kemal, "15 Temmuz Kontrollü Darbe Girişimidir", April 3, 2017; http://www.bbc.com/turkce/haberler-turkiye-39478777.

Koçak, Recep. "Alev Alatlı'nın Söyledikleri," *Milat,* December 15, 2014.

Kökçe, Halime. *AK Parti ve Kürtler,* Kopernik Kitap, Istanbul, 2017.

Kuzu, Burhan. "Nasıl Bir Seçim Sistemi: Siyasi Parti Görüşleri Adalet ve Kalkınma Partisi," http://www.anayasa.gov.tr/files/pdf/anayasa_yargisi/anyarg23/kuzu.pdf.

Mahçupyan, Etyen. *Yüzyıllık Parantez,* Söyleşi: Şener Boztaş, Mehmet Âkif Memmi, Profil Yayıncılık, Istanbul, 2014.

—. "AK Parti ve Yeni Milliyetçilik," *Akşam,* February 24, 2014.

Mert, Nuray. *Merkez Sağın Kısa Tarihi,* Selis Kitaplar, Istanbul, 2007.

Micklethwait, John, and Arian Wooldridge. *God is Back: How the Global Revival of Faith is Changing the World,* Penguin Press, New York, 2009.

Morris, Chris. *The New Turkey: The Quiet Revolution on The Edge of Europe,* Granta Books, London, 2006.

Nesin, Aziz. *Zübük,* Nesin Yayınları, Istanbul, 2005.

Olçok, Erol. Interview: "Yüzde 60 Oya Neden Ulaşmayalım?", *CNBC-e Business,* Issue: 65, March 2012.

Oran, Baskın. *Türk Dış Politikası: Kurtuluş Savaşından Bugüne Olgular, Belgeler, Yorumlar (2001-2012)*, İletişim Yayınları, Vol. 3, Istanbul, 2013.

Örmeci, Ozan. "Recep Tayyip Erdoğan," http://ydemokrat.blogspot.com/search?q=tayyip.

Özkan, Fadime. "PKK-HDP muhataplıktan nasıl düştü?" *Star*, November 11, 2015; http://www.star.com.tr/yazar/pkkhdp-muhatapliktan-nasil-dustu-yazi-1068893/.

Özkan, Abdülkadir. *Modern Zamanların Hasan Sabbahı: Fetullah Gülen*, Kopernik Kitap, Istanbul, 2017.

Özkan, Ayşegül Büşra. "Türkiye'nin Avrupa Birliği Macerası: 2002-2015 Döneminde Yaşanan Gelişmeler," BİRSAM Report, 2015.

Özkök, Ertuğrul. "Tarih size öyle bir manşet atacak ki," February 19, 2014; hurriyet.com.tr/tarih-size-oyle-bir-manset-atacak-ki-25840227.

Öztürk, Mustafa. "Dünü ve bugünü itibariyle İslâmcılığın kısa hikâyesi," *Sebilürreşad*, June 2017.

Önay, Günseli. "Kan dökülecek, fıstık gibi olacak," May 9, 1997; http://arsiv.sabah.com.tr/1997/05/09/f08.html.

Pipes, Daniel. Washington Institute, *Policy Watch*, Vol. 746, April 10, 2003.

Peterson, Scott. "In Turkey, Erdoğan fans an Islamic nationalism to build Ottoman-style influence," *The Christian Science Monitor*, February 2, 2017.

Popper, Karl R. *The Poverty of Historicism*, Beacon Press, Boston, 1957.

Poyraz, Fahrettin. *Millî Nizam Partisinden AK Parti'ye İslâmî Hareketin Partileri ve Değişim, İttihat ve Terakki'den Günümüze Siyasal Partiler*, Turgay Uzun (ed.), Orion Kitabevi, Ankara, 2010.

Roy, Olivier. *The Failure of Political Islam*, I. B. Tauris & Co Ltd, New York, 1994.

Rumsfeld, Donald. *Known and Unknown a Memoir*, Penguin Group, New York, 2012.

Said, Edward W. *Covering Islam: How the Media and the Experts De-*

termine How We See the Rest of the World, Vintage Books, New York, 1997.

—. *Şarkiyatçılık: Batının Şark Anlayışı,* Metis Yayınları, Istanbul, 1995.

Sarıbay, Ali Yaşar. *Türkiye'de Demokrasi ve Politik Partiler,* Alfa Yayınları, Istanbul, 2001.

Schward, Jonathan. "Lie After Lie After Lie: What Colin Powell Knew Ten Years Ago Today and What He Said," 2013.

Sever, Metin. "Merkez Sağ Geleceğini Arıyor...(5)," *Radikal,* October 17, 2002.

Şafak, Erdal. "Erdoğan'ın Gömleği," *Sabah,* January 4, 2006.

Şen, Mustafa. "Türk-İslâmcılığının Neoliberalizmle Kutsal İttifakı," Dipnot Yayınları, Istanbul, 2006.

Talbot, Valeria. *The Uncertain Path of The New Turkey,* ISPI, New York, 2015.

Taşkın, Yüksel. *AKP Devri: Türkiye Siyaseti, İslâmalık, Arap Bahan,* Birikim Yayınları, Istanbul, 2013.

Türk, H. Bahadır. *Muktedir, Türk Sağ Geleneği ve Recep Tayyip Erdoğan,* İletişim Yayınları, Istanbul, 2014.

Uzgel, İlhan. "AKP: Neoliberal Dönüşümün Yeni Aktörü," *AKP Kitabı: Bir Dönüşümün Bilançosu,* Phoenix Yayınevi, Istanbul, 2009.

Yavuz, Hakan. *Secularism and Muslim Democracy in Turkey, "Introduction: what is an Islamist party? Is the AKP an Islamist party?"* Cambridge University Press, Cambridge, 2009.

—. "Introduction, *The Emergency of a New Turkey: Democracy and the AK Parti,*" University of Utah Press, Salt Lake City, 2006.

Yalçın, Soner. *Kayıp Sicil: Erdoğan'in Çahnan Dosyası,* Kırmızı Kedi, Istanbul, 2014.

Yeşilyurt, Nuri, and Atay Akdevelioğlu, "AKP Döneminde Türkiye'nin Ortadoğu Politikası," *AKP Kitabı: Bir Dönüşümün Bilançosu,* Phoenix Yayınevi, Ankara, 2013.

Yetkin, Barış. *Bir Siyasal İletişim Tarzı Olarak Popülizm: Turgut Özal'ın "İcraatın İçinden" ve Recep Tayyip Erdoğan'in "Ulusa Sesleniş"*

Konuşmaların Karşılaştırılmalı İncelemesi, Yüksek Lisans Tezi, Akdeniz Üniversitesi, 2010.

Yıldız, Nuran. *Türkiye'de Siyasetin Yeni Biçimi: Liderler İmajlar Medya,* Phoenix Yayınevi, Ankara, 2002.

Yılmaz, Nuh. "İslâmcılık, AKP, Siyaset," *Modern Türkiye'de Siyasî Düşünce İslâmcılık,* İletişim Yayınları, Vol. 6, Istanbul, 2014.

Yılmaz, Turan. *Tayyip: Kasımpaşa'dan Siyasetin Ön Saflarına,* Ümit Yayıncılık, Ankara, 2001.

Yürük, Tuğba. *Siyasal İslâmcılığın Dönüşümü: Tunus'ta en-Nahda Hareketi,* Post-Graduate Dissertation, Ankara Üniversitesi, 2017.

Zürcher, Eric Jan. *Modernleşen Türkiye'nin Tarihi,* İletişim Yayınları, Istanbul, 2015.

MINUTES

Supreme Election Council Decision, *Resmî Gazete,* Issue: 21038, pp 34-35, November 1, 1991.

AK Party Afyon Meeting Minutes, August 1, 2001.

Virtue Party Congress Minutes, May 14, 2000.

Virtue Party Congress Minutes, May 14, 2000-2.

National Salvation Party Congress Minutes, October 15, 1978.

Grand National Assembly of Turkey Resolution Minutes, March 1, 2003.

CHP Group Meeting Minutes, May 4, 2007.

NEWSPAPERS AND MAGAZINES

Milliyet, November 6, 1983.

Sabah, July 1, 1985.

Tercüman, July 1, 1985.

Milliyet, August 28, 1992.

Hürriyet, February 18, 1994.

Milliyet, March 28, 1994.

Milliyet, July 14, 1996.

Hürriyet, December 9, 1997.

Milliyet, July 10, 1997.

Radikal, September 24, 1998.

Akşam, April 23, 1998.

Radikal, April 25, 1998.

Hürriyet, April 23, 1998.

Hürriyet, February 15, 2000.

Zaman, July 20, 2000.

Milliyet, August 15, 2001.

Turkish Daily News, January 31, 2004.

Yeni Şafak, January 13, 2009.

As Safir, January 30, 2009.

Radikal, October 21, 2009.

Taraf, April 4, 2011.

Taraf, December 28, 2013.

Bugün, July 20, 2014.

Yankı, July 8-14, 1985.

ONLINE REFERENCES

eski.yerelnet.org.tr/secimler/il_secim.php?ilid=34&yil=1989

rusencakir.com/30-YILDAN-HATIRLADIKLARIM7-20-Ekim-
1991-Genel-Secimleri-Baraja-karsi-Erbakan-Turkes-ittifa-
ki/5110

http://www.birikimdergisi.com/birikim-yazi/3956/fazilet-kon-
gresi-demokrasi-virusu-fp-ye-de-sizdi#.WNO-BDvxg_U

http://rusencakir.com/30-YILDAN-HATIRLADIKLARIM8-
27-Mart-1994-yerel-secimleri-Medyaya-ragmen-ve-medya-
sayesinde-RPnin-zaferi/5118

http://www.aljazeera.com.tr/portre/portre-recep-tayyip-erdogan

http://www.surecanaliz.org/tr/article/sener-akturk-kurt-cozu-
mu-acilimin-sebebleri-sonuclari-ve-sinirlari

yerelnet.org.tr/belediyeler/belediye_secimsonuclari.php?y-
il=1989&belediyeid=128393

https://www.youtube.com/watch?v=Mffx_KREx5A

http://www.hurriyet.com.tr/geriye-o-sozler-kaldi-tak-emrediyor-
sak-yapiyoruz-27387374

http://gazetearsivi.milliyet.com.tr/Arsiv/1992/08/27

http://www.radikal.com.tr/politika/16-yilinda-mumcu-suikasti-hl-sir-918404/

http://www.ysk.gov.tr

http://odatv.com/erbakanin-basarili-havuz-sistemi-neden-bir-daha-uygulanmadi-1712141200.html

http://www.milligazete.com.tr/bir_iftira_daha_son_buluyor/293177

http://www.hurriyet.com.tr/28-subatin-ustunden-14-yil-gecti-17143455

http://www.milliyet.com.tr/o-generali-de-acikladi-gundem-1537413/

http://www.hurriyet.com.tr/burada-bitmez-39039785

Hürriyet, "Demokrasiye Bak," May 14, 2000, http://www.hurriyet.com.tr/demokrasiye-bak-39154160

http://www.hurriyet.com.tr/demokrasiye-bak-39154160

http://www.yenisafak.com/gundem/abdullah-gulun-darbe-komisyonuna-yaniti-bu-yapiyla-iliskim-olmadi-2591575

http://www.milliyet.com.tr/2003/05/22/siyaset/asiy.html

http://www.yeniasya.com.tr/2007/07/21/haber/h3.htm

http://www.hurriyet.com.tr/siyasal-İslâm-bitti-yasasin-yeni-İslâmcilik-128061

http://www.hurriyet.com.tr/son-dakika-avrupadan-flas-turkiye-karari-13-yil-sonra-bir-ilk-40437890

https://www.youtube.com/watch?v=D337eO8tBB0

http://www.gazetevatan.com/rusen-cakir-491426-yazar-yazisi-erdogan--demokrasi-tramvayinda-ihtirasli-bir-yolcu/

http://www.milligazete.com.tr/bu_yaziyi_mutlaka_okuyun/112583

http://www.hurriyet.com.tr/erdogan-ideologdan-cok-pragmatik-bir-kapitalist-14363856

http://t24.com.tr/haber/sabah-oslo-gorusmeleri-yabanci-bir-ajan-tarafindan-cemaate-servis-edildi,250598

http://www.aksam.com.tr/dunya/vatan-haini-can-dundari-yerine-dibine-sokan-verheugen-turkiyeye-garanti-verilmeli/haber-606012

https://tr.sputniknews.com/politika/201701051026642300-per-incek-bati-erdogan/

http://www.cnnturk.com/dunya/erdoganin-sanghay-beslisi-aciklamasina-rusyadan-ilk-yorum

http://www.ntv.com.tr/dunya/cinden-turkiyenin-sangay-beslisi-ile-is-birligi-aciklamasina-destek,_ssF5DpbPkGkzuCt-G19XTw

http://www.globalresearch.ca/plans-for-redrawing-the-middle-east-the-project-for-a-new-middle-east/3882

http://sahipkiran.org/2016/09/11/buyuk-ortadogu-projesi-bop/

http://armedforcesjournal.com/peters-blood-borders-map/

http://www.globalresearch.ca/plans-for-redrawing-the-middle-east-the-project-for-a-new-middle-east/3882

http://www.haber7.com/siyaset/haber/642749-davutoglu-erdogan-bop-es-baskani-olmadi

http://www.washingtontimes.com/news/2015/jan/28/inside-the-ring-gen-james-mattis-criticizes-obama-/

http://www.trthaber.com/haber/turkiye/buyukanitin-27-nisan-e-muhtirasina-iliskin-ifadesi-222976.html

http://www.hurriyet.com.tr/genelkurmaydan-cok-sert-aciklama-6420961

http://www.dailymotion.com/video/xvhrbx_cemil-cicek-ten-27-nisan-e-muhtirasina-cevap_news

http://www.aljazeera.com.tr/portre/portre-vecdi-gonul

http://www.milliyet.com.tr/karar--font-color-red-bugun-mu---font--aciklanacak--siyaset-972729/

http://www.haberturk.com/gundem/haber/1398471-basbakan-basdanismani-abdulkadir-ozkan-feto-dolmabahcede-bitecekti

http://www.cumhuriyet.com.tr/haber/diger/57056/Beykoz_daki_kazida_silâhlar_bulundu__.html

http://www.ntv.com.tr/turkiye/basbug-poyrazkoy-silahlari-tsk-ya-ait-degil,nkbvmfx2-k6NUCDnYOL2kg

http://www.sabah.com.tr/gundem/2012/08/06/basbugdan-erdo-gana-tesekkur

http://www.hurriyet.com.tr/devlet-kurtleri-ne-asimile-etti-ne-ink-r-etti-sadece-bilincli-olarak-goz-ardi-etti-10094707

http://www.haberturk.com/gundem/haber/626064-bu-ulkede-artik-kurt-sorunu-yoktur

http://www.cumhuriyet.com.tr/haber/siyaset/231433/Erdogan_agiz_degistirdi__Ne_Kurt_sorunu_ya_.html

https://www.haberler.com/dengir-mir-mehmet-firat-ak-parti-bogulma-emareleri-6604089-haberi/

http://www.haberturk.com/gundem/haber/1182321-kilicdaro-glundan-erdogana-elestiri-sen-bu-yemini-niye-ettin

http://www.haberturk.com/yazarlar/nihal-bengisu-kara-ca/1117505-neden-buzdolabinda

http://www.adanapost.com/cemil-bayik-buyuk-savas-olur-32654h.htm

http://www.radikal.com.tr/politika/paketten-yasam-tarzi-cik-ti-1153298/

http://www.iktibasdergisi.com/catismasizlik-nasil-sona-erdi/

http://www.cumhuriyet.com.tr/haber/turkiye/9947/Erdogan__Cezaevlerinin_bosaldigini_gorecegiz_.html

www.milliyet.com.tr/kandil-den-tehdit-gibi-aciklama/gundem/detay/1802013/default.htm

http://www.radikal.com.tr/turkiye/ocalan-bu-atese-benzin-tasi-mayacagiz-1170417/

http://www.bbc.com/turkce/haberler/2014/03/140315_kck_akp

http://www.karar.com/gundem-haberleri/pkk-ve-hdp-cozum-su-recini-boyle-bitirdi

http://rusencakir.com/Ocalan-tamam-degil-devam-dedi/2592

http://www.sabah.com.tr/gundem/2014/06/02/en-onemli-re-alite-surecin-yeni-asamaya-gelmesi

http://www.sde.org.tr/userfiles/file/SD_EYLUL2015_SAYI70_BASKI.pdf

http://www.hurriyet.com.tr/2-hava-kuvvetleri-komutanliginda-
ki-bayragi-indirdiler-26575475

http://www.bbc.com/turkce/haberler/2014/08/140816_ocalan

http://www.diken.com.tr/ocalan-kobani-duserse-cozum-sure-
ci-biter/

http://www.milliyet.com.tr/pkk-icindeki-derin-ayrilik-gun-
dem-2100900/

haber.sol.org.tr/turkiye/cemil-bayik-isidin-gercek-halifesi-el-bag-
dadi-degil-erdogan-104569

http://m.turkiyegazetesi.com.tr/yazarlar/yildiray-ogur/587467.as-
px

http://www.mynet.com/haber/guncel/rakamlarla-7-yilda-ter-
or-ve-cozum-sureci-2425443-1

http://www.diken.com.tr/demirtastan-cozum-aciklamasi-
na-ic-guvenlik-paketi-uyarisi-demokratiklesme-bu-paketle-ol-
maz/

http://odatv.com/sorun-cozulmeden-pkk-silah-birakacak-de-
mek-demagojidir-aldatmaktir--2802151200.html

http://www.star.com.tr/acik-gorus/catismasizlik-nasil-sona-er-
di-haber-1050354/

http://dirilispostasi.com/a-1851-ocalan-tarihi-mektuptan-cikar-
di-mi.html

http://www.aljazeera.com.tr/haber/erdogan-dolmabah-
ceyi-de-10-maddeyi-de-elestirdi

http://www.sozcu.com.tr/2015/gunun-icinden/pkkdan-silah-bi-
rakma-sartlari-823658/

http://www.radikal.com.tr/turkiye/kck-silah-birakma-iradesi-bi-
ze-ait-1378056/

http://www.hurriyet.com.tr/bedeli-ne-olursa-olsun-engel-olaca-
giz-29394009

http://www.radikal.com.tr/turkiye/karayilan-rojavaya-muda-
hale-olursa-savas-cikar-1387653/

http://www.aksam.com.tr/guncel/cemil-bayik-silahl-anin-tunel-kazin/haber-424316

https://firatnews.com/kurdistan/hpg-2-polisi-apocu-fedai-timi-cezalandirdi-51114

https://www.dunya.com/gundem/mhp039den-huku-mete-habur-tepkisi-haberi-105911

http://t24.com.tr/haber/haburda-pkklilar-icin-kurulan-mahke-menin-hakimi-fetoden-tutuklu,369619

http://www.radikal.com.tr/dunya/dunya-basini-da-vos-sokunu-boyle-duyurdu-919321/

http://www.ntv.com.tr/dunya/davostaki-moderator-kendi-ni-savundu,cS0iQb3yHU-QPZsk7N2I0w

http://www.aljazeera.com.tr/haber/erdogan-dunya-5ten-buyuk-tur

http://www.haaretz.com/israel-news/netanyahu-phones-erdo-gan-to-apologize-for-deaths-of-turkish-citizens-on-gaza-flo-tilla.premium-1.511394

http://www.tuicakademi.org/arap-bahari-ve-nedenleri/

"Muslim cleric Gulen: Coup bid in Turkey could have been staged"
    http://www.reuters.com/article/us-turkey-security-gulen-re-marks-idUSKCN0ZW11D

http://www.bbc.com/turkce/haberler-turkiye-39478777

http://www.takvim.com.tr/guncel/2017/05/01/yuzu-maskeli-ter-oristlerden-erdogana-olum-tehdidi

https://tr.sputniknews.com/avrupa/201704241028201391-erdo-gan-oldurmek-kaliyor-fransiz-siyaset-bilimci-sorusturma/

http://www.foxnews.com/opinion/2016/07/16/turkeys-last-hope-dies.html

http://www.sabah.com.tr/gundem/2014/12/03/alev-alat-li-konustu-erdogan-gozyaslarini-tutamadi

http://tr.euronews.com/2017/01/04/erdogan-turki-ye-de-hic-kimsenin-hayat-tarzi-tehdit-altinda-degildir

http://www.hurriyet.com.tr/erdoganin-yazarlarla-bulusmasin-da-yaptigi-konusma-14448731

http://www.haber7.com/ic-politika/haber/1035100-gezi-par-ki-temsilcilerinin-hukumetten-7-talebi

http://fgulen.com/tr/turk-basininda-fethullah-gulen/fethul-lah-gulen-hakkinda-dizi-yazilar-dosyalar/fethullah-gulen-web-sitesi-ozel-dosyalar/9897-merhum-turgut-ozal

http://odatv.com/guleni-bitirme-plani-2004-mgkda-alin-di-2811131200.html

http://www.hurriyet.com.tr/guleni-bitirme-iddiasina-ak-par-tiden-art-arda-aciklamalar-25228969

http://www.radikal.com.tr/turkiye/hukumet-mgknin-2004te-ki-cemaat-eylem-planini-uygulamis-1163747/

http://www.hurriyet.com.tr/basbakan-erdogandan-onem-li-aciklamalar-25048293

http://www.hurriyet.com.tr/gunaydan-insanlik-aniti-aciklama-si-16726377

http://www.milliyet.com.tr/basbakan-konustu-bakan-gu-nay-yikildi-siyaset-1338681/

http://www.radikal.com.tr/politika/akpli-kocak-ihrac-edil-di-784707/

http://www.milliyet.com.tr/son-dakika-cumhurbaskani-erdo-gan-siyaset-2433585/

http://www.hurriyet.com.tr/erdogan-sert-yanit-suursu-zlar-5753501

http://www.gazetevatan.com/-velhasil-onlar-vurdu-biz-buyuduk-kardesim--300413-gundem/

http://www.cumhuriyet.com.tr/haber/siyaset/88985/Erdogan_iki_bilezigi_hic_unutmadim.html

Fatih Altaylı, "En beyaz Türk Michael Jackson kadar beyazdır", http://www.haberturk.com/polemik/haber/822746-en-beyaz-turk-michael-jackson-kadar-beyazdir

http://www.haber7.com/dis-politika/haber/2320458-yuzu-maske-li-teroristlerden-erdogana-olum-tehdidi

http://www.ntv.com.tr/turkiye/esref-bitlisten-ozala-son-mek-tup,Kh57CMBp2EKPtdupFftg5g

http://www.bbc.com/turkce/haberler/2013/12/131225_mus-luman_kardesler

http://time100.time.com/2013/04/18/time-100/

http://www.bbc.com/turkce/haberler-turkiye-39582101

www.herkul.org/herkul-nagme/391-nagme-egitime-darbe-plani

http://www.haberturk.com/gundem/haber/850438-fethullah-gu-lenden-gezi-parki-aciklamasi

The most common problem Erdoğan has experienced throughout his political life is the issue of his wife and daughter's headscarves.

Erdoğan's critical visits while president transpired as the AK Party's search for legitimacy.

Erdoğan's speech at the AK Party's founding meeting had the characteristics of a manifesto, so to speak, and changed the registry and mentality of politics.

A critical detail that should be considered is the unity of Western politics that, since the beginning, has chosen to maintain a distance with Erdoğan.

DER SPIEGEL

Nr. 30
23.7.2016

Diktator Erdoğan und der hilflose Westen

Es war einmal eine Demokratie

Nato-Leaks
Das geheime Netzwerk von General Breedlove

Berlin, München, Hamburg...
Kurzurlauber verdrängen (Ur)einwohner

Bestsellerautor Peter Wohlleben
„Das Elstermännchen: ein Schwein wie du und ich"

It is quite serious that Der Spiegel, one of German media's most important outlets, has directly targeted both Erdoğan and Turkey in its publications with a systematic plan.

Erdoğan's Kurdish Opening, which challenged the intrinsic system of tutelage, would come to an end with the involvement of a hidden hand.

The crisis in Davos was Erdoğan's first open clash with global powers with Davos as the first disease vector for Erdoğanophobia.

DOUBLE ISSUE
NOVEMBER 28, 2011
The Year's 50 Best Inventions
Euro Crisis: A Critical New Phase
Why Chinese Factories Can't Pay Their Bills
Russia's Olympic Dreams
TIME
Turkey's pro-Islamic leader has built his (secular, democratic, Western-friendly) nation into a regional powerhouse ...
... but can his example save the Arab Spring?
ERDOGAN'S WAY
BY BOBBY GHOSH
www.time.com

The Western media took no time to release various publications to turn antagonism of Erdoğan into fear. This frightening presentation of Erdoğan should be considered an outward expression of a much deeper subconscious rather than everyday political reflexes.

Erdogan explains to the dominant powers at the United Nations General Assembly that the world is bigger than five.

Erdoğan's conceptualization of the "Turkish Rabia" is "one homeland, one state, one nation, one flag."

Although Erdoğan's political discourse overlaps with Mustafa Kemal Atatürk's definition of nationalism, it is clear that it has a paradigmatic differentiation in general meaning.

Erdoğan's emotional side is regarded as a sign of his authenticity and sincerity..

The West encoding Erdoğan as a sultan or dictator is an important paradigm that must be understood within orientalism and the thesis that political Islam has failed.

Sultan
Tayyip Erdogan

Selbstherrlich baut der türkische Premier sein Land zu einer Wirtschaftsmacht und
zu einem Modell für die arabische Welt aus. Die Demokratie kommt zu kurz

The West's definition of Erdoğan as a sultan is the clearest indication that the Western
paradigm continues to see him as a serious threat and danger.